CORPS = 2 DIVISIONS
DIVISION = 16 BATTALIONS

THE RUSSIAN ARMY IN WORLD WAR I

ABOUT THE BOOK

The Good Read story of the great battles, the personalities, the campaign strategies of our Russian ally in World War I. Ten million Russians died in the War. Although Britain and France distrusted Russia and despised her corrupt and despotic government, they were ready to sacrifice Russia's armies to ensure their survival. Tsar Nicholas accepted their constant urgings for fresh military adventures in order to prove his trustworthiness. Here is the story of how the battles were planned, how they evolved and how they affected the whole nation and changed the course of history.

ABOUT THE AUTHOR

Ward Rutherford was born in Richmond, Surrey, in 1927. He was educated on the island of Jersey where he lived through the German Occupation and was imprisoned for listening to BBC broadcasts on a home-made crystal-set.

In 1962 he joined the management of Channel Television and from there went to the BBC where he was a regular broadcaster on television and radio.

He has written two crime novels, *The Gallows Set* and *Great Big Laughing Hannah*, as well as history and military history *Kasserine Baptism of Fire, The Fall Of the Philippines, Genocide: the Nazi Persecution of the Jews*, and *The Untimely Silence.*

Ward Rutherford

THE RUSSIAN ARMY IN WORLD WAR I

GORDON CREMONESI

Designed by Heather Gordon-Cremonesi
Produced by Chris Pye
Set by Preface Ltd, Salisbury
Printed in Great Britain by The Anchor Press Ltd

ISBN 0-86033-002-8

Gordon Cremonesi Publishers
New River House
34 Seymour Road
London N8 0BE
England

Contents

DATES

All dates herein are given in the Gregorian reckoning, introduced into Russia in 1918. Before this the Julian calendar, which was thirteen days behind the Gregorian, was in general use there.

MAPS

I   The Eastern Front: the summer campaign of 1915

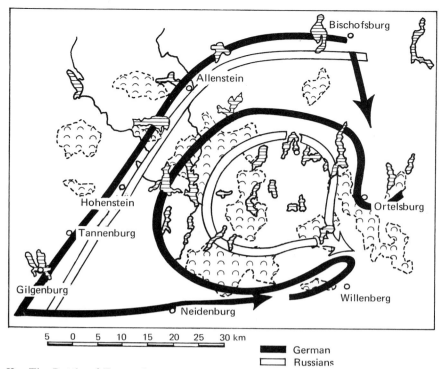

II The Battle of Tannenberg

III The breakthrough at Brzeziny in the Battle of Lodz

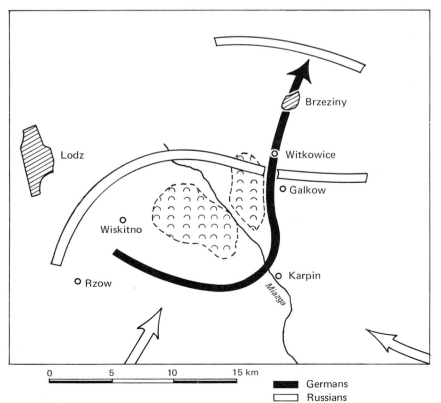

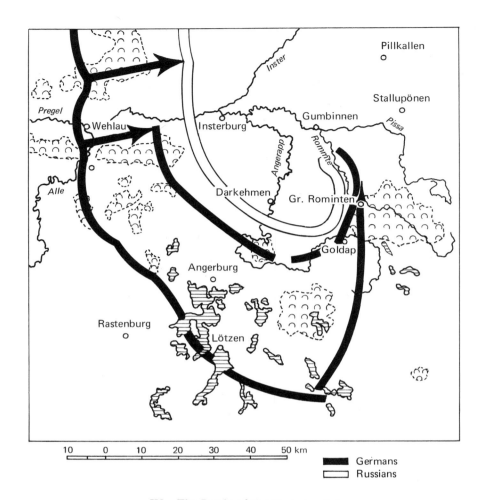

Pillkallen

Stallupönen

Inster

Pregel

Wehlau

Insterburg

Gumbinnen

Pissa

Angerapp

Rominte

Alle

Darkehmen

Gr. Rominten

Goldap

Angerburg

Rastenburg

Lötzen

| 10 | 0 | 10 | 20 | 30 | 40 | 50 km |

■■■ Germans
☐ Russians

IV   The Battle of the Masurian Lakes

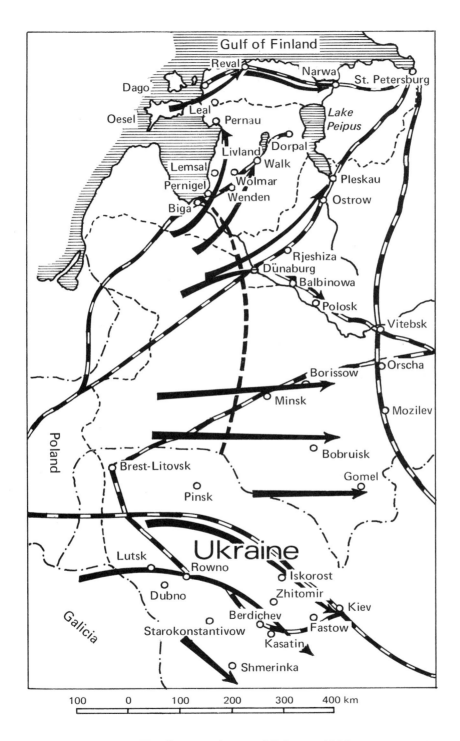

V   The German advance of February 1918

Chapter 1

War Fever In St Petersburg

On Monday 20 July 1914, with the guns of St Petersburg reverberating in salute, the French president, Raymond Poincaré, arrived in the Gulf of Finland aboard the battleship "France" for a three-day visit to Russia.

It was a particularly hot day even for that hot summer which had brought drought to Russia, as well as to the rest of Europe. Sometimes, when the wind blew down from the Gulf of Finland, it carried the smell of burning pinewood from forest fires.

Poincaré was a grey-haired, neatly bearded man who, even in the nondescript costume affected by republican heads of state, looked as if he might have been chosen by his country to typify its provincial bourgeois — honest, prudent, complacent and well-nourished. A lawyer-turned-politician from Bar-le-Duc on the Meuse, his career had progressed by orderly degrees from deputy for his home town to junior minister, minister and prime minister, and he had succeeded Clement Faillières the previous year. This was, therefore, his first presidential visit to the country which had now been allied with his own for almost a quarter of a century, and whose sovereign head, Nicholas II, Autocrat of All the Russias, now stood beside him in the bows of the royal yacht "Standarte", which was bearing them down the Neva to the Peterhof Palace.

The Franco-Russian Treaty which brought the two men together had originated in the antipathy of Tsar Alexander III towards the "garçon mal élevé", Wilhelm II of Germany, who had acceded in 1888, and in the Kaiser's consequent refusal to renew the Bismarckian "Treaty of Reinsurance" which extended the 1881 Drei Kaiser Bund of Russia, Germany and Austria-Hungary.

Alexander had thus been left unaligned in Europe, while Germany and Austria-Hungary formed the Triple Alliance in combination with Italy. As Alexander was convinced his vast country was more than a match for all comers, the need to guard

1

against checks in the flow of desperately needed foreign development capital was more important than the defensive purposes for which the alliance was formed. Forced, therefore, to look elsewhere for this, his eye had alighted on France and, swallowing his own and his government's distaste for this nation of republicans and regicides, in 1892 he had signed a treaty of economic and commercial co-operation. Not until a year later was a secret convention subjoined whereby the partners undertook to render each other military assistance in the event of German attack. So it was that the military clauses of the compact, which was to have so cataclysmic an effect on Europe, could be said to have come into existence as an afterthought, though on the French side this was carefully contrived.

The Franco-Prussian War of 1870 had shown France, isolated in Europe, her need for supporters, but every country she turned to was already committed. The opportunity for an alliance with Russia had therefore been seized upon as the first breach in this cordon sanitaire. A further breach occurred in 1905 through the Entente Cordiale with Britain. France was now the common partner in two alliances, which were converted into a complete triangle when the British King, Edward VII, met Alexander's son Nicholas at Reval in 1907, and Russia too joined the Entente.

Still menaced by the Triple Alliance — whose leading member, Germany, was plainly antagonistic — France had worked assiduously to perfect the detailed arrangements for defensive co-operation among her associates; this was what had brought Poincaré to Russia in 1914, and had also taken him there two years previously as foreign minister.

To commentators who had watched the growth of two opposed European blocs with misgiving, and whose alarm seemed justified by the series of confrontations between them, the French could at last point to some success for their policies in the long, brilliant summer of 1914. Since Poincaré's 1912 visit tensions had slackened, agreements having been reached between individual member-states of each side on a number of minor but hitherto intractable issues. In Germany, forced to retreat from her bellicose stance during the Agadir Incident, more moderate counsel seemed to have prevailed, and settlement had been reached with France over Morocco. Britain and Russia had already resolved a number of matters between themselves and Germany, and the Berlin government had brought influence to bear on its Austrian ally when the latter was about to go to war with Serbia over the annexation of Albania, so avoiding a conflict in which Russia would inevitably have been involved.

In the rough and ready balance of power which had been achieved, largely by French efforts, both sides seemed to have begun to appreciate that more could be gained from co-operation than hostility. There were even signs of positive goodwill abroad: only two months before the "France" sailed into the Gulf of Finland she had visited Germany with the navies of her other allies to participate in the international celebrations marking the opening of the widened Kiel Canal. Despite Russian encouragement, the French had been unwilling to participate until the Germans, in a goodwill gesture, agreed to exclude from the assembled fleets any vessel bearing the name of a French defeat of 1870.

Poincaré's arrival in Russia was therefore regarded with feelings of mutual satisfaction by the treaty-partners, and whereas − during his 1912 visit − he had been received with a coldness bordering on hostility by the "St Petersbourgeois," in 1914 they greeted him warmly − or at least as warmly as was possible in a city paralysed by large-scale strikes.

The numerous potential points of international friction had by no means been totally eliminated, though when the president and his host, the tsar, broke off the round of receptions, banquets and parades for informal talks on the second day of the visit, they could feel that none of the matters coming within their province posed an immediate threat. True, relations between Greece and Turkey were strained, and they also considered the motive behind an Austrian princeling's visit to Albania; the tsar promised to rectify difficulties which had arisen with Britain over the Anglo-Russian agreements on Persia, and they discussed the politics of the Scandinavian states Poincaré was due to visit after leaving Russia.

Another matter touched upon, albeit fleetingly, was an occurrence in Austria's recently-annexed province of Bosnia: the murder of the heir to the throne of the Dual Monarchy, Archduke Franz Ferdinand, and his morganatic wife. While both deplored Austria's attempt to hold Serbia responsible for the crime, they agreed that the death of a single couple, even when one was heir to an imperial throne, was not sufficient to disturb − much less imperil — the new climate of confidence. Germany, they considered, could only be bluffing in supporting the Austrian démarche against Serbia. In any event, the tsar at least felt his present domestic problems to be more urgent and pressing than an assassination in an Austrian provincial capital.

Although external relations had improved since 1912, this had been counteracted by a deterioration in the internal situation and there was every indication that 1914 would replicate 1905, the year of the Bloody Sunday Massacre and the consequent January Revolution. This had forced the tsar to issue the Constitutional Manifesto, and also to institute the first Russian parliament, or State Duma, whose existence had irritated the government ever since.

The ostensible spark for the present troubles was an incident at the British-owned Lena goldfields in Siberia in April 1912 when workers protesting peacefully about the quality of the food were fired on by the police, over a hundred being killed or wounded. An official inquiry placed the blame firmly on the shoulders of the company whose monopoly had been broken, while improvements in working conditions were immediately introduced. However, consequent growth of continuing industrial protest throughout the country evidenced deeper dissatisfactions, and the strike movement began to include textile workers who were generally regarded as among the least militant. Between 1912 and 1914, the number of strikers rose from 725,000 to 1,450,000. Tempers, too, became increasingly frayed, and as in 1905 this unrest took on an openly political character, agitators declaring that there could be no permanent amelioration of the workers' lot without fundamental changes in the régime.

To the government's embarrassment, these demonstrations continued throughout the French presidential visit, despite strong police measures, and increased during succeeding days with rioting and shop-window smashing in the working-class Vyborg area of St Petersburg. All this was meticulously reported to Berlin by the German ambassador, Count Pourtalès, where the Kaiser seized on it to support his thesis that Russia had fallen into the "mood of a sick tom cat."

By late July, barricades were going up across some of the Vyborg streets. On the evening of 1 August, when Pourtalès drove to the office of the Russian Foreign Minister, Sergei Sazonov, handed over the German Declaration of war and immediately burst into uncontrollable tears, there were rumours that the Soviet of Soldiers' and Workers' Deputies, formed in 1905 as a rival government, was about to reconvene itself.

That night, as news of the declaration of war reached the streets, the mood changed. Barricades were pulled down, the demonstrating workers joined cheering crowds outside the French, Belgian and Serbian embassies, waving their flags or the double-headed Russian eagle, breaking into the anthem of republicanism, the "Marseillaise", for the first time without risk of arrest; marching up the Nevsky Prospekt, past the classical façades, to the square in front of the Winter Palace where, as the French ambassador Maurice Paléologue recalled in his diary, they had been mown down in 1905. Now they fell on their knees when the tsar and tsarina appeared on the balcony, breaking spontaneously into the national anthem, "Bozhe Tsaria Kranie".

A war fever, as delirious as that which seized Berlin, Vienna and Paris, had infected the city where revolution seemed so imminent that Pourtalès had declined an offer to have his personal art collection kept for the duration in safe custody at the Hermitage, being convinced the building would be blown up by insurgents.

At that time Mikhail Rodzianko, president of the State Duma, returned to a capital he had heard was in turmoil. Asking a cheering workman what had become of their previous grievances, he was told: "That was our family dispute . . . But now all Russia is involved."

In the Duma itself, the country's young and precarious parliament, there was a one-day session on 8 August when members of the contending parties vied with each other in declaring their unity in the struggle with the government they had recently been attacking; thus, in Kerensky's view "sorrily submitting to the incompetent and criminal tsarist government" in the belief that they were inaugurating a "union sacrée" of the parties such as was enacted in Britain and France. This typified the nine-year history of the Duma, where each successive election, thanks to government gerrymandering and alterations to the electoral law, increased the representation of the right until they now (in the Fourth Duma, elected in 1912) represented a majority.

The heady mood continued. On 15 August, the tsar drove to the cathedral of Our Lady of Kazan to swear before the miracle-working ikon his determination "not to make peace so long as there is a single enemy on Russia's soil".

Two days later, the crowd vented its feelings against Germany by breaking into the deserted German embassy, a huge ornate building surmounted by bronze chargers on twin domes. They tore down tapestries and destroyed the pictures, bronzes and marbles of Pourtalès' private collection which he had refused to commit to safe-keeping.

At court, the official German titles were replaced by their Russian equivalents, and at the end of August, the tsar issued a ukase changing the name of the capital from the German St Petersburg to the Russian Petrograd.

In his diary, Paléologue wrote: "The bad days of 1905 seemed to have gone from the memory of all. The collective soul of Holy Russia has never manifested itself so forcibly since 1812." Below his window an ikon-carrying procession shouted "Vive La France!", reappearing so regularly that even he suspected police collusion, if not inspiration, behind it. "This way of expressing hatred does seem a little puerile," Poincaré commented in Paris when he heard of the renaming of St Petersburg, "and one wonders whether in order not to be suspected of pro-Germanism we should have to change the names of Strasbourg, Cabourg, Bourg en Bresse and all the other Bourgs in France." Thus he missed the key to Russia's changed mood after the declaration of war and to the country's enthusiasm for the conflict. As the tsar's aunt, the Grand-Duchess Maria Pavlovna, said, "it was a duel to the death between Slavism and Germanism".

There were 170,000 German subjects in the empire, compared with 10,000 French and 8,000 British, but in addition, some 2 million German immigrants lived in the Baltic countries, the Ukraine and the Volga valley. They had always exerted a disproportionate influence on the population as a whole, and for 150 years the Baltic provinces had produced the Tchinovniki, or titled bureaucrats, the "Baltic barons" who operated the machinery of state and whose readily identifiable names were to be found in the highest ranks of the government, civil service, the Okhrana (secret police) and the army.

To the peasants they were the tsar's reactionary servants who could turn his "yes" into their "no". To the workers they were the financiers, owners and managers of industry, the alien exploiters. The Russian hereditary nobility considered them obstacles to advancement and advantage, and many were turned away from the régime. The intelligentsia saw them as interposed between themselves and the liberal democracies of France and Britain, a constant deadweight dragging Russia away from western culture and freedom of thought towards the autocracies of Germany and Austria-Hungary. Conservative opinion, convinced that they remained loyal to their nation of origin, saw them as the agents of Russia's downfall, as a result of whose intrigues corruption was allowed to thrive, and through whose activity funds which even the police believed came from Germany, were distributed to political agitators. It was also noticeable that left-wing political exiles, such as Lenin, Trotsky, Zinoviev, Rykov and Martov, found havens among the Germanic nations.

These sentiments, equally apparent in the vandalism at the German embassy and the kneeling crowds before the Winter Palace, made the Russian people feel that they had entered an era not merely of strife with an external enemy, but of self-liberation, and a new and fruitful relationship between themselves and their tsar, the White Father of All the Russians.

All this feeling would be expressed through the purgation of a war, victorious and brief — brief because all wars were. Napoleon's campaign of 1812, the Franco-Prussian War, the Russo-Turkish War and the Russo-Japanese War had all lasted less than eighteen months. Now the enormously increased economic resources and vaster armies could only lead to an even shorter, though perhaps more violent, struggle. It was upon this thesis that all the nations had prepared themselves for action: the Germans with their Schlieffen Plan, the French with Plan Seventeen, the Russians with the twin plans "A" and "G".

So the army, which the tsar had hesitated to mobilise and which earlier would have been reviled as the epitome of state repression, now marched past enthusiastic crowds. White-uniformed bands were followed by great columns of infantry; artillery and limbers rattled over the cobbles, succeeded by ambulances, transport wagons and the endless tinkle and clatter of cavalry. The citizens poured from the shops to cheer, office workers leaned from their windows to wave and call encouragement; families ran out to thrust gifts upon them. Thousands of young men rushed to volunteer, while the women and girls of Russian society, not to be outdone, queued up to work in the hospitals. It was "as if we were going to the Crusades," wrote Pavel Rodzianko, officer nephew of the Duma president.

It had been difficult to dissuade the tsar, a slight, bearded man, from personally leading this "crusade". Instead, on 2 August, he had appointed his uncle, the Grand-Duke Nicholas Nicholaievich. The "True Russia" of whose latent existence the tsar had always been convinced, was on the march and, to keep its mission undefiled, he temporarily banned the sale of vodka throughout the empire. Intended to match the French prohibition on absinthe, this embargo was later extended for the duration of the war.[1] In the sanctified atmosphere of the time, however, there was little excess drinking even among officers who could buy brandy and wine from the army cooperatives. "The war is too serious for that," one officer told Major-General Knox, British liaison officer.

On 18 August, taking with them the French ambassador and his British colleague, Sir George Buchanan, the tsar and royal family went to Moscow, the ancient capital, to offer the traditional prayers for victory at the Kremlin. There were more scenes of jubilation, but with the city's bells still echoing in his ears Buchanan found he was asking himself "how long this national enthusiasm would last." Paléologue, too, recalled that "every war has brought the Russian people a deep domestic crisis." Yet beneath all the manifestations of eagerness for the struggle, all the exalted hopes for a new Russia to come, the more discerning could detect signs of a half-buried anxiety. The huzzas of the people of St Petersburg, Moscow, Odessa, Novogorod, and the eager anxiety of young officers who feared only that it would be over before they reached the front or that they would be sent to fight the inferior Austrians rather than the Germans, was not necessarily echoed among the soldiers marching through the streets or filling the trains.

Both Meriel Buchanan, the British ambassador's daughter, and Major-General Knox saw crying wives and children accompanying reservists, seeking to defer the moment of parting. Paléologue recalled a very young, fair-haired Russian peasant girl, striding out to keep up with a soldier in one of the columns, holding a baby to her breast: "They did not exchange a word, but gazed at each other with loving, haggard eyes."

Paléologue had a strange visitor in Count Sergei Witte, chairman of the Council of Ministers from 1905 to 1906, who had persuaded the tsar to accept a draft constitution for his people. Bitter and disillusioned with his fellow Russians and with a régime he had called "a tangle of cowardice, blindness, craftiness and stupidity", he absented himself from his native country with increasing frequency. In March 1914 he caused some misgivings among the French when the leading St Petersburg newspaper published a series of interviews with him, the purport of which was that Russia should not heedlessly incur German enmity even to please present allies. Already mortally sick (he died of a cerebral tumour the following spring), he had spent the summer in Biarritz, returning to Petrograd when war became inevitable. Just after its outbreak he went to Paléologue with criticisms of every aspect of Russia's participation.

The championing of the Serbian cause was nothing but a "romantic, old-fashioned chimera." The Serbians were not even Slavs that Russia – greatest of the Slav nations – should feel obliged to stand by them; they were Turks "christened by another name," who were about to receive the chastisement they deserved at Austria's hand. He went on to discuss the profits and rewards the war might bring. "Constantinople, the cross on the Santa Sophia, the Bosphorus, the Dardanelles? It's too mad a notion to be worth a moment's consideration." What would an Allied victory bring? The end of German domination, yes, but with it the proclamation of republics throughout Europe and the end of the Russian monarchy.

"My practical conclusion," he ended, "is that we must liquidate this stupid adventure as soon as possible."

Paléologue pointed out that this was now impossible, whereupon Witte asked with incredulity bordering on horror: "So we've got to go on fighting? "

However, in the third week of August the bells rang out once more, this time to celebrate a victory gained over the Germans in East Prussia by the First Army of the North West Front, under the command of the bold and dashing General Pavel K. Rennenkampf. In an encounter at Gumbinnen, some twenty miles over the Prussian side of the border, the German Seventeenth Corps under von Mackensen had broken in panic and their First Corps had been forced to retire to avoid envelopment. The towns of Stallüponen and Gumbinnen were in Russian hands and a steady trickle of prisoners and war-booty was sent to the rear, including a German machine-gun which Rennenkampf sent as a personal gift to the tsar.

The war was living up to its expectations.

Chapter 2

The Veil Of Suspicion

Witte's acrid denunciation of the war revealed threads of that veil of mutual suspicion — not to say antipathy — through which the eastern and western Allies viewed each other. The Russian alliance was not, Poincaré sighed in his diary after his 1912 visit, "always an easy machine to handle."

Re-reading those lines later, he must have been amazed at his restraint, and envied the situation of those against whom that alliance was primarily directed: Germany and Austria-Hungary. Geographically united and familiar to each other, sharing language, race and culture and having similar systems of government, they seemed to possess every attribute to make them natural allies.

In contrast, the eastern and western partners of the Triple Entente were unnatural allies on all these scores, thrown together by nothing more than circumstance — on the one side, a need for capital; on the other, for a defensive alliance at all costs.

Firstly, there was the brute fact of their separation by the landmass of Central Europe which contained not only their potential enemies, but also the whole constellation of Balkan states whose goodwill was uncertain. Still worse, except for ports in the far north and on the Pacific, Russia's only connection with the outer world and hence the west was by way of the Black Sea and, via the Dardanelles, the Mediterranean.

This separation had also led to the development of two dissimilar cultures originating in the religious bases of the two societies; the Christianity of western Europe came from the Roman stream, that of Russia from Orthodox, eastern origins. Differences not only of language but of phonetic system had contributed to maintaining this separation, with the result that each possessed an impression of the other devoid of middle-tones, simplified to the point of crudity, so coloured by myth and half-truth as to border on superstition.

To Westerners, the Russians were inhabitants of a primitive,

11

snow-clad land, oriental, devious, complex and barbaric; the Russians conceived themselves, however, as the "Holy Russia" of the devout, long-suffering and self-sacrificing "mouzhik", sole repository of the true faith in a world of secular materialism.

Cultural differences were reflected in political systems. French and British liberalism saw in Russia only a repressive despotism, the direct antithesis of all they stood for, a state dichotomised between rulers and ruled, the "two Russias" in which one was determined at all costs to retain its dominion over the other, excluding from its counsel that section from which the western politicians were mostly drawn — the middle-class intelligentsia.

To its Russian advocates, however, the system appeared to provide a unifying permanence through its structure of inter-dependent tiers: tsar, nobility and toiling masses, at one in the Orthodox faith. The topmost ranks gave their time and effort without hope of reward or mass-adulation and, since they were spared the necessity of courting as well, could make decisions disinterestedly, "for the good of Russia". A country which had undergone no political, religious or industrial revolution, needed a benevolent despotism to carry it forward, they might have argued, even if it meant certain imperfections and injustices.

To Nicholas II who stood at the apex of the pyramid and declared himself its dedicated upholder, this had nothing to do with a taste for personal power. Indeed, subsequent events in Russia are only comprehensible if one realises that the country was led by a man who heartily detested the power thrust upon him. His reaction on finding himself tsar at the age of twenty-six was one of undisguised alarm, and he confided to his brother-in-law, the Grand-Duke Alexander, within hours of his father's death: "I'm not prepared to be tsar. I've never wanted to be one. I know nothing about the business of ruling."

Throughout his reign it was clear that his deepest and only abiding interest lay in his family and home. By temperament the antithesis of the Titan public figure Russia so needed and had found in Alexander III, the manifold virtues of his character were those private qualities which were disadvantageous in public life. Those who came to know him personally were charmed by his warm-hearted sincerity, integrity and sensitivity; in company he was overcome by a chronic and endemic shyness.

Given this background, it was hardly surprising that the Franco-Russian Treaty encountered hostility from both sides at its inception. In France, in 1892, the employment of republican credit to bolster monarchical repression was denounced as a betrayal of the principle of the revolution. In Russia, Leo Tolstoy pamphleteered against the pact as a slamming of the door by France on the plight of Russian progressive opinion.

To the Russian right, conscious of rebellion constantly simmering beneath the surface of the system, this new entanglement represented nothing but danger to their country. Never having outgrown that terror of revolution which seized all Europe after 1789, they were convinced that they faced engulfment in the tide of republicanism, atheism and — worst of all — parliamentary democracy. Feeling against the treaty was such that, when the military protocols were added a year later, Alexander insisted they be kept secret, a request the French were not averse to granting.

The fears of Russian conservatism were increased rather than alleviated when Russia became associated with Britain through the extension of the Entente. "Constitutional monarchy" appeared a mere euphemism for the crown's feeble surrender of its obligations and prerogatives. "I can understand a republic . . ." Nicholas I had once said. "I can understand an absolute monarchy . . . But what I cannot understand is a constitutional monarchy. It's a government of lies, fraud, corruption, and rather than adopt it I'd withdraw to China." His successor would have supported his views, and it was against the spectre of "constitutional monarchy" no less than against parliamentarianism, that the Autocrat of All the Russias strove throughout his reign.

The troubles which attended the birth of the Alliance had, as Poincaré's exasperated comment explains, persisted throughout its life. France and Britain were uncertain of the tsar's devotion to a partnership in which he was the odd man out.

Both countries were dismayed by the Björkö Fiord incident. From the moment when he had allowed his dignity to get the better of him in the matter of the Reinsurance Treaty, Wilhelm II had regretted it and sought to mend the damage wrought by his impetuosity. In 1905, when he and Nicholas II met aboard their respective yachts in the Finnish Björkö Fiord, he so far succeeded in persuading the tsar that his natural habitat was among the other imperial autocracies that he actually signed a treaty with Germany, by which the two monarchs would render mutual aid in the event of war. This was, of course, a clear repudiation of the Franco-Russian Treaty, as prime minister Witte pointed out to Nicholas after his return to St Petersburg, and the pact had to be allowed to lapse.

The west was fully aware of the activities of the pro-German "Baltic barons" in the Russian government which continued to plead the cause of Russo-German détente right up to the outbreak of the war and beyond it. To the tsar, the arguments in favour of joining those with whom he felt a close political kinship could not fail to sound convincing. It was pointed out that Russian and German interests did not conflict: Germany's future was on the seas, a sphere where Russia – necessarily the most continental of the great powers – had no interest at all. As far as contemporary events were concerned, Germany had only felt obliged to back Austrian aims when she saw Russia drawing closer to England and thereby conniving at German isolation and encirclement, the "Einkreisung" so terrifying to her leaders.

As Sazonov, the Russian Foreign Minister until 1915 expressed it, relations with Britain over two centuries had produced "an endless series of political misunderstandings, of mutual suspicion and open hostility." These were scarcely dissolved in the period of under a decade during which the two nations were associated through the Triple Entente. Russia had been the enemy in the Crimean War, and over Afghanistan and Persia there had been long-standing conflict. In 1904 the Dogger Bank incident occurred, when Russian warships fired on British trawlers (allegedly because there were Japanese torpedo-boats among them)[1] and a sense of grievance remained against Britain because she supported Japan during the Russo-Japanese war.

On the British side there was not only this unhappy history of Anglo-Russian relations, but also the detestation felt by intellectuals of the ruling Liberal Party for both Russian autocracy and German militarism. The pragmatists of government recognised that any realistic world alliance must include one nation or the other, although German anglophobia and rivalry made it difficult to look in that direction. When, however, in 1907 they adopted the only possible alternative, the Cabinet felt itself to be courting criticism and national unpopularity. As Lloyd George declared in his memoirs published in 1933, to the British people the Russian régime was "almost as unpopular . . . as Bolshevism is today"; it was, he said, identified with Siberian political prisons, pogroms and "the massacre of workers whose only crime was the presentation of a petition for the redress of their undoubted wrongs." A massacre of workers, which had occurred only two years before the signing of the Entente, was still fresh in the British public mind, and at the time the tsar had been reviled as a red-handed murderer by the press and at public meetings.

To the British people, however, ignorant of German rivalry, the Germans were kindred, and the Kaiser remained a popular figure whose visits always drew enthusiastic crowds. Both Britain and France were aware of Russia's imperialistic ambitions, not least her openly expressed desire to expel the Turks from Europe. Any attempts to realise these ambitions would destroy the image of altruistic concern for international justice which they wished to present before the neutral nations, the most powerful of which — the United States — had already indicated her misgivings about Russia's presence in the Triple Entente and consequent difficulties in persuading the American people to support the war. Nor could Turkey be unaffected by the establishment of a power bloc containing Russia; she was being driven into the willing arms of the Triple Alliance, away from Britain, her traditional ally. A hostile Porte would hazard Russia's shortest line of communication with the west.

Russia, in turn, suspected the west of carrying their antipathy towards her political system to the length of conspiring with dissident elements in the country. Early in the war an exile named Bourtsev, a member of a group who conspired against the life of the governor of Moscow, Grand-Duke Sergei, returned to Russia in an effort to end subversive activity for the duration. When he was promptly arrested and sent to Siberia, both French and British ambassadors interceded for him. The tsar granted him the pardon they requested, but told Paléologue, "I don't remember my ambassador in Paris intervening to secure the pardon of any French political criminal," and commented to Sazonov on the interest taken by Britain and France in Russia's internal affairs.

After their various meetings, both tsar and French president expressed to third parties their mutual liking and respect, but the Russian monarch must have realised that the ending of his régime would remove the greatest stumbling block to the British and French public accepting the Russian treaty.

More practical misunderstandings arose from the fact that the eastern and western politicians were bred in entirely different political nurseries. Among the Russians were men like Ivan Logginovich Goremykin, chairman of the Council of Ministers, who regarded himself as no more than the pliant instrument of the tsar's will; General Vladimir Sukhomlinov, the War Minister, who inspired immediate distrust among his western counterparts; or Alexander Isvolski, the Russian ambassador in Paris, who was regarded by the French as so egotistic and devious that at one time they demanded his removal from the French capital. Following dismissal as Foreign Minister in 1908 after the Bosnia-Herzegovina incident in which Austria annexed these two Serbian provinces behind Russia's back, thereby devaluing the latter's standing as champion of the Slavs, Isvolski was to boast in August 1914, "This is my war! My war!"

A further twist to the intricacies of day-to-day east-west relations was imparted by the tsar's habit of dismissing his ministers just when it seemed to their western colleagues that a rapport had been established. To fail in their job was not necessary — an equally certain road to downfall was to support the Duma or, even worse, to earn the dislike of Rasputin, the court mystic. It was for both these reasons that in February 1914, just after completing negotiations for a new loan from France, Vladimir Kokovtsov — a man thoroughly trusted by the west — was dismissed as chairman of the Council of Ministers and replaced by the aged Goremykin, who combined reverence for Rasputin with a hearty contempt for the Duma which he ridiculed at every opportunity. At the moment when Russia most needed dynamism, the country's political leadership was entrusted to a man so old that, in his own words, "he ought to have been put into his coffin long ago." Sir Arthur Nicholson, the British ambassador before Buchanan, met him during his first period as chairman of the Council of Ministers in 1906, and found him, "an elderly man with a sleepy face and Piccadilly whiskers," reclining on a sofa in his office surrounded by French novels.

While the west regarded Russian politicians as difficult to

handle, their opposite numbers questioned whether they could rely on the word of British and French politicians who had to submit their intentions to the arbitrament of the mob and of parliament. "In Russia", Isvolski told Poincaré, "the tsar is all powerful and so France may be sure of us, while in France the government is impotent without parliament . . . What guarantee have we that in a general outbreak your parliament would follow your government's lead and recognise for itself the sanctity of obligations entered into? "

These uncertainties as to the behaviour of the French, who were at least committed to Russia by treaty, were immeasurably multiplied in the case of Britain whose sole link with both France and Russia was the loose tie of the Entente. The tsar's efforts, through France, to have this converted into a formal agreement drew no response from Britain, despite his pointing out that this reluctance increased the difficulties of his own position in supporting the alliance with the west against the pro-German faction about him. Germany had declared her willingness to sign a treaty at any time. However, with every indication that international tensions were easing after 1912, the Liberal government felt disinclined to risk further unpopularity by so strengthening Britain's ties with Russia that in the event of a Russo-German war – regarded by the British public as a not unwelcome "contest between autocracies" – Britain would automatically be involved.

France next attempted to persuade Britain to sign a naval convention with Russia, similar to her own agreement whereby the Royal Navy would assume responsibility for guarding the Channel, leaving the French navy to deploy its entire strength in the Mediterranean. Should it be possible to secure a similar arrangement in the Baltic, the Russians could concentrate on safeguarding the Black Sea and keeping their western approaches open. King George V thought this would be "a capital thing," but the British Foreign Minister, Sir Edward Grey, while personally not opposed, expected strong resistance from his party to "an alliance with an autocratic government."

In the end, the British were won over, and in the autumn of 1914 Prince Louis of Battenberg, the First Sea Lord, who was related to the British Royal family, should have visited St Petersburg to sign an agreement on behalf of the British government. However, this was prevented by the outbreak of war.

The three Entente powers thus moved ineluctably towards the greatest conflict the world had yet known, with the member whose presence was regarded as vital to the Alliance's invincibility was attached to the other two by an informal association from which it could easily escape.

In so far as the arrangements had already been tested, the French might have considered Britain to be a more reliable ally than Russia. In June 1911 the German gunboat "Panther", to give force to the Kaiser's demands for "a place in the sun", appeared off the coast of Morocco at Agadir, then controlled by France and Spain under a treaty co-signed by Germany. The Russians had hesitated about giving the French support, Isvolski declaring that his country "would never go to war over some strips of colonial territory," but a somewhat different interpretation was given in St Petersburg where support was promised. However, in view of the difficulty of persuading public opinion that Russia should take the field over such an issue, France was urged to keep open its "pourparlers" with Germany. Britain, on the other hand, gave unconditional support, which was instrumental in forcing the Kaiser to withdraw his threat.

The Agadir incident, however, had posed a straightforward issue between Germany and France, whereas the present crisis principally involved Russia and Austria, with the Germans and French only concerned as seconds. There were alarming indications that Britain proposed to use this as an excuse to avoid becoming embroiled in a war which would be unpopular among the people. Jules Cambon, the French ambassador, reported from London on 31 July that there was a marked lack of enthusiasm about entry into the war if this involved coming in on the Russian side. To the French this was particularly frightening, since the massing of German troops along the borders emphasised that the Kaiser's intentions were what they had always anticipated: a settlement of differences between the two nations. Believing the eastern partner of the Triple Entente to be incapacitated because of its domestic disputes, and with Britain showing signs that she intended to remain neutral, he could well feel that he would have a free hand in bringing about this final and long-postponed reckoning.

In any case, Britain — like Russia — was torn by a domestic crisis: the Curragh Mutiny in Northern Ireland when a group of officers, encouraged by the Conservative Party, threatened to resign when it was suggested — quite falsely — that they might be used to enforce the Liberals' 1913 Irish Home Rule Bill. The incident, unimportant in itself, nevertheless caused the British government, mindful of Ireland's tempestuous history, to panic to the extent of delaying implementation of the Bill fearing that to do so might precipitate civil war.

While Germany declared war on Russia on 1 August, and on France on the following day, Britain remained neutral — and in St Petersburg Buchanan found himself besieged in his embassy by angry Russians. Germany herself spurred the nation to decision by violating Belgian neutrality which both she and Britain had guaranteed, and on 4 August Britain delivered an ultimatum to Germany demanding withdrawal of all forces from Belgium. At eleven o'clock that night, no answer having been received, the third party of the Entente entered the war.

There is no evidence that any of the leaders of that partnership actually made any resolution during these dramatic days as to the future conduct of inter-Allied relations. Had they done so one might venture to guess, from the internal evidence, that for the French and British this would have taken the form of a determination to see that Russia fulfilled her obligations at whatever cost, while nevertheless treating her with the utmost suspicion. On the tsar's side, there would surely have been an equal determination to prove himself an impeccably trustworthy ally — at whatever cost.

Chapter 3

". . . For Faith, Tsar and Country"

However shaky and riven by reciprocal suspicions the Triple Entente might be, it possessed one indisputable trump card: the sheer size of the Russian army. Under a law passed in 1874 all fit twenty-year-old male members of the empire's 167 million population had to serve in the forces for a period of three to four years (according to the army to which they were drafted). This was followed by thirteen to fifteen years in the reserves and a further five or six years in the Opolchenie or national militia. Thus, a regular army strength of 1,423,000 was multiplied to 6,800,000 by mobilising the reserves and the Opolchenie in time of war.

The size of the army had been increased as recently as 1913, when France and Russia jointly introduced measures to match the German expansion of their own forces. In France, this took the form of the Three-Year Military Service Law, pushed through a reluctant parliament with difficulty, while in Russia the period of national service was increased by three months. This not only enlarged the peace-time force, but provided an overlap during the critical period between the recall of one class and the call-up of the succeeding one.

In 1914 the total Russian army amounted to 114 infantry divisions, plus a further 36 of cavalry,[1] compared with Germany's 87 and Austria's 49 infantry divisions. Moreover, Germany and Austria had other fronts and enemies to occupy them.

Such legions could not, of course, be organised in five minutes, especially in a country the size of Russia, but once assembled it seemed that no opponent, whatever his material or technical resources, could stay their forward impetus, Hence they came to be known as "the Russian steamroller" to the French and British press, and to that of Germany and Austria as "the Asiatic hordes". The mere thought of those great clouds of shouting and sabre-brandishing Cossacks,[2] or of the automata-like advance of uncountable waves of grey-clad infantry, was enough to excite a comforting glow or chill of terror — according to which side they were on — among Europeans who had never come within a thousand miles of the Steppe.

The fact was, however, that to the people and governments of Britain and France, statistics of manpower resources formed almost the sum total of their knowledge of the Russian army. In military, as in other matters, their partner played his cards close to his chest and even the French, with whom they had been in treaty-relations for twenty-two years, were largely kept in the dark.

On the credit side, the peasant-infantrymen who formed the primary units of these large forces were known to be brave, stubborn, frugal, hardy, obedient and uncomplaining, perfectly willing to offer their lives for the mystical troika of "faith, tsar and country". On the debit side was the fact that, alone of the Entente nations, Russia had suffered a recent defeat, by the Japanese in 1905. In the subsequent nationwide unrest the army, though less disaffected than the navy, had nevertheless been shaken by scores of mutinies including that of the Kronstadt garrison. The consensus of opinion among foreign observers was that the defeat had been brought about through poor leadership combined with lack of modern equipment, but it was also pointed out that the nation had by no means exerted its full strength.

Acknowledging their army's defects, the Russians had supposedly devoted themselves to their subsequent correction and achieved miracles in this respect. A group of General Staff officers who had come to be called "The Young Turks," and among whose members were the Grand-Duke Nicholas Nicholaievich and Generals Vassili Gourko, Alexeiev and Polivanov, had coalesced round Alexander Guchkov, ex-soldier, deputy of the Conservative Octobrist Party in the Duma and the acknowledged parliamentary expert on military affairs. Despite his surly and retiring nature he had acquired an almost legendary reputation and — now a wealthy Moscow businessman — had abandoned all his interests at the start of the century in order to fight for the Boers in South Africa.

Nevertheless, despite the enthusiasm of this "ginger-group", information available at government and general staff level in the west can scarcely have indicated that the Russian army had so reformed since 1905 as to be capable of meeting any foe. There was a critical shortage of railways in the country, although it was generally admitted that these had become an essential element of troop movement. As early as 1900 General Alexei Kuropatkin (then Minister of War and later to become commander-in-chief against the Japanese) had officially stated that, while the Austrian and German railway systems would enable them to place 1½ million men on Russia's western doorstep within days of mobilisation, the Russian armies would have to travel on foot. Concerned at this state of affairs, the French had lent Russia millions of francs for the specific purpose of building railways and when Poincaré went to St Petersburg in 1912, he conveyed pleas from French General Headquarters to their Russian counterparts on the necessity for doubling and re-doubling the number of lines. Despite these efforts, by 1914 Russia's track mileage was still only a twelfth of Germany's.

There was further concern on the French side because much of the track running towards the western frontiers was not of the wider gauge in general Russian use, but of the same gauge used on the Austro-German railways. This meant that if the Russians had to transport troops to these points, they would need to transfer them to other rolling stock to complete the journey, while the German trains carrying invading troops could use the tracks as "a through line". Rolling stock was insufficient even for the existing lines, nor was this compensated for in other ways: there were only 679 motor vehicles in the entire army, plus 475 civilian vehicles which the army had the right to requisition.

Unfortunately the western Allies were so hypnotised by the astronomical numbers of Russia's forces that they virtually dismissed the overwhelming evidence that tsarist Russia in 1914 was incapable of maintaining even a fraction of her vast manpower resources as a field army under conditions of modern war.

The overall equipment situation represented the outcome of efforts by the Russian War Ministry to make good the deficiencies of the Russo-Japanese War. They calculated average figures for the various requirements of the forces in a war of unspecified but comparatively short duration, but once these figures had been achieved the factories were closed down and their workers dismissed. No plans were made for their recall in an emergency, nor was there any provision to keep equipment in step with increases in army manpower.

The Russian army had only 4,652,000 rifles although, with the calling-up of the 1914 class, the army would number 7,480,000. Allowing for fresh drafts, wear and tear and battle losses, the estimated rifle requirement was for 11 million, leaving an actual deficit of over 6 million. Those that were being issued were the cumbersome Mosin-Nagant 7.62 cm. rifles manufactured to a 1891 pattern and weighing nearly 10 lb. Therefore the size of the army was to all practical intents no more than a numerical concept.

Other equipment was equally scarce. Field guns totalled 48 per division, half the proportion in the German army and, compared with Germany's 381 batteries of heavy guns, the Russians had only 60. Supplies of shells had only reached 800 per gun by the beginning of the war, as against a target figure of 1500; whereas other belligerent armies which possessed 2–3000 were all to find themselves under-provided to some degree. The output of cartridges was about 50 per cent of the known requirement.

There were 263 aircraft, mostly French, and an output of only five aero-engines a week from the "Gnom" factory in Moscow. The embryo Russian aviation industry had been almost entirely devoted to the development of the world's largest aircraft, the four-engined "Ilia Murometa" type designed by Sikorski. Built to carry twelve passengers or a large bomb-load, insuperable technical difficulties prevented it from ever taking the air against the enemy. A few additional dirigibles combined to make up an air force which one army commander described as "beneath criticism" but equally beneath – or perhaps above – criticism was its commander, Grand-Duke Alexander Mikhailovich, brother of the tsar. Rodzianko discovered that orders for aircraft supposedly placed with France during the war had never left the grand-duke's desk, and one Minister of War had been forced to ban discussion of the air force at meetings on the grounds that criticism reflected badly on the royal house.

To combat enemy air activity there was only one anti-aircraft battery. This was kept at Tsarskoe Selo (literally: Tsar's Village), fifteen miles south of Petrograd, where the tsar and his family were living for safety, and its only break from guarding the royal household was on the rare occasions when its commander brought it to the front in order to give it a little practice.

Following an initial burst of zeal, the reformation of the Russian forces had also proceeded slowly in other spheres, and by 1914 had virtually ceased despite the retirement of some 341 generals and 400 colonels as inefficient. Some reforms described by contemporary writers on the "New Russian Army", such as the replacement of the old feudal structure by a system enabling any promising soldier to earn the imperial commission, came from an earlier reformer in the 1870s, Dmitri Alexeievich Miliutin.[3]

Regarded by his superiors as "a natural warrior", the Russian recruit was not thought to need much formal training. Apart from basic weaponry instruction, a modicum of drill and the inculcation of sufficient discipline to enable him to participate in the "crowd rushes" and bayonet charges which were the principal feature of all attacks, further training was considered neither necessary nor – in view of the average soldier's illiteracy – practicable.[4] The training camp was merely a brief pause on the journey from depot to front, where discipline was harsh and brutal, enforced by kicks, blows, floggings and hangings.[5]

To foreign observers the soldier's unschooled rustic simplicity made him appear as "just a great, big-hearted child," "cheery" and "wonderfully patient," but they recalled that only fifty-three years earlier he had been a serf and this subjection had so leeched from his nature every vestige of personal initiative that he was more dependent on leadership than any other European soldier. Yet, there was little to indicate that such leadership was available. Despite considerable financial inducements, there was such a scarcity of NCOs that once the effect of casualties began to be experienced, regiments had to establish their own training schools behind the lines where crash courses for putative "unterofitsers" and "feldfebels" could be organised. There was an average of two NCOs per company in the Russian army compared with six in the French army and twelve in the German.

Officer-recruits for the cavalry and guard regiments were never lacking, but at the outbreak of war artillery and line-infantry were 3,000 below par. Training still followed the Prussian lines of the 1870s, and officer-cadets were called "junkers". In the great "officer academies" with whitewashed barrack-rooms, pictures of the tsar, lamplit ikons and bare floorboards, they learned to march and countermarch or to slash through cones of unbaked clay with sabres while riding at a gallop, and attended lectures on history and tactics. No scientific instruction or training in the use of firepower was given. In spite of attempts to make the army a "carrière ouverte aux talents,"[6] officers as a whole were apathetic, lazy and unenterprising.[7] towards their profession. They cared little for the well-being of their troops or the enforcement of discipline, substituting for studiousness and serious devotion to duty a wild bravado which caused them to scorn all regard for personal safety in battle. Their reckless behaviour continued despite appeals from everyone in authority up to the tsar, in consequence of which they were killed in droves, further reducing their numbers.

Lethargy and professional apathy were to be found at all levels of command, though the more extreme form this took in higher ranks was one of the factors which automatically restrained efforts to reform the army. Even by current European standards, Russian commanders were old. Some, like General Wenzel von Plehve who commanded the Fifth Army until 1916, were not so much past retiring age as actually dying. In fact, he handed over his command only weeks before his death. The senility and total lack of imagination of Russian senior officers was accompanied by hidebound bureaucracy, the endemic disease of totalitarianism.

Moreover, in their efforts to maintain autocracy's rule, the secret police adopted a policy of dividing any force which might conceivably constitute an opposition to the system; this effectively discouraged any measures which could have helped to build an esprit de corps.

There was little attempt to achieve continuity by re-forming regiments which had been broken in combat and survivors were simply dispersed among other units. There was, therefore, no fostering of the competitive spirit which, for good or ill, increased effectiveness in western armies.

Yet another factor which stifled all efforts to modernise and adequately equip the Russian army was the corruption and venality running like a poison through every level of official life. The ease with which the plans of the Russian General Staff could be bought was a standing joke among the Germans, who consequently knew more about the Russian army than did its allies.[8] One notorious incident concerned a Colonel Miassoiedev, chief of the railway police on the frontier with East Prussia, who held no less than five German decorations. Publicly accused of being in German pay by Guchkov, a member of the Duma, with whom he fought a duel, he was ultimately arrested and charged with espionage by the Russian authorities in 1912. However, such was the influence brought to bear on his behalf by War Minister General Sukhomlinov, his protector and patron, that he was not only acquitted but given a new and more responsible assignment organising the secret surveillance of army commanders. Miassoiedev was alleged to have been the lover of the General's wife, and was not the first spy to find his way into the War Minister's domestic circle. In 1906, at the age of fifty-eight, Sukhomlinov had pursued and won, after a titillating divorce case, the twenty-three-year-old wife of a provincial governor. Among those who provided evidence for him was an Austrian named Altschiller, later discovered to have been Austria's principal agent in Russia.

Sukhomlinov exhibited total irresponsibility and frivolity of mind while in office. In November 1912, for example, during the Russo-Austrian crisis over Serbia, he appeared at the Council of Ministers with a plan for partial mobilisation of the armies.[9] This proposal (to activate only those forces on the Austrian frontier) was overruled by the council, but amazed ministers who questioned his declared intention to leave for a holiday on the Riviera after putting forward plans which could entail war, were asked "Why not? A mobilisation doesn't have to be conducted by the Minister of War in person."

While freely embezzling public funds he passed on all his own work to subordinates, and on meeting the Duma's Armed Services Commission he displayed to the assembled civilian deputies an ignorance of current military matters far greater than their own. Russia's allies found it impossible to obtain from him any reliable information on which to base their plans for assistance.

Nonetheless, this was the man of whom the tsar said to Poincaré (who distrusted him on sight): "His looks are not in his favour, but he is an excellent minister and I trust him entirely." Had any gossip about the War Minister's conduct chanced to reach the palace, it would no doubt have been dismissed by the Autocrat of All the Russias as disdainfully as the stories about another court favourite, Rasputin, and Sukhomlinov's uncompromisingly right-wing conservatism, combined with his refusal to co-operate with the Duma — so hated by the tsar and tsarina — was undoubtedly another point in his favour. His conservatism extended even to military matters. He maintained that warfare had not changed since 1877 and boasted that he had not read a military manual for twenty-five years. His notions on the use of firepower were summed up by his habit of quoting the aphorism of the eighteenth century Russian military idol, Aleksander Suvorov: "The bullet is a fool; the bayonet is a hero". Thus the Russian infantryman kept his long, quadrangular bayonet permanently fixed while on the front, leaving his scabbard behind him. A more far-reaching consequence of his beliefs, however, was the grudging provision of artillery and ammunition; although 200 million gold roubles of the funds allocated for this purpose remained unspent.[10]

The tsar had only been restrained from leading the armies personally by pressing arguments that the initial lengthy retreats might tarnish the image of autocracy. Sukhomlinov, one of the most ardent advocates of this course, notwithstanding a scandalous reputation, a known preference for the Germans and an idiosyncratic military philosophy, fully expected to become commander-in-chief. However, the fifty-eight year old Grand-Duke Nicholas Nicholaievich was appointed in his stead. A very tall thin-faced man "quite absorbed in his profession, who knew theory and practice," hot-tempered and given to forthright and sometimes profane turns of speech, he was regarded by the troops as the "noble champion of truth and the ruthless enemy of falsehood," "severe and just to all" and, in particular, alive to the needs of the rank and file. His deep suspicion of the Germans endeared him to the French, and his energetic, quick-moving and vigorous characteristics were combined with the more typically Russian ones of emotionalism and piety.

His appointment was a triple blow for Sukhomlinov. Not only had he been superseded in a post which according to recent precedent should have been his as Minister of War,[11] but the man chosen was a sworn personal enemy whose conscientious devotion to duty was in sharp contrast to the minister's culpably irresponsible attitude. Furthermore, until then he had reason to think that Nicholas Nicholaievich no longer constituted a threat to his career, since in 1907, following criticism in the Duma, the grand-duke had resigned active command and left Sukhomlinov a clear field. The latter had been quick to exploit the tsarina's known hatred of her uncle-by-marriage.

The grand-duke's wife was the Princess Anastasia, daughter of the king of Montenegro, a pocket state which abutted Albania along the Adriatic coast, and had become a monarchy only in 1910. To marry him she had to divorce her first husband, the

Duke of Leuchtenberg. Anastasia and her sister, Princess Militsa had first introduced Rasputin into the imperial household, but later — realising he was a charlatan, drunkard and lecher — they had tried to undeceive the tsarina only to have their warnings cursorily dismissed. From then on, the "Montenegrin nightingales" (as they were nicknamed) and the grand-duke were barely tolerated as enemies of the "Friend".

There was, however, a still greater reason for the tsarina's loathing. After the events of Bloody Sunday, Witte, as chairman of the Council of Ministers, had presented the tsar with an ultimatum: either he must grant a constitution and national assembly, or Russia must be ruled through a military dictatorship. The tsar had, not unexpectedly, opted for the second course and selected his uncle for the post of strong man. The grand-duke not only promptly and unequivocally rejected the appointment but urged his sovereign to accept the constitution instead, which in these circumstances he was reluctantly compelled to do. The tsarina never forgave him and, when the troops of the St Petersburg garrison were due to leave for the front on 14 August under the grand-duke's command, she dissuaded her husband from going to Warsaw Station to take leave of them; this act was characteristic of the creature who was to be the chief instrument of Russia's ruin.

Accompanying the Russian generalissimo on his journey to forward headquarters at Baranovichi, midway between the southern and northern extremities of the western front, were his two principal aides: Generals Yanushkevich and Yuri Danilov, respectively chief of staff and quartermaster general. The grand-duke would have preferred Alexeiev and Polivanov, both "Young Turks," and the former regarded as the best strategist in the army, but the tsar had insisted on these two nominees of the War Minister, thus putting the Russian commander-in-chief under an immediate handicap.

Yanushkevich, described by Sukhomlinov as "still a child", had received his early military training in Germany, and his attainment of high office at the age of forty-eight was due to influence rather than ability. Attracting the tsar's attention when a captain of the palace guard, he had no field experience whatsoever and had never commanded anything larger than a company. Yet he rose from height to height and in 1913 was appointed commandant of the Nicholas Academy, the Russian staff college. Although in this position for barely a year, he nevertheless dismissed five of the academy's best professors for teaching the heresy of firepower in opposition to the creed of the bayonet as maintained by his patron Sukhomlinov.

Danilov, nicknamed "the Black" partly to distinguish him from other Danilovs and partly because of his dour personality, was described by Knox as "a hard worker with a good brain," though General Brusilov found him "narrow and stubborn." He had served on the Supreme Directorate of the General Staff and had studied the strategy of the western frontier, but although accused of "hidebound" strategy, the intense dislike felt for him by army and corps commanders may have stemmed from his strict and un-Russian insistence on discipline, exacting eye for detail and uncompromising personality.

On receiving the imperial commission, the grand-duke was said by a colleague to have wept "because he did not know how to approach his duties", and one reason for this could well have been the defensive problem confronting his unprepared forces. Drawn up at the Congress of Vienna, exactly a hundred years earlier, the western frontier might have been designed to test Russian defensive skill to the uttermost by giving every advantage to its opponents. About 1,500 miles in length, its longest section was on the vast salient formed by the boundaries of Russian-Poland bordered by enemy territory on three sides. Silesia was to the west, the Austrian Polish province of Galicia to the south and East Prussia to the north. Russian armies within the Polish salient therefore had two flanks to protect and were open to a combined Austrian and German attack which could envelop them by slicing through their rear and lines of communication.

Defence devolved upon two groups of armies called "Fronts" by the Russians: the North West front facing East Prussia and comprising the First and Second Armies, and the South West, facing Silesia and Austria and made up of the Fourth, Fifth, Third and Eighth Armies. The number of armies was increased as mobilisation gathered momentum and early in 1915 the centre was taken over by a third army group: the West Front, to which the First and Second Armies from the North West, the Third and Fourth Armies from the South West and the additional Tenth Army were transferred.

The Russian General Staff had drawn up two plans for overall defence: Plan "A" was to be employed if Austria attacked, when the armies of the South West Front would take the field against her. Plan "G" was to be adopted if the Germans concentrated for an attack. The defensive forces of the North West Front could then fall back through the Polish salient to the line of fortresses on either side of Brest Litovsk. A second line of fortresses further west were considered so out of date as to be virtually useless against modern artillery attack, thanks to Sukhomlinov's modifications on modernisation plans.

Ultimately, it was thought, the armies of the North West Front could resort to a "Kutuzov" strategy like that of 1812, operating a scorched earth policy as they retreated into the depth of the country, hoping to stretch enemy lines of communication to the point where he could be caught off balance and defeated.

The effect of Plan "G" was therefore defensive rather than offensive in nature, and rested on the correct supposition that in a war with France the Germans would want to remain on the defensive in the east. Both plans, drawn up in 1910, were said to represent the whole gamut of Russian strategic thinking throughout the war. Events moved too speedily for other plans to be formulated, let alone acted upon, and in fact prevented the full development of either "A" or "G".

Chapter 4

Movements On the Battlefield

In the mind of the Russian public there was only one clear reason for going to war: to frustrate the Austrian attempt to dragoon the southern Slavs of Serbia. Austria was a traditional enemy and, apart from any other considerations, shared with Russia a reciprocal envy towards those parts of Poland falling within one another's hegemony.

Galicia, which abutted on Russia, was the largest and most easterly province of the Austro-Hungarian Empire, covering some 30,000 square miles and with a population of 8 million. The capital, Lemberg (Lvov), a splendid city with its own university and music conservatoire, contrasted with the province as a whole which Octavian Tăslăuanu, who served there as an Austrian officer, described as one of the "most poverty-stricken regions in the world". In the countryside, home, barn and stables coexisted under one roof, with a hole in the ceiling for the chimney. The basic diet was milk and potatoes, supplemented on holidays and feast-days by unappetising loaves of blackish bread made from a little corn grown and ground by the peasants.

Russian Poland, although suffering from the defensive disadvantage of being a salient, was larger in population and area: 14 million inhabitants and 40,000 square miles, with the capital in Warsaw. In some respects the condition of the rural populations was more advanced than in Galicia, with a great deal of industry, including highly developed textile manufacturing, centring on the second city, Lodz.

Austrians and Russians alike were aware of active Home Rule movements within their dominions, also of the desire for reunification in a country partitioned among foreign occupiers since 1772 and now shared between Russia, Germany and Austria. Both sought to convert these nationalist sentiments into weapons.

On the whole, the Poles had fared better under the Austrians than under their German or Russian masters. Austrians and Poles were united in common membership of the Catholic Church and the Hapsburg empire retained sufficient feudalism for the Polish aristocracy to find a place for themselves once they were prepared to accord it their allegiance. The Polish provinces within the Dual Monarchy therefore possessed some measure of independence.

The tsarist occupier, on the other hand, had set about the systematic obliteration of the Polish national identity. The country was renamed "the Vistula Provinces"; efforts were made through the schools to make Russian the "official" language; the Catholic Church and Polish aristocracy were singled out for special hostility; and a combination of civil and military rule employed to maintain passivity.

In these circumstances, the Austrians expected the Poles to greet them as liberators, an illusion shared by the Germans even through their occupation — particularly since the accession of Wilhelm II, an acknowledged Slavophobe[1] — had been as oppressive as that of the Russians. The partitioning of their country and the years of ineffectual struggle certainly led to the splintering of the various Polish Home Rule and reunification movements. On the whole, however, Polish sympathies were with France and Britain, which led them to support their Russian ally in the hope that after the war the two western countries would be influential in helping Poland to get her freedom.

The Russians, however, were too alarmed at the prospect of dealing with rebellious populations in the areas where vital battles might be fought to reverse their previous policies, despite the grand-duke's advocacy of Polish autonomy. In a proclamation to the people, published in the "Warsaw Gazette" on 16 August, he declared "A century and a half ago, Poland's body was torn to shreds, but her soul lives on . . . May the Polish people find their unity under the sceptre of the Tsar! Under this sceptre Poland will be born anew, perfectly free as to her faith, her language and her internal administration . . ."

As a good republican, Poincaré was quick to spot the expression "under the sceptre of the Tsar" and see in it the dark hand of Russian annexations which might "prejudice the conditions for peace". He was also suspicious of the fact that the proclamation had come from the grand-duke rather than the tsar, and that there was no intimation from Petrograd of its acceptability there. There was some foundation for his disquiet. Although the proclamation had been enthusiastically received in Poland, a delegation of Poles residing in Paris (including Marie Curie) who asked Isvolsky, the ambassador, whether it had the tsar's support, were given an "evasive and ambiguous answer". Their subsequent plea to the French government for public ratification of the grand-duke's pledges brought no response.

The tsar's lack of authority had caused the whole "Polish question" to be thrown into the melting pot and he was, in any case, reluctant to commit himself publicly when uncertain whether he would still be in favour of autonomy in a year's time. Moreover, the tsarina, prime minister Goremykin and Minister of the Interior Maklakov were among those vehemently opposed to Polish autonomy even under the imperial sceptre and who saw that the proclamation, having been issued under the grand-duke's name, provided an escape clause.

The immediate response of the Polish people, however, was to declare for Russia, and the troops were welcomed as "little brothers" in both Russian and Austrian Poland. Although some of Pilsudski's Sokoly (Falcon) legions were formed to fight under the Austro-German banner, the Galician Poles as a whole not only offered passive resistance to the Austrians, but provided the Russian commanders with a first-class intelligence service. Moreover, there were no protests when, on 9 September, it was announced that any members of the Sokoly legions who fell into Russian hands would be treated as traitors and executed.

The Russians had been forced to move quickly on the Polish question because they anticipated an early and massive Austrian invasion, which the public would expect to be halted and converted into a victory. Plan "A" was therefore put into action at the outbreak of hostilities and there were thus no fewer than four Russian armies in this sector as distinct from two facing the Germans. To anticipate the expected attack, the commander of the South West Front, General Nicholas Ivanov, had drawn his forces up in a reverse-chevron shaped formation covering the corner of the Galician border. The Fourth Army, under Evert, and the Fifth under Plehve, were mustered before Lublin and faced south; the Third under Ruszki, and the Eighth under Brusilov, faced west. His own plan of attack was for Brusilov and Ruszki to keep the Austrians occupied along the river Weszyca; the other two Russian armies would then sweep down behind the defenders, enveloping their armies, and rapidly defeating the Austrians so decisively that they would perhaps be forced to make peace.

This plan came very near to realisation.

The stumbling block was the existence of the obligations entailed by Russia's alliance with France, as Rennenkampf's victory at Gumbinnen served to demonstrate.

French aid had covered the sphere of moral aid to them in addition to technical and financial help. Tired of being on the defensive against Germany for over forty years, the French army had seized avidly on the gospel of General Foch (director of the École Supérieure de la Guerre) who preached the importance of will as a fundamental prerequisite of victory. Colonel Grand-maison (director of the Bureau of Military Operations) declared its practical expressions to be "l'offensive à outrance" — offensive to the uttermost — beside which firepower, numerical superiority, mobility, tractics and strategy were insignificant. The Prussian teachers who insisted on such dully solid military virtues as organisation and planning, derived from Clausewitz and the elder Moltke, aroused the antipathy of their Russian pupils, but in the French military credo the latter found something corresponding with their own tastes, history and contemporary situation.

The French, however, required some evidence of Russian conversion. Under the terms of the military convention of 1893, while France put an army of 1,300,000 men in the field against Germany as soon as possible after mobilisation, the Russians' slower mobilisation was to muster 7–800,000 men. In 1911, a time limit laid down that the 800,000 Russians were to take the field on the fifteenth day of mobilisation. Thus, France sought to ensure that her ally marched against the enemy without delay.

Although aware that the undertakings could not be realised, the Russians had accepted this at the time as the price of continuous French technical assistance, trusting that there would in fact be no war. That they had no intention of fulfilling their obligations is demonstrated by the arguments employed to dissuade the tsar from taking personal command of the armies, and Sazonov, then Russian Foreign Minister, confirms in his memoirs that an offensive against the Germans on M-15 formed no part of the Russian

General Staff's plans.

Indeed, the practical difficulties involved appeared insurmountable, one of the main problems being the time needed for Russia to establish herself on a war footing. In a land with few railways or even good roads, a man called to colours had to travel an average distance of 700 miles from home to depot compared with 130–200 miles in Germany.

Pre-war estimates, generally considered improbably optimistic, put the time needed for concentration of the armies at three months, during which time the standing forces would be incapable of effective offensive action.

In the last days of peace, the tsar's desire to appear conciliatory to Germany had further aggravated this situation, and on 29 July (the day after the Austrians began to bombard the Serbian capital of Belgrade) the most he was prepared to grant in response to his generals' pleas for the ukase of mobilisation was – as in 1912 – the partial step of mobilising the forces on the Austrian border. Despite protests from his generals about the effects on the entire mobilisation time-table, it was not until twenty-four hours later that he was persuaded to allow a general mustering of reserves.

An additional complication was the fact that the call-up coincided with the gathering in of the harvest, needed not only to feed the Russian people, but to earn essential foreign currency by way of exports. Only a month earlier, during his visit to St Petersburg, Poincaré had been told by Sazonov that if "the worst came to the worst", it would be difficult for Russia to combine mobilisation and harvesting. The Russians did all they could to hasten the process and subsequently shared the general astonishment at their own achievements in respect of both harvesting and mobilisation. Progress was the more striking in view of the fact that there were no exemptions for any particular groups in the community, and farm and industrial labour was called up with equal impunity.

Unlike the Russians, the French took their agreement seriously. It had always been France's contention that she would be the first victim of a German attack, this being a matter of sheer military expediency quite apart from the declarations of intent made by Germany and the Kaiser. As events in the Serbian crisis moved from the diplomatic to the military sphere this assumption proved justified. An attack upon Germany from eastern France had always formed an essential part of Plan Seventeen — drawn up before the war to counter a possible German sweep into France by way of Belgium — which proposed that the German right and centre be allowed to move unimpeded, while the French and, it was hoped, their British allies would hurl themselves on the German left wing. According to peacetime calculations this was where the enemy line should be weakest and the shortest route to Germany would be opened. However, this move could only be successful if the Germans were sufficiently engaged on the eastern front to prevent their utilising internal rail connections to reinforce their left.

As early as 1 August Count Ignatiev, head of the Russian military mission in France, telegraphed that the French Ministry of War was "seriously suggesting that Russia invade Germany and advance on Berlin in the direction of Warsaw". "Considering the respective strength of the forces that would meet," comments the Russian General Golovin, "such a request was equivalent to asking Russia to commit suicide, in the full sense of the word; and repeated several times by the French Government it was a request that put the Russian High Command in a very difficult position."

Four days later Paléologue paid a personal call on the tsar and begged him to order that his troops speedily take the field against Germany. If they did not, "the French army would have to face the formidable onslaught of twenty-five German corps" and there was a danger it would be crushed. The tsar promised that, the moment mobilisation was completed, an advance would be ordered.

Paléologue then drove out of the city to the Znamenka Palace on the Gulf of Finland where Grand-Duke Nicholas still had his headquarters. When Paléologue broached the subject of an offensive against Germany, the grand-duke explained his plans for advances by the armies of the North West Front against East Prussia, and those of the South West Front against Austria. At the same time there was to be a mass concentration in the Polish salient to "bear down on Berlin as soon as the armies succeeded in 'holding up' and 'fixing' the enemy."

The French ambassador, knowing that by this he meant Austria, asked when the advance against Germany was to begin.

"Perhaps I shan't wait even until the concentration of all my corps is complete," the Russian generalissimo, carried away as it seems by the emotions of the moment, told him. "As soon as I feel myself strong enough I shall attack. It will probably be 14 August."

He proved as good as his word and orders sent from the General Staff to North West Front the following day said it was essential to prepare for an "energetic offensive against Germany at the earliest possible moment, in order to ease the situation of the French . . .", adding, however: "But of course only when sufficient strength has been made available."

The Russians proved correct in their expectation of an early Austrian invasion of Poland.

The nominal commander-in-chief of the Austrian armies was the jovial, paunchy Archduke Frederick, but he had as his chief-of-staff — and therefore executive commander — Franz Conrad von Hötzendorff. Conrad, now sixty-two, was a slight figure whose severely military demeanour was somewhat lessened by a facial tic. Protégé of the assassinated Archduke Franz Ferdinand, his patron's death led him to urge mobilisation against Serbia even when it became increasingly obvious that this would impel Russia into taking similar steps. He believed Serbia to be militarily insignificant, and felt no fear of Russia so long as Austria had Germany as an ally and, in the event of war, as comrade-in-arms. To this, he assured himself, Germany had pledged herself.

His allies, however, saw matters somewhat differently. In 1909 the German commander-in-chief had acquiesced to a proposal made by Conrad for a combined strike from East Prussia and Galicia upon the flanks of the Polish salient. Although German intentions in the east had since altered, and they now had in mind a purely defensive war, they had not only failed to apprise Conrad of this but even encouraged his aggressive intentions.

In July 1914, the German commander-in-chief, Helmuth von Moltke and Conrad had met at Carlsbad, where the former annually took the waters. Moltke pointed out that Germany proposed to subdue France before turning elsewhere, and when Conrad not unreasonably asked how long this was expected to take, he answered: "We hope in six weeks from the start of operations to have dealt with France, and then to attack in the east with overwhelming force."

Conrad returned to his own headquarters considering how best to occupy himself during this crucial period, his mind working on the lines of an all-out offensive after having crossed the Danube. He regarded himself, with some justification, as a considerable strategist, and offensive action would give him the best opportunity to display his virtuosity. Furthermore, it would be highly satisfying to greet the Germans, when they arrived, with the news that victory was won.

Unfortunately, as Sir Basil Liddell Hart has pointed out, the weapon which fate had put into his hands to achieve this desirable end was wholly unfitted for the task. This was largely due to the character of the Austro-Hungarian empire itself. Fewer than half of its 50 million inhabitants were Austrian or Hungarian, while the forty-nine divisions of the army (totalling 4,320,000 men) were made up of no fewer than ten nationalities; more than half owed only a grudging allegiance to the Dual Monarchy, while the numerous Slavs regarded the Russians as their ethnic kin.

The Austrians were even worse off for equipment than the Russians, whose immensely larger country had at least a basic national unity and whose equipment, although deficient in quantity, was less obsolete. Austria's few field guns were of short range; two-thirds of the rifles were twenty-five years old and so few in number that before a month had passed troops in the Carpathian passes had to be issued with single-loaders. There was little transport and farm-carts often had to be pressed into service.

However, none of this deterred Conrad. He was the author of the army's infantry manuals and felt that this alone should ensure success. He anticipated a Russian blow from the north, and hoped to disrupt it by moving in that direction himself, taking advantage of Russia's notoriously slow mobilisation. The speedier assembly of his own forces had begun on 25 July, and he expected to be on equal terms with the Russians by 18 August; by 30 August, however, they would outnumber him by five to four.

Conrad assembled two of his best armies along the northern border of Galicia in the area of the Forest of Tanev and the River San — the First under Dankl on the left, with the Fourth under Auffenberg next to it. These two armies were to advance simultaneously northward on Lublin. The subsequent task of guarding the right flank of the Fourth fell to the Third Army, facing east, which was drawn up in front of and guarding Lemberg, the

Galician capital. As the Fourth advanced, the line of the Third Army would thus become stretched and Conrad proposed using the Second Army, which he withdrew from the Serbian front, to reinforce it. In any case, he was convinced that the Russians would attack from the north that he felt no qualms for his eastern frontier. Unknown to their commanders, the opposing armies were actually facing one another, and the Russians, who had concentrated against Austria prior to general mobilisation, actually had four armies to the Austrian three and were assembling their forces far more speedily than anticipated.

Although the grand-duke had explained the political and military considerations compelling him to deal with the threat to his own left flank, and the Austrians were planning an invasion which could disastrously affect Russian morale, the French remained obdurately opposed to the present Russian concentration of forces, deploring any dilution of effort against the main enemy, Germany. They were harried by the fixation that an easy victory against Austria might cause Russia to lose interest in the more formidable enemy, and were oblivious to the effect that the defeat of Austria would have on the security of Germany's southern frontiers.

The grand-duke, refusing to be shaken from his conviction that Austria must first be neutralised, nevertheless tried to placate his ally by hastening preparations for the South West Front's campaign, with the result that units were sent forward without adequate supplies of arms and ammunition, and before the call-up of infantry reserves had been completed.

Even so, each day increased the exigence of French appeals. Pre-war estimates of the strength of the German forces that would come through Belgium had discounted the possible use of reserves in an offensive rôle because they themselves were convinced that "l'offensive à outrance" demanded the cream of active troops at the peak of training. The Germans had no such inhibitions; and, as in 1870 when their armies far exceeded French estimates, they were bringing up double the "twenty-five corps" whose "formidable onslaught" Paléologue had pictured to the tsar in such horrifying terms.

On 14 August the offensive against the heart of Germany was

launched through Lorraine, to be met by a full-strength defence. The German commander-in-chief, Moltke, had departed from the original Schlieffen Plan to the extent of doubling his forces there, and once the French had left the safety of their own frontier fortifications they were decimated by the Germans securely entrenched behind theirs. They made some gains through sheer élan, but by 24 August their advance had been held. The battle to liberate the French provinces, annexed in 1870, turned into defeat, each day increasing the suspicion that the earlier débâcle was about to be repeated with its attendant horrors of annexation, indemnities and possibly civil war. This time, however, France was not without allies. On 9 August, Poincaré wrote in his diary: "It is surely time for Russia to get to work to relieve the pressure on Belgium and ourselves."

The French General Staff openly blamed the Russians for failing to attack Germany in force and thereby being responsible for the defeat in Alsace-Lorraine. This was a mere excuse for, as the war was to demonstrate, attempts to throw troops onto a well-entrenched enemy equipped with modern weapons caused heavy losses and were doomed to failure. Nevertheless, this defeat critically affected the French situation and the French commander-in-chief, General Joffre, was urging the grand-duke to "move forward as quickly as he possibly can". In Russia itself, Paléologue and General le Marquis de Laguiche, the French liaison chief, were adding to these appeals.

At Baranovichi, the Russian headquarters was exactly midway between the two extremities of the front. This might seem to be an ideal location and would have been had the front not been so long and had communications been less utterly primitive. As it was the field-telephone system was many times worse than the enemy's, itself notorious. Often letters sent by special messenger was the most reliable way of conveying orders.

The headquarters was no more than a collection of rail coaches drawn up fanwise and hurriedly converted into offices, messes and sleeping accommodation. It had been set so deeply in pinewoods outside the town that only the occasional Cossack sentry in fur hat and with long rifle betrayed the presence of a military concentration.

The grand-duke's room was scattered with bearskin and Eastern rugs and in his bedroom the walls were covered with ikons, about a hundred on Paléologue's computation; otherwise there was no luxury and in fact little comfort there. In summer the sun beat down on the carriage roofs and in winter they were icily cold – though the Russian stove in the grand-duke's personal office so overheated it, according to the tsar, that he could not "endure it above an hour". To add to his discomfort, the grand-duke's height caused him constantly to hit his head on door lintels and other projections, so that they all bore, pinned to them, scraps of papers as warnings to duck. Later the carriages were roofed over and a little wooden chapel was added, but these were the sole concessions.

In one corner was a fenced off sandpit in which areas of the front were modelled and where the ancient and solemn generals of the Russian army came to have strategy explained to them by the grand-duke himself or by one of his entourage, using a walking stick.

To this place he gave, when he arrived there on 14 August, the name "Stavka", after the camp of a Russian warrior-chieftain. There was a strange, if unconscious appropriateness about the choice of name. Not only did it possess exactly that makeshift character, but it was also an anachronism, as if indeed some Genghis Khan or Tamurlaine had marched into the 20th Century and were now gathering in cavalry and bowmen, oblivious of the modernity and overwhelming technical superiority of the enemy on whom he proposed to loose them.

By hindsight it is easy to be shocked that none warned them, gave them the least intimation from which they could have drawn new conclusions or pulled back before it was too late. The truth was they would have listened to no such warnings. They would have rejected them as merely insulting to the bravery and skill of the warriors and to national pride.

It was not that in science Russia was necessarily behind other countries. They had made a formidable contribution to the world's repository of knowledge. And when it came to the actual struggle they were not lacking in men of ingenuity, though they did not have a developed industry to apply their ideas. They were, for example, among the first to realise that the lock of trench warfare could be broken only by some mechanical contrivance and devised a species of tank, named after the tsar, to do it, though it was never used. It was rather that everyone, including the scientists themselves, shared in the belief that such enormous hosts, so willing to die, must be invincible. It was all summed up in one of their innumerable proverbs: when it came to war, they said, "Mother Russia has sons enough". They could, in these circumstances, conceive of no weapon which could not simply be overrun. Nor could they think of those masses being pinned down helpless in trenches.

Given all this, Stavka at Baranovichi was all that was required in the way of a headquarters.

Upon his arrival, the grand-duke immediately telegraphed Joffre that "with full confidence in victory he would march against the enemy with the flag of the French republic flying next to his own". That day he also issued orders for "the quickest possible advance against Germany", dropping the proviso that this was not to be attempted "until sufficient strength was available". This became what David Lloyd-George has called "little more than a chivalrous improvisation to save France from the blunders of her generals". No attempt was made to modify Plan "A" because of the new orders, and the armies were once more committed to battle without adequate preparation before the call-up of reserves was completed.

And all this into an area — East Prussia — in which, because of inadequate intelligence, they had no reliable idea of what lay ahead.

Chapter 5

The Chivalrous Improvisation

Not temperamentally cautious, Conrad could nevertheless see the
risk inherent in committing his limited military resources before
first ascertaining that the enemy was disposed as he imagined.
Since Austrian intelligence (like Russian) was negligible, and there
were only forty-two aircraft in his entire forces — of which still
fewer were serviceable — the only way to investigate enemy
activity was by reconnoîtring with the cavalry; with 100,000
horsemen, this was the one section of his army with which he was
copiously provided.

In 1914 the drab uniforms later to be adopted had not yet been
introduced. The Russians and Germans were in grey, the British in
khaki, but the French cavalry still wore shining cuirass and helmet,
and their infantry marched in "pantalons rouges," kepi and blue
overcoat. When the Austrian cavalry sallied out on 15 August
uniformed in red and blue, this brilliance only made them easier
targets for the enemy who merged into the landscape. Although
the reconnaissance operation involved penetrating as much as 100
miles into enemy territory along a 250 mile front, little information was garnered by the weary survivors who struggled back.
Nevertheless, Conrad interpreted the limited intelligence as supporting his own thesis that the Russians would strike from the
north, and declared that there was "no sign of any Russian
movement from the east against his right flank".

On this basis he ordered his offensive to proceed.

The vast distances involved, and the lack of adequate internal
communications rendered the commanders on both sides uncertain of the disposition of their own forces, let alone those of the
enemy. The ensuing battle therefore became a quadrille of increasing complexity, as the armies weaved in different directions.

The Austrian First and Fourth Armies began advancing northward on 20 August; Krasnik and Komarov lay ahead, and beyond
them Lublin their first objective. After three days' march the First

accidentally encountered the Russian Fourth Army, drawn up before Krasnik, which had been sent forward before mobilisation was complete despite protests from Ivanov, the South West Front commander. Outnumbered by the Austrians under their commander, Dankl, the Russian Fourth was driven back.

The Russian negotiator who signed the undertaking to mount an offensive by M-15 had been the elderly, "generally unpopular" General Zhilinsky, appointed as chief-of-staff in 1910 as the climax to a career which had included undistinguished service in Manchuria and command of a cavalry division in Poland. His reason for acceding to French demands, on his country's behalf, could have been the likelihood of his retirement before the offensive began, since it was explicitly understood that Russia could not consider embarking on a war sooner than 1917.[1] However, a year before the war, he was relieved as chief-of-staff at his own request and appointed commander of the Warsaw Military District. When war broke out, he was given command of the North Western Front and replaced as head of the Warsaw Army by General Alexander Samsonov. It was ironic that he became directly responsible for executing the undertakings with the French into which he had entered so lightly.

East Prussia, as a counterpart to Russian Poland, also formed a natural salient projecting into Russian territory and was flanked along most of its northern boundary by the Baltic. The name was misleading, since its inhabitants were ethnically Slavonic, although the region had been under continuous German rule for 700 years. From the practical viewpoint, its value to the Germans was as an area of rich farmland where Holstein cattle were reared and where cavalry horses were bred on the stud farms. Swamps, marshes and lakeland provided a natural moat, with broad stretches of the Masurian Lakes in the south-eastern corner. Both sides had left this region unreclaimed on account of its defensive value, though the Germans had built roads and railway lines on causeways for faster movement.

The Russians only had half the promised 800,000 men at their disposal for the campaign but this still gave them a two-to-one advantage over the defenders. The 400,000 Russian troops were divided into two armies: Rennenkampf's First and Samsonov's

Second. Rennenkampf, sixty-one years old, and with a reputation as a ladies' man, was a cavalry general with particular skill in handling the brave but unruly Cossacks. The boldness and tactical flair he had shown in various campaigns — during the Chinese Boxer Rising and the Russo-Japanese War — had been sullied in the public mind by his activities after the 1905 Revolution when he had led a punitive expedition from Manchuria to Siberia, enforcing order with executions and mass floggings.

Samsonov, six years younger and bearded like his tsar in the tradition of Russian officers, first took up the sword on behalf of his country at the age of eighteen when they were fighting the Turks in 1877. He became a general at forty-three, commanded Siberian Cossacks in Manchuria and had been governor of Turkestan until his move to Warsaw. A man with a "simple, kindly nature", beloved by his men and idolised by his staff, he suffered from the dual disadvantage of being new both to his command and to the region, his secondment having been gazetted on 12 August when he was in hospital for chronic asthma.

The two attacking armies were to advance on either side of the Masurian Lakes — a plan Samsonov had criticised from the beginning since it entailed separation for a crucial period during which they would be unable to assist one another. Rennenkampf was to start three days before Samsonov, another aspect of the plan disliked by the Second Army commander because his own army, which had much further to travel, would not have time to get into position. The First Army's task was to push the defenders westward toward the River Vistula, where Samsonov was to cut them off and surround them. As a secondary but vital task, Rennenkampf was to seize railway rolling stock and telegraphs to make good the Russians' deficiency in communications.

Activity against East Prussia had in fact begun on the third day of the war, when Rennenkampf sent a detachment of Cossacks on a reconnaissance foray. Pre-war Russian intelligence services, being almost non-existent, had to resort to cavalry scouting as the principal method of gathering information despite its intrinsic disadvantage of giving notice of impending attack.[2] These reconnaissances, however, had one effect which might have influenced the Russians' future conduct of the war had they known Newspapers in Germany, seizing the opportunity to match the Allies' atrocity stories which were already circulating throughout the civilised world, published lurid, highly embellished and supposedly eye-witness accounts of Cossack brutalities. This stimulated such panic throughout Germany, especially in those areas near the Russian border, that thousands of inhabitants began streaming from the frontier zones and indignant deputations sought assurances that, as loyal Germans, they would be adequately protected. German rolling stock and telegraphs were cleared from the border and an early-warning system was organised to inform them of any further Russian incursion.

On 16 August, Poincaré wrote: "The constant pressure on our front compels Joffre to stir up anew his Russian colleagues."

The next day, Rennenkampf's First Army began its advance proper, marching along the dusty summer roads into German territory, under conditions seeming to seal the campaign's doom from the beginning. That this doom was delayed was due to the remarkable behaviour of the Germans themselves. Because of the needs of the Western Front, defence of the region had been left to some 200,000 men, made up into three regular and one Landsturm or militia corps; but in keeping with German practice, they were gathered from the area so as to have a vested interest in its defence. They constituted the German Eighth Army, commanded by the corpulent General Max von Prittwitz und Gaffron, a personal fried of the Kaiser, whose appointment had been made in face of Moltke's opposition.

Although the Germans did not anticipate the Russians being capable of early offensive action, with characteristic thoroughness their General Staff had tried to predict its reactions in such an eventuality. The omniscient Field Marshal Alfred von Schlieffen had forecast that the Russian attack could only emanate from either side of the Masurian Lakes. His defence formula, therefore, was to exploit the natural advantages of the region, while simultaneously preparing to deliver a stroke "with all available strength at the first Russian army which came within reach".

Although the Russians obligingly behaved exactly as von Schlieffen had predicted, a series of disasters shook the German Eighth Army commander's nerve. First, Stallüponen, just over the East Prussian border, fell to Rennenkampf's advance guard; then there was the flight of the Seventeenth Corps from Gumbinnen, followed by the realisation that the intelligence network had failed to warn them of the approach of Samsonov's Second Army which, by 20 August, was pushing von Scholtz's Twentieth Corps before it.

When giving him his command, Moltke had told Prittwitz to keep the Eighth Army intact; to avoid being hemmed into the fortress of Königsberg; and to hold the Vistula, though in dire extremity he could abandon the region east of it. If, therefore, Rennenkampf pursued the broken Seventeenth Corps in its flight from Gumbinnen, the remaining German forces would be split and those on the left forced to take refuge at Königsberg, so precipitating the exact situation Prittwitz had been ordered to avoid. Since, at the same time, Samsonov's advance threatened to sweep over their Vistula positions if these were not speedily consolidated, this seemed to constitute the emergency referred to by the commander-in-chief, and the Eighth Army commander accordingly ordered a rapid withdrawal behind the Vistula.

There was an immediate protest from General Hermann von François, commander of the First Corps which had already engaged Rennenkampf twice, and from two members of Prittwitz's staff, General Grünert and Colonel Max Hoffmann. Hoffmann, in his forties, was Prittwitz's head of operations, and like his commander, projected the image of the rotund good fellow who likes nothing so much as good living. However, appearances were deceptive for he had a cool, decisive brain and was constantly alert for opportunities for self-advancement. Having been a German military observer during the Russo-Japanese War, he not only understood Russian weaknesses but knew of the famous quarrel between Rennenkampf and Samsonov in which they had come to blows. He had returned from the Far East to join the General Staff under von Schlieffen as its expert on Russian affairs. British and French observers in Manchuria insisted that the introduction of trenchlines had been unique to the Russo-Japanese action and that future conflicts would be fought on the traditional lines of Boer and Franco-Prussian Wars. However, Hoffmann made a number of recommendations based upon trench warfare, including the suggestion that the German Army should adequately equip itself with machine-guns; it thus became the first and, in 1914, the only army to do so.

It seemed to Hoffmann that the rôle of the German forces in

the east was likely to be less passive and defensive than had been envisaged when Prittwitz was first entrusted with the command of the Eighth Army. His conclusion was based principally on the failure of German diplomacy to secure Japanese neutrality. Japan's declaration for the Triple Entente had released the Russian armies in the Far East which could logically be launched forthwith against their western enemies.

Not wishing the Eighth Army to fail at the first test, he pointed out to Prittwitz that since Samsonsov was nearer to the Vistula than were the defenders, he would be able to cut off the greater part of their forces if they retreated. They should therefore adopt François' suggestion to drive home a further attack on Rennenkampf, before turning in full strength on the Second Army. Prittwitz would brook no discussion and left Count von Waldersee, his chief-of-staff, to argue the question while he telephoned Moltke at Koblenz. Moltke was horrified to be told by a depressed Prittwitz that, since the Vistula was at low ebb and would not hinder a determined force, he doubted his ability to hold even this line without reinforcement. If the Russians crossed the Vistula they would threaten not only Germany, but also the guardian of their southern flank, Austria. But where could reinforcements be found? To disengage any unit on the Western Front would give the French, Belgian and British armies the advantage. In this appalling predicament he could only hope that Prittwitz was exaggerating the gravity of the situation, and therefore ordered his staff to obtain an exact picture by personal telephone consultations with the Eighth Army corps' commanders.

When Prittwitz returned to the discussion, he found von Waldersee converted to the opposing point of view. The critical question was: could Rennenkampf pursue the Seventeenth Corps? Hoffmann, like François at the front, believed that had this been possible he would have done so, and the passage of time seemed to support this view. Now Prittwitz's own hopes revived and he was persuaded to halt the retreat to the Vistula and order Scholtz's Twentieth Corps to attack Samsonov's left flank next day, with the objective of gaining time and space for manoeuvre.

By the morning of 21 August, a cheerful Prittwitz was told that Samsonov had been brought to a standstill, while the forces on Rennenkampf's front had successfully disengaged and were not being pursued.

Unhappily, the one flaw in his improved situation was that, although his new orders had been conveyed to all those directly concerned with their execution, no one else had telephoned Koblenz to inform Moltke of the changed circumstances. That morning Moltke's staff, who had unsuccessfully tried to contact Prittwitz's subordinates by field telephone, concluded that the crisis, though serious, was not so grave as had been indicated. So far as Moltke was concerned, this was the coup de grâce to the Eighth Army commander's military career, and the search for his successor began: someone able to transform a calamitous situation into a victory. Such a person was found in forty-nine-year-old General Erich Ludendorff, who by seizing command of the broken Fourteenth Brigade during the battle for Liège had re-formed it into a force which, aided by heavy Austrian siege guns, destroyed the Belgian fortress line in days. However, if appointed as a commanding general, Ludendorff's lack of title would prevent him from being on equal terms with his brother commanders and many of his subordinates who possessed the mandatory "von".

With a stroke of genius, Moltke remembered the retired sixty-two-year-old General Paul von Hindenburg und Beneckdorff, who had applied for employment when war seemed imminent. He was a Junker, had served on the General Staff under von Schlieffen, had connections with East Prussia and was by chance Prittwitz's cousin. Since Moltke never saw Hindeburg as anything but a figurehead, he did not bother to offer him the appointment as commander until six hours after Ludendorff had received his as chief-of-staff. By evening, the two were en route for East Prussia in a special train, Ludendorff having been briefed by Moltke and the Kaiser at Koblenz and having issued preliminary orders by telephone, which merely confirmed those already given by Prittwitz, who was unaware of the new arrangement.

On the arrival of the new Eighth Army commander, Prittwitz left without, according to Hoffmann, "a word of complaint at his treatment".

Meanwhile, on the Western Front, the "offensive à outrance" in Alsace had achieved nothing, the German advance continued unchecked through Belgium and sooner or later would swing into France.

The French, aware of the Russian offensive in East Prussia, were concerned that this was not affecting the Germans' western campaign. Under the strain, French approaches to their Russian ally changed from the polite urgings of diplomacy to the tone a commander might use to a recalcitrant subordinate.

On 21 August, Paléologue reported back to Paris: "The Grand-duke is determined to advance with full speed on Berlin and Vienna, more especially Berlin [sic!], passing between the fortresses of Thorn, Posen and Breslau."

On the 22nd, General de Laguiche, who had mistakenly been told that Austrian troops were actually in Alsace, again urged on the grand-duke "the importance of an offensive to relieve pressure on the west". Two days later in Paris, Minister of War Adolphe Messimy claimed (again falsely) that two active corps from the eastern front had been identified on the western front. The Russians must, he telegraphed Paléologue, prosecute their "offensive à outrance" in the direction of Berlin. "Inform the Russian government and insist."

Not only was the Russian air force small and ill-equipped, but its pilots were exposed to the double risk of contending not only with the enemy but also with the hazards of their own infantry who — either because they saw so few planes or because they could not believe their countrymen capable of mastering an intricate flying-machine — fired off their rifles at any they saw.

In mid-August and early September, virtually the whole of this force was on the South West Front, against Austria — a solitary plane occasionally taking the air over East Prussia. On 25 August, five days after Gumbinnen, a Russian aviator saw what he took to be transport wagons moving behind the German lines. Descending for a closer look, he saw that every conceivable kind of vehicle was being used, including buses and taxis. He was witnessing the German army's response to the obligingly revealed Russian intentions.

The haste with which preparations for the East Prussian campaign were made not only prevented the Russians from advancing with adequate supply trains, but also left them short of telegraph wire for communications. Since the Germans had frustrated their hope of commanding existing telegraph lines in the region, they were driven to using radio for relaying orders and maintaining communications between corps. The simplest possible code was chosen in order to be within the scope of their operators, hence the Eighth Army intelligence cryptologist found it so simple to break that a trick was suspected until the messages were confirmed by actual Russian troop movements.

The Germans learned from these intercepted messages that Hoffmann and François had been right in presuming the First Army to be incapable of pursuit. Rennenkampf was dogged by supply problems, had suffered heavy losses and was unaware of the rout of the German centre at Gumbinnen, though this in fact had been a strategic victory for his army. His cavalry scouts had observed crowds of refugees streaming westward which, accompanied by an absence of defending forces, led him and Zhilinsky to conclude that the Germans were abandoning the whole of East Prussia. Thinking that his pursuit would only hasten this and so baulk Samsonov of his prey, he halted while the Second Army was ordered to execute "a most energetic offensive" to cut off the enemy before he reached the Vistula and safety. This Samsonov was endeavouring to do, in face of the greatest difficulties. Even before he crossed the frontier, his line of march lay along sandy tracks which were brutally fatiguing to men and horses and where guns and limbers were constantly bogged down.

The further he advanced the more his supply shortage told, and once over the border there was no chance for men or horses to live off the country because the civilians, terrified of the dreaded Cossacks, had driven all before them in their flight.

Nevertheless, Zhilinsky continued to goad Samsonov from his headquarters at Bialystok. "Hurry up the advance of the Second Army and hasten your operations as energetically as possible," he ordered the day before Samsonov crossed the frontier, adding: "Delay in the advance of the Second Army is putting the First in a difficult position", a statement which was entirely without foundation. The First Army was in no difficulty and Rennenkampf had not even attempted to move his left wing southwards to join up with Samsonov. The Second was not only on schedule but was pushing the German centre, Scholtz's Twentieth Corps, steadily in front of it, in one case charging entrenched machine-gun positions with bayonets. None the less, Zhilinsky not only deprived Samsonov of his Second Corps and sent it to Rennenkampf, but also removed the Guard Corps from his command.

By the end of 23 August, the Germans were retreating along the whole of the Second Army front, and Soldau and Neidenberg were in Russian hands, albeit at a cost of 4,000 casualties. Samsonov was now becoming aware of hardening resistance which he reported to Zhilinsky. The latter, still convinced that the bulk of the German defence was fleeing before Rennenkampf, telegraphed: "To see the enemy where he does not exist is cowardice. I will not allow General Samsonov to play the coward!"

Zhilinsky's constant harrying, coupled with the need to form a continuous line by joining his right wing to the First Army's left (while Rennenkampf made no move to lessen the gap between them) caused Samsonov to so extend his front that communication between centre and wings became uncertain.

On the night of 24 August, still on schedule, Samsonov issued the next day's orders to his corps commanders. Since not all the commanders had each others' codes, he was compelled in desperation to send out uncoded instructions. German monitors who picked these up could scarcely believe their ears, and Ludendorff needed all Hoffmann's assurances to persuade him they were genuine. Rennenkampf was simultaneously sending out his own orders in the code the Germans had broken, from which they gathered that instead of moving south to close the gap between his own and Samsonov's army, he was actually moving north toward Königsberg in the belief that here lay the greater part of the German defence.

The north-to-south movement of German forces observed by the Russian pilot on 25 August was their response to this intelligence; leaving only a thin screen in front of Rennenkampf they hastily moved all their available forces to Samsonov's front, whereafter Zhilinsky – in urging Samsonov forward – was simply pushing him deeper into the trap the Germans were about to lay for him. At Koblenz, Moltke was still in the throes of conflict. Wondering whether, by sending Ludendorff and Hindenburg to East Prussia, he had done everything possible to save the situation there, he still believed that any reduction of German forces on the Western Front would be perilous. In the end he ordered his staff to carefully examine the situation on the Western Front with the

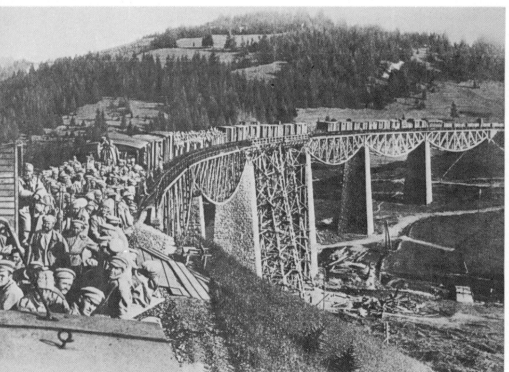

The Battle of Tannenberg. (*above*) Russian infantry ford a stream, better equipped than was usual in the War. (*Popperfoto*) (*below*) The Germans used their strategic railways to tremendous advantage. Here Russian prisoners are taken away from the front after the Battle of Tannenberg (*Popperfoto*)

Some of the greatest achievements of the Russian Army were in the Carpathian Mountains, where natural obstacles were near-overwhelming. A Russian machine-gun detachment makes a stiff climb in 1914. (*Mansell Collection*)

(*top left*) Russian infantry in extended order before a battle in 1915. (*Mansell Collection*) (*middle left*) Russian Troops stop for a hot meal on the way to the front in April 1915. Hot meals, or any meals at all, became a rarity as the War continued. (*Mansell Collection*) (*bottom left*) Russian barbed wire entanglements laid near Warsaw in January and February 1915. Supplies of barbed wire were always short. (*Mansell Collection*) (*bottom right*) A view of the summit of the Dukla Pass. The crest was finally captured by the Russians early in February, 1915. (*Mansell Collection*)

The Cossacks regiments were a source of terror throughout Eastern Europe Here a group of rough-and-ready Kuban Cossacks just before the War. (*Popperfoto*)

Cossack scouts were able to operate in the taxing conditions of the Russian winter. (*Mansell Collection*)

A detachment of Russians on the Vistula near Warsaw. (*Novosti Press Agency*)

The Struggle for Warsaw involved all the hazards of winter warfare. Here Russian Soldiers are breaking ice on a Polish river so that it can be used for transport. (*Mansell Collection*)

Some of the most ruthless fighting took place on the Turkish front. (*Imperial War Museum*)

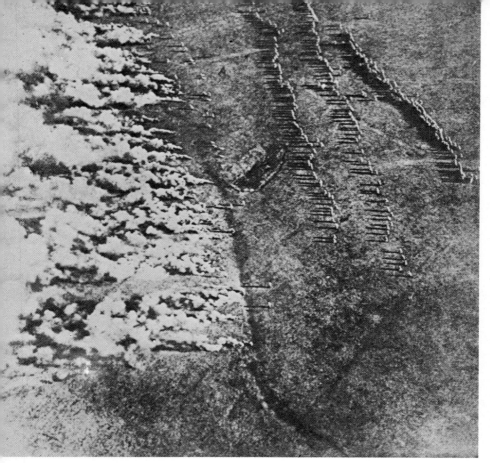

A Russian aerial reconnaissance photo of a German gas attack. Lines of Germans are waiting behind the billows of gas until the fumes have done their work. (*Mansell Collection*)

After the spring mud dried, choking dust became a serious problem. Here a German detachment advances to the front. (*Mansell Collection*)

(*top left*) A Russian bayonnet attack on the Germans, Polish front, 1915. (*Imperial War Museum*) (*bottom left*) Russian cavalry driving a German cavalry regiment into a trap, Polish front, 1915. (*Imperial War Museum*) (*top right*) Brusilov's break-through on the southwestern front in May–July 1916. A Russian charge. (*Novosti Press Agency*) (*bottom right*) Russian troops in Buchach in June 1916 during Brusilov's advance. (*Novosti Press Agency*)

The Russians made use of every form of manpower. Here peasant women dig trenches behind the Russian lines. (*Novosti Press Agency*)

Recruits became younger as the War wore on. (*Mansell Collection*)

Lieutenant General Mikhail V. Alekseyev. (*Novosti*)

General P. Lechitsky who led the capture of Chernovitsy. (*Novosti*)

General A. N. Kuropathkin. (*Novosti Press Agency*)

(*top left*) The Battles of the Masurian Lakes. German Soldiers with their machine-guns. (*Popperfoto*) (*bottom left*) The Masurian Lakes. Barbed-wire entanglements. (*Popperfoto*) (*top right*) Russian prisoners taken by the Austrians. (*Mansell Collection*) (*bottom right*) A scene in the streets of Petrograd after the abdication of the Tsar. Discipline gradually became impossible. (*Mansell Collection*)

The women's brigade, called the "Battalion of Death", could not offset the desertion rate among the men. (*Popperfoto*)

A meeting of soldier delegates from the Armies at the front in the Duma. Had the supplies situation not been so desperate, their on-the spot knowledge of the combat situation might have helped to turn the tide. (*Mansell Collection*)

(*above*) Bolsheviks holding the end of a street with an armoured car during the street fighting in Petrograd in 1917. (*Mansell Collection*) (*below*) October 1917, a street battle in Petrograd. (*Mansell Collection*)

object of finding areas from which troops could safely be withdrawn and sent east. When these were located he ordered his Operations Chief, Colonel Tappen, to telephone the Eighth Army. Treating Central Headquarters with customary wariness, Ludendorff asked Hoffmann to pick up an extension telephone "so that you can hear what Colonel Tappen wants and what I answer him". Astonished to hear that three army corps and a cavalry division were being sent from the west, he explained that these were not really needed; Tappen insisted, however, on sending two army corps and one cavalry division: the Guard Reserve Corps from von Bülow's army, the Eleventh Corps from von Hausen's army and the Eighth Cavalry Division.

As he advanced, Samsonov became increasingly concerned about the attenuation of his line, the far right now being about fifty miles (two days' march) from the vanguard of the army. Having decided on the night of 25/26 August to change his orders and close up the ranks by bringing in the corps on the right, fear of the consequent effect on the flank made him change his mind. However, the corps was already on the march, soon clashing with German forces thought to be fleeing from Rennenkampf's front. In fact it was Mackensen's re-formed Seventeenth Corps, one of the units rushed from north to south, which fought so fiercely that a second Russian corps became embroiled. Both were pushed back and, by the end of the day, a six-mile gap had been torn in Samsonov's line between his centre and the Masurian Lakes. The Russian Twentieth Corps, under Artamanov, was ordered overnight to fill this gap, but came under heavy artillery fire and the troops, weary and half-starved, broke and fled.

The Germans were now round the Russian right flank. Meanwhile, at the other end of the line, François' First Corps, newly arrived from Rennenkampf's front, prepared to move against the Russian left. A heavy artillery bombardment launched at Usdau, near the Russian frontier, caused the Russian forces to break and flee before the infantry attacks began. François, now wanting to push eastwards behind the Russian centre, was once more forced to wheel southwards towards the Russian border by an attack on his left flank from a relief column under Sirelius, sent out to reinforce Samsonov. Its intervention was brief; having grossly overestimated François' strength in this first encounter, they had retreated by 28 August back across the frontier and the Germans were able to concentrate once more on Samsonov's centre.

Having finally realised that the Germans, far from retreating in disorder, were concentrating all their forces against the Second Army, Zhilinsky ordered Rennenkampf to go to its aid. Unaware of its location, Rennenkampf began moving in precisely the opposite direction, and since he was not told how critical the situation had become he did not order forced marches. The Germans, who had a nasty moment when the First Army's radios pronounced that he had begun to move, soon realised that he could not possibly reach the battlefield in time.

Meanwhile, Samsonov, unaware of the precise situation, was actually advancing, pushing Scholtz's Twentieth Corps before him, with Mackensen on his open right and François coming round his centre rear.

Chapter 6

"We Owed This Sacrifice To France"

The Russians whom Dankl's First Army had encountered and beaten at Krasnik confirmed Conrad in his belief that their attack was coming from the north, and that the danger had now been obviated. The way to victory was open.

Ivanov, on the Russian side, was equally deceived and believed that the main Austrian attack was to be eastwards. The only explanation for the presence of forces at Krasnik, therefore, was that they were a flank guard for this offensive. His response was to direct Plehve's Fifth Army, standing on the left of the retreating Fourth, to wheel westwards so as to meet and aid any other forces marching in that direction.

This opened the Fifth's flank to Auffenberg's Austrian Fourth Army which, advancing parallel with Dankl, attacked it at Komarov on 26 August. Because of the abominable communications, Ivanov at his headquarters in Kiev remained ignorant of this encounter so long that he continued to order the move westward while Auffenberg was actually pushing Plehve's left wing southwards so that the whole line was becoming bent upon itself and in danger of Austrian encirclement.

Unknown to Conrad, while this battle was proceeding further south and roughly at right angles to Krasnik and Komarov, the Russian Third and Eighth Armies were advancing from the east toward Lemberg. Apart from the threat to the Galician capital, they were approaching Auffenberg's line of communication.

Conrad, hearing only of the Fourth Army's success at Komarov and its anticipated envelopment of the Russian Fifth, decided to draw three divisions from the Third Army shielding Lemberg and send them to reinforce Auffenberg. When he finally heard of the Russian approach he understood it to be a small force, and ordered the remainder of the Third Army to leave their prepared positions and repulse it.

The Second Army, which was to reinforce the guard on the west flank, had now arrived from Serbia, though at that moment it was still at Stanislau almost a hundred miles south of the battlefield.

The Third Army began advancing in a south-easterly direction, roughly towards the advancing Russian Eighth Army on the Zlota Lipa. Finding that, instead of being the small force reported, the Russians outnumbered them five-to-one, they were thrown back on the Gnila Lipa, some twenty-five miles from Lemberg. The Austrians were now engaged in two big battles: south of Lemberg, between the remains of the Austrian Third and the Russian Eighth, shortly to be joined by the Third; and in the north round Krasnik and Komarov, between the Austrian First and Fourth and the Russian Fourth and Fifth Armies. In the second, the advantage still lay with the Austrians; in the first with the Russians, but the success of either would determine the outcome of the other. The following day, 27 August, Conrad was compelled to acknowledge the crisis in the south to the extent of ordering the Third Army to fall back on Lemberg; he also had to ask Auffenberg to return the three divisions sent to assist him in enveloping the Russian Fifth Army.

Ivanov, however, remained so convinced in his delusion that the forces which had struck at the Fourth and Fifth were mere flank guards for an army advancing eastwards, that he believed the insignificant forces from the Third Army, parried so easily, represented the advance of the Austrian mass. He therefore halted to collect his own forces for a set-piece battle on the Gnila Lipa – not knowing that this had already been evacuated by Conrad.

At Baranovichi, the grand-duke had made a more accurate assessment and ordered the advance on Lemberg to continue forthwith. But Ivanov's hesitancy in pressing his attack had given Conrad fresh hope and, persisting in his belief that the whole situation could be changed by a victory in the north, he allowed Auffenberg to retain his three divisions.

Of the two Russian armies on Austria's eastern side, the nearest to Lemberg was the Third, commanded by Ruszki, a brisk sixty-one-year-old, but the assault on the city was to be made in conjunction with the army on his left. This was the Eighth, commanded by Alexei Alexeievich Brusilov, now moving southward to clear the way for an assault on Lemberg from the flank. Brusilov was a slight, irascible man, his grey stubble of hair and sharp-tipped Cossack moustache giving him a military mien contrasting with the almost feminine grace of his gestures and the way he held the long, Russian cigarettes he smoked. He had particularly deep-set eyes and a way of squinting with one of them, which both Knox and the Empress felt gave him a "cunning look". The same age as Ruszki, he also came from the Russian nobility which traditionally supplied the army with its officers, but differed from the general run in his professional dedication. He had been appointed to his present command after a frustrating career trying to push through the modernisation of the army after the Russo-Japanese War. In it he had earned both the devotion of his troops, especially the Cossacks, by a tireless concern for their welfare and the implacable loathing of his brother-officers by his acid and outspoken criticism of the follies and incompetence he saw about him. Their malevolence was in no way diminished by the successes on which he now embarked.

After secretly moving his troops forward, he launched a series of actions which fully utilised the ability of the fast-moving Cossack bands (armed with their own light artillery) who not only fought with ferocious bravery but spread such terror and demoralisation among the Austrians that, as both Tăslăuanu and the Official History admit, the cry "Cossacks are coming" was enough to create a panic. On 27 August he took Tarnopol, seventy-five miles south-east of Lemberg, and from here went slightly southward to take the former Galician capital. Halicz, on the Dniestr on the 29th. On 1 September he swung northward to participate with Ruszki - now advancing in a westerly direction – in the double advance on Lemberg.

During this time, Auffenberg's Fourth Army was still trying to encircle the Russian Fifth away to the north. Since the Austrian army formed a large horseshoe round the Russians, Conrad had on 30 August granted Auffenberg the two days he requested to complete the envelopment.

Plehve, the sixty-five year old commander of the Fifth Army, unpopular and exacting but of indomitable will, was seeking a way of escape, and on 30 August had ordered a withdrawal, Auffenberg had anticipated this and provided for the two corps on either side of the open horseshoe to close in. Unfortunately, one of Austria's few aircraft, reconnoîtring that morning, reported cavalry divisions advancing on either side; although these were only patrols, the closing ends of the horseshoe were pulled apart as the units turned about to meet the new "threat", and Plehve quickly withdrew his army.

Anxious to minimise their error, the Fourth presented the ever-optimistic Conrad with a picture of a routed Russian army whose shattered survivors were fleeing in panic, a picture he unhesitatingly accepted. Now, with the Fifth Army "destroyed", Auffenberg was to wheel about and pounce on the Third and Eighth while the Second Army, from Serbia, was to be sent against the flank.

Had Conrad learned to listen to Russian radio messages – which here, as in East Prussia, were sent out uncoded[1] – he would have heard that the disposition of the Russian Third and Eighth Armies had already changed and they were rapidly moving northwards in pursuit of the forces following Plehve. Therefore, instead of hitting the Russian Third on its flank, Auffenberg met both armies head-on. Moreover, Ivanov was bringing yet another army to the battlefield – the Ninth, under Lechitsky, which was to be principally concerned with the battle round Krasnik in which the Austrian First Army had been engaged since the offensive began. Lechitsky was to slip behind the Austrian First and Fourth, cutting off their line of retreat. Since neither Conrad, Ivanov, nor their army commanders had a clear picture of their opponents' position, the subsequent action took the armies twisting across the plains like so many snakes, the Austrians generally getting the worst of encounters against the numerically stronger Russian forces.

In East Prussia, Samsonov had now discovered that instead of enveloping the Germans he faced this hazard himself. It was too late. François had placed all available troops in a line of outposts spread west to east from Neidenberg to Willenberg barring the Russian retreat, and Samsonov's order for a general withdrawal simply pushed his troops against this. In forest and swamp, confused and scattered men lost themselves in the rising mists, falling prey to François' machine-guns along the causeway roads whenever they came within range.

At the crisis of the battle, Samsonov had said to Knox, "The enemy has luck one day. We will have luck another." On the 28th, he slipped away into the forest and shot himself, unable to face the disgrace of "failing his tsar". His death was not established until Guchkov — who had fought the duel with Miassoiedev — crossed the lines as Red Cross plenipotentiary and questioned the Germans.

Of the five and a half army corps with which Samsonov had marched to battle, two and a half were wiped out. The Germans took 90,000 prisoners. Russian losses during the four weeks of their invasion of East Prussia were 310,000 men and 650 guns, "a force equivalent to seven and a half corps". This was the flower of the Russian army, and throughout the remainder of the war, she would be trying to make good the losses of this one battle.

At Baranovichi General de Laguiche, having got the offensive his country wanted, went immediately to commiserate with the grand-duke on its outcome. "Nous sommes heureux de faire de tels sacrifices pour nos alliées," the grand-duke told him.

In Petrograd, Sazonov expressed himself in almost identical terms to Paléologue: "We owed this sacrifice to France, as she has shown herself such a perfect ally."

German Eighth Army headquarters had been moved for the climax of the battle to the little village of Frögenau, near Tannenberg. Ludendorff was about to send off his despatch when Hoffmann, catching the word "Frögenau", reminded him that they had just avenged a 500-year-old defeat (when the Russians defeated the Teutonic Knights in 1410) and suggested he substitute "Tannenberg".

In contrast with the speed with which the victory of Gumbinnen became known, the Russian public were not told what had happened for almost a week, information then being restricted to a three-line communiqué: "In the south of East Prussia, the Germans disposing superior forces, have attacked two of our army corps which have sustained considerable losses. General Samsonov has been killed." According to Paléologue, this laconic message failed to deceive and rumours became rife. Efforts were also made to keep the news from the Allies, so that Knox found himself a virtual prisoner at the North West Front headquarters at Bialystok for four days after the action.

This suppression of news accounted for Poincaré writing on 30 August, that the Russians were "developing their offensive toward Berlin". Coming through General de Laguiche, this information relieved the general gloom brought about by the advance of the German right under von Kluck and von Bülow to within twenty miles of Paris. The capital had been within reach of German aircraft since 30 August, and on 2 September the government left for Bordeaux.

In Russia it was being publicly suggested that France would be compelled to make peace, while the commanders of the tiny British Expeditionary Force were so alarmed at the possibility of French collapse that they were in full retreat, and there was talk of merely retaining a bridgehead on the Channel coast until this could be reinforced.

In fact, the crisis was now past its peak — though French Headquarters had withheld the fact from their own government, let alone their Russian allies. Joffre, who had already heard of Tannenberg via a monitored radio message, was cheered by a report from French intelligence that thirty-two troop trains had passed eastwards through Berlin. Moltke, having assigned detached units for surveillance on the Belgian army cornered at Antwerp, further weakened his forces by sending two corps east.

The reduced columns of the advancing German right thus lacked sufficient force to contain the strong Paris garrison and continue the march according to the timetable it was essential to keep, in order to prevent the French army from escaping the noose. Von Kluck, on the extreme right, had to decide whether to bypass Paris to east or west. His final solution was to take the easterly route, detaching part of his forces to guard his uncovered flank as they made the turn. Gallieni, military governor of Paris, took the opportunity to send his Sixth Army to attack this flank on 6 September, whereupon von Kluck was forced to move more and more men from left to right, leaving only a cavalry screen to cover the gap between himself and von Bülow.

At this moment the British finally felt able to go over from retreat to the offensive. Having pierced the cavalry screen, they were astonished to find themselves advancing into a thirty-mile gap between von Kluck's left and von Bülow's right, just where the

Guard Reserve Corps (now on the way to East Prussia) should have been. Suspecting a subterfuge, they slowed the advance — which could have split two German armies — to a crawl.

Von Kluck, however, attacked on the right by Gallieni and threatened on the left by the advancing British, felt he had no option but to retire, forcing von Bülow to conform.

By 11 September the entire German army had retreated. The French and British had won the Battle of the Marne. Paris, for whose salvation the Russians had made such sacrifices, had been saved. "The tsar's army and the Grand-Duke Nicholas have a right to France's undying gratitude," Joffre has declared.

The Russian delay in issuing their Tannenberg communiqué until 2 September enabled them to offset the defeat by announcing that air reconnaissance had established the Austrians to be evacuating Lemberg.

The jealousy felt by other commanders against Brusilov is evidenced by Ruszki's despatch announcing this victory which omitted his name. Moreover, when the grand-duke sought decorations for both men from the tsar, he requested the Cross of St George Fourth Class for Brusilov, while Ruszki was recommended for the First Class in that order.

In East Prussia, however, the battle was not yet over.

The Russian army's rudimentary organisation and primitive personnel had one merit which, combined with its colossal manpower, gave it an advantage over its more efficient and technically-complex adversaries. There was no supporting stem as was necessary to western forces, and the limited technical services depended upon a few regulars or trained specialists on the reserve list. Battles mainly consisted of moving men from one place to another to kill or be killed, after which survivors could be quickly re-formed or assigned to other units.

The Germans, accustomed to appalling reorganisation difficulties in the wake of defeat, therefore supposed that following the disaster at Tannenberg, the Russians would long be occupied in licking their wounds.

On 2 September, Zhilinsky had told Rennenkampf that with

Samsonov defeated the "enemy was at full liberty to turn on him". The First Army commander began, therefore, to regroup his forces into a defensive line stretching from Labiau on the Baltic Coast down to Angerburg at the northern end of the Masurian Lakes, a line which Zhilinsky ordered him "to hold at all costs".

Although Rennenkampf had suffered heavy casualties, and the loss of half the Second Army reduced the original two-to-one superiority to well below parity, this deficit was being made up by three corps from Turkestan and Siberia which had joined North West Front, plus returning Second Army stragglers.

The Germans had also been reinforced with arrivals from the west and had improved their existing artillery superiority by borrowing from neighbouring units early in the campaign.

To demonstrate that the defeat at Tannenberg left the way open for a German invasion of Russia, on 4 September Ludendorff had taken the border town of Mlava in Russian Poland, which goaded Zhilinsky into ordering Rennenkampf to recommence offensive action immediately. Once again uncoded Russian orders betrayed their intention, and Hindenburg and Ludendorff decided that they too must act.

They divided their forces into six groups, scheduled to move with the ultimate aim of enveloping the First Army as completely as the Second. On 7 September, the town of Bialà on the Masurian Lakes was captured by François' First Corps, which then began moving successfully against Rennenkampf's flank. On 9 September other German forces began frontal attacks but the Russians were well entrenched and repulsed the corps on the German right, inflicting heavy losses.

François' progress against the Russian flank compelled Rennen-kampf to order a general retirement which degenerated into a rout when he abandoned control of the battle and drove back to Kovno. From here he reported to the grand-duke on 14 September: "All corps have now broken off the battle."

Next day they began crossing the frontier back into Russia, the East Prussian campaign at an end Ludendorff had been appointed chief-of-staff of the Southern army Group, now hastily being concentrated at Breslau in Silesia, hence the pursuit into Russian territory devolved upon Hindenburg alone, accompanied by Hoff-mann. The Russian towns of Augustovo and Suwalki were taken, and the Germans advanced towards the line of the River Niemen, but Hindenburg was then transferred from the battlefield to join Ludendorff at South Army, leaving Hoffmann — promoted to chief-of-staff of the Eighth Army — to continue with Prince Leopold of Bavaria as his nominal commander-in-chief.

On the Russian side recriminations began as the campaign ended. Because of Rennenkampf's German ancestry and name, it was even suggested that his failure to support Samsonov was treason, a verdict more consistent with current spy-mania and anti-German hysteria than with any evidence. The grand-duke's wrath fell mainly on the frail shoulders of Zhilinsky, who was replaced in command of the North West Front by Ruszki. Later in the war he obtained a job as liaison officer at the French Grand Quartier Général.

The menacing situation in the south was the reason for Hindenburg and Ludendorff's removal from East Prussia and the urgent preparations in Silesia. By 8 September, the Austrians had been brought round into a single line facing east, while the Russians were tipped northwards. Conrad's troops were tired and dispirited and the struggles in which they had been involved were totally beyond their capabilities. They suffered such a high casualty rate that the burial parties were unable to cope. Bodies were left to rot under the hot summer sun, thus creating a health hazard. In addition, the troops' mixed racial origins caused constant problems.

Nevertheless, Conrad continued and mounted two attacks; the first ended in a bloody stalemate and the second, at Lemberg, was a disaster. The Austrian First Army in the north west was still trying to hold the Russian Fourth and Ninth, but on 9 September Dankl, the First Army commander, had to fall back to the River San, his original jumping-off point. Moreover, Conrad was unaware that Plehve's Fifth Army — supposedly routed by Auffenberg — was cutting round Dankl's flank towards his rear, in accordance with the original plan for Austria's defeat.

It was then that the Austrian High Command — realising that a great deal could be learned about Russian intentions by listening to their radio messages — discovered Plehve's plan. On 11 September, at the last possible moment, Conrad ordered his troops to disengage and retired hastily behind the San. Events had already overtaken this order, however, and the Austrians were retiring as quickly as was practicable.

The long summer drought had broken into torrential rains, dirt roads becoming a morass into which, says the Austrian Official History, artillery sank to its axles; men trudged with bowed heads; and cavalry in "molten confusion".

Russian pursuit became difficult through this quagmire, and the Austrians made full use of their opportunity to tap Russian radio messages in order to evade their hunters. Nevertheless, the retreat became increasingly disorganised. Of the army which went forward as the instrument of Conrad's optimistic plan, only two-thirds reached the San; when the first Russian forces overtook them they had to be moved again, this time to the River Dunajec further west. Behind him, Conrad had left the besieged fortress of Przemysl which was to menace the Russians for months to come.

Out of 900,000 men, Conrad lost 350,000 including 30,000 prisoners most of whom surrendered. The remnants of the Austrian forces had now retreated 150 miles, leaving much of Galicia to be subjoined to the tsar's empire.

Although it was this situation which led to Ludendorff and Hindenburg's transfer south, the Austrian disasters before this compelled the Germans to act. Since there were no troops available, ships of the German Baltic Fleet had been sent out on a naval diversion intended to deceive the Russians into believing their coast was about to be invaded. However, this manoeuvre failed to frighten them into stripping the Galician front and a further action on 26 August resulted in the German light-cruiser "Magdeburg" grounding in fog off Odensholm Island in the Gulf of Finland. A Russian naval boarding party, which took the German crew by surprise, seized the ship and also discovered code books which, passed to the Allies, enabled the Royal Navy to keep up with German naval codes for the rest of the war.

Despite the East Prussian victory the position of the Austro-German confederation looked very black. The war had run for six weeks and there was no sign of France being so crippled as to enable the Germans to move their armies from west to east in the "overwhelming force" Moltke had promised Conrad. With Serbia still unbeaten, the Austrian armies were recoiling from Russian blows and could only expect to be driven further back in the event of fresh attacks. The terror of Russian occupation now spread to the plains of Hungary, beyond the wall of the Carpathian Mountains. Istvan Tisza, liberal premier and "ablest and calmest of the Hungarian statesmen", had opposed the Dual Monarchy's rush to war and, in the German view, could now be expected to influence the aged Emperor Franz-Joszef in support of peace. If this came about, instead of the Triple Alliance outflanking Russia on either side of the Polish salient, Germany would find herself outflanked in the south, with the rich industrial province of Oppeln at the tip of a narrow and militarily untenable salient.

Nor had the threat to East Prussia been ruled out. The Russian First Army, although forced back on the line of the Niemen, had been reinforced there and had not only prevented the Germans from crossing the river but, by 22 September, had compelled them to withdraw. At the Second Battle of Augustovo they were defeated and lost 60,000 men before pulling themselves back across the East Prussian border. Should this rich farmland area — where Cossack raiding parties were again causing havoc — be lost, German resistance to the mounting British blockade would be reduced.

The defeat of the Marne, combined with the deteriorating situation on the Eastern front, had led to the ailing Moltke's replacement as commander of the armies on 14 September. His place at Koblenz had been taken by the tall, elegant Erich von Falkenhayn, at fifty-three a comparative child among generals who, it was hoped, would bring a youthful zest to the critical situation.

The armies of the tottering tsarist regime caused a crisis in the enemy coalition far more serious than any on the Western Front, and the Germans were confronted by the dreaded "war on two fronts". Austria's increasingly desperate position necessitated immediate emergency help. Under Falkenhayn's orders, therefore, a new Ninth Army was scratched together at Breslau, commanded by Hindenburg, with Ludendorff as chief-of-staff. This included three corps from East Prussia, a cavalry division, and a detachment of Landwehr under General von Woyrsch. The Ninth was to be placed as near to Cracow as possible, to guard the Austrian left flank and provide increased cover for the industrial regions.

Chapter 7

Forward — To Berlin

Unaware of the alarm inspired among the enemy, news of the Russian success in Galicia was received without excitement by Russia's allies. In the short term, "France's undying gratitude" was manifested in representations to Baranovichi for further military initiatives including an attack on Silesia. Poincaré commented, when shown the grand-duke's telegram, "It appears ... that Russia, contrary to our repeated requests, is making her chief effort against Austria, as if the surest way to beat Austria were not to begin by beating Germany."

On 14 September, when the last tired rearguard of Rennenkampf's army crossed the Niemen back into Russia, Paléologue visited Sukhomlinov to plead his government's case for a new assault on Germany. The War Minister reminded him that "we lost 110,000 men at Soldau when trying to help the French", and indicated that it would be some time before the grand-duke was ready for fresh adventures. Paléologue answered (if his diary tells the truth): "We would have made the same sacrifices for the Russian army, but it isn't our fault if the faintheartedness of one of your corps' commanders suddenly left the flanks of the Russian army in the air."

The French and British were only aware that Russian mobilisation was reaching full flood and the depots were crammed with soldiers which the grand-duke would not commit to battle. The subsequent British proposal through Buchanan, that Russia send three or four army corps west by way of Archangel was not turned down out of hand, but failed to develop because of the Russian shortage of transport.

The stalemate in the west raised extravagant hopes: "With the Austrian armies hors de combat in Galicia", Poincaré wrote on 20 September, "it only remains to annihilate the German forces to institute a new European régime which would guarantee peace for many a long year."

Notwithstanding Sukhomlinov's comment to Paléologue, the grand-duke had every intention of keeping his promises as a faithful ally. Some of the North West Front's corps, earmarked for the "advance on Berlin" prior to the East Prussian campaign, were assigned positions from which it was supposed they could influence that battle while being available for the greater offensive to follow. Zhilinsky's conviction during the actual battle that the defenders of East Prussia were in inextricable disarray, led him to deny Samsonov two of his corps so that they too could be used for this purpose.

French insistence on the Silesian operation had been such that at Baranovichi there was an almost tangible sense of guilt about the way the task of defeating the invading Austrians was approached; this led to the armies of South West Front being concentrated for the battle with undue haste and to its less than decisive result which, in turn, led to large sections of the Austrian army escaping.

At this time, plans had been completed for an advance on Silesia along "a wide front in the direction of Posen and Breslau", for which purpose 2 million Russian soldiers were concentrated in seven armies in a line from Warsaw to the confluence of the San and Vistula waiting for orders to move once the Galician campaign was won. The massing of these forces was no small achievement considering the problems dogging the Russian command. Although the depots were overflowing with men, they lacked almost every essential necessary to convert them into fighting units. Even contemporary accounts, normally reticent in this respect, admitted that right from the start the Russians were short of everything from "clothing to great guns".

The men were still in summer uniforms throughout the torrential September rains. Boots were so scarce that many had only their bast peasant shoes, and once these gave out they had to march barefoot through the Galician mud. Rifles were in such short supply that, as early as 24 August, Sukhomlinov wrote to Yanushkevich, the grand-duke's chief-of-staff, begging him, "in God's name" to issue orders for the collection of rifles from the field of battle, a perilous operation in which many lives were lost. There was no improvement in the artillery shortage and too few shells for existing guns. Having repeatedly appealed to Sukhomlinov about this, on 8 September the grand-duke complained to the tsar that operations would have to be postponed until shell stocks had been increased from twenty-five to one hundred per gun. Yet on 25 September, when Joffre asked if Russia had sufficient shells, Sukhomlinov could not admit his own failures and assured him there was "no cause for alarm on that score". The troops, driven to desperation, improvised weapons out of empty food tins, shell cases and gas pipes, and exactly a month later, on 26 October, Ivanov reported from the South West Front that ammunition was completely exhausted; unless replenishments arrived, all action would have to be "broken off and the troops retired under difficult conditions". The total shell output from the Russian munitions factories was 35,000 per month, while expenditure was running at the rate of 45,000 daily.

Experience of battle had shown how far artillery requirements on both fronts fell below estimates. In East Prussia the Russians guns had fallen silent in the middle of battle for lack of fodder, and at other times the infantry had been compelled to endure enemy bombardments while their own guns were silent.

German air superiority made it impossible to use balloons for aircraft spotting and, even if they had been adequately trained in entrenching, the shortage of barbed wire would have prevented the Russians from making their defences as impregnable as those they were required to attack.

Among other deficiencies illuminated in the flaring lights of battle was the failure of the Russian army's admirable system of field bakeries to operate because flour supplies did not arrive, and in one case troops were given an extra allowance of 50 kopeks a day to buy bread wherever they could. More appalling still was the total incompetence of the medical services, and the position of the wounded was, said Brusilov, "pitiable in the extreme". Enduring bombardments in open trenches without artillery of their own to silence the enemy guns, assaulting machine-gun positions with mere bayonets, meant casualties were very much heavier than the most pessimistic pre-war calculations had predicted. Yet, even by these standards, army medical services were insufficient: few proper ambulances; no medical appliances; insufficient doctors with no clear idea of their duties and insufficient hospitals. One hospital supposed to be capable of taking 3,000 wounded proved to have fewer than 400 beds; yet had to cope with 3,500 Russian and an unknown number of Austrian wounded.

Mikhail Rodzianko, president of the Duma, who visited the front at that time, saw 17,000 battle-casualties at Warsaw station; lying in the cold and mud just as they had been taken from the carts which brought them in, they were crying out for their wounds to be dressed. Many had been there for five days and there was no one to tend them.

Difficulty in moving the wounded because of the scarcity of rail-line and rolling stock was only one aspect of the Russia's transportation problem. What really troubled the grand-duke's headquarters in planning their new offensive was that in Russian Poland there was only one line west of Lodz and none at all running laterally. Troops being massed for the assault on Silesia could only reach their concentration points by marching through puddles and mud along unmade roads — hence the War Minister's caveat that it would probably be some time before the attack could be launched — while troop movement along the wide front could only be carried out in the same way.

The commander-in-chief was concerned that since the battle of the Marne in early September, there had been no intimation of any future action by the French; he therefore asked for clarification of their intentions. Did they propose merely to throw the Germans out of France? Or did they intend to push on into the heart of Germany? Joffre, who replied with platitudes and vague promises did not, however, see that the lack of action on his front was any good reason for the Russians adopting a similar policy and, on 15 September, Paléologue extorted an undertaking from Sazonov that "as soon as the Austro-Hungarian armies in east Galicia are put out of action, a direct offensive of the Russian armies against Silesia will be developed." However, the tsar decided to override the proviso in this formula and ordered an immediate offensive, whereupon the grand-duke philosophically directed his southern armies to hold their lines before the collapsing enemy.

The Third, Eleventh and Eighth Armies, presently engaged on the South West Front, were therefore left to accomplish several objectives which could change the course of the war: the final destruction of an Austrian army still capable of rallying; the clearing of enemy-occupied Galicia and then the forcing of the Carpathian passes which would enable the Russians to debouch upon the Danubian Plain. Their chances of a substantial victory were nullified by the need to provide a flank guard on the advancing armies of the centre. Ivanov was particularly critical of the situation but there was no gainsaying the tsar's orders and the grand-duke never disobeyed his sovereign nephew.

On 26 September, the Marquis de Laguiche reported from Baranovichi that the "advance on Berlin" had begun. The Russian High Command had promised that no troops would be diverted from this to the Austrian battlefield.

Notwithstanding the urgency of Austria's situation, the Germans were taking steps to keep the confederation and their own borders inviolate. On 29 September, while the Russians were still struggling along the almost impassable roads to their concentration points, some sixty German battalions began to cross into Russian Poland from four centres: Thorn and Cracow in the north, and Kalisz and Czestochova in the centre. Part of these forces were to engage the Russians concentrated in the chain of fortresses bisecting the Polish salient, while the rest made a two-sided assault on the Polish capital and postponed the threat to Silesia by rendering innocuous whatever Russian forces were assembling in the area.

The Germans had hoped for Austrian collaboration in this effort, but Conrad was only prepared to offer token support. With so much of the enemy engaged by his allies, he intended to relieve his troops besieged since the Russian advance at the largest Galician fortress of Przemysl and re-establish prestige by retaking Lemberg. It was the Germans' first experience of campaigning in the region and they soon found out for themselves the characteristics of Galician mud, which put a brake on their advance towards the enemy.

On the Russian side, once the grand-duke was aware of the German moves he made his own offensive plans and defensive dispositions. The main body of his forces were to hold the German thrusts southward along the Vistula, tempt them into an attack on Warsaw by moving back, and then cut round their left. The effect of what Hindenburg later called "the grand-duke's greatest plan" was somewhat diminished when certain orders fell into German hands and they also discovered that the Russians were opposing some 224 battalions against their own sixty. Although Russian radios helped them once more, it was hardly encouraging to discover that Siberian units armed with Japanese artillery were moving along the Vistula. Having presented themselves as the saviours of Austria, they now had to ask for aid, but their allies were only prepared to help by taking over the Vistula line themselves to avoid the mingling of commands about which they were so particular. With the troops thus freed, the Germans buttressed their lines before Warsaw.

However, the Russians were also moving up reinforcements taken from Galicia into this sector of the front, marching their army along appalling roads with some divisions completely without bread for six days — an achievement which as Cyril Falls says, "few other troops in the world could have made in the time". Despite their apparently complete exhaustion they were in combat within days, fighting with their customary tenacity and courage.

Meanwhile, Conrad's operation in Galicia had advanced as far as the San, and on 9 October he relieved Przemysl. Railway lines to the fortress were hurriedly repaired and 128 supply trains sent in, for he rightly feared his hold might only be temporary. On 18 October Hindenburg and Ludendorff, sent east to relieve Prittwitz but believing Mackensen's Seventeenth Corps on the left to be threatened with envelopment, abandoned "the battlefield of Warsaw to the enemy" and retired to their own frontier, jeered by the Austrians who now had to take over that part of the German line in front of the fortress of Ivangorod, fifty miles south of Warsaw. The Germans blamed their allies' failure to secure victory in the part of the line they had previously taken over, but their position was doubly humiliating because they had begun making plans for the future government of Poland, even bringing the client-king of Saxony (whose titles included "King of Poland") to a convenient spot for installation at Warsaw — a plan which was much criticised as there was no evidence that subjugation to yet another foreign sceptre would in any way placate the Poles.

At this time the British and French ambassadors at Petrograd made joint complaints concerning lack of information from the eastern battlefronts, and were promised that Joffre and Kitchener would in future be kept properly informed. Although Poincaré concluded in mid-October that "a long time must elapse before the Russian army can move against Berlin", in fact that army was once more engaged in fighting. Hindenburg and Ludendorff realised that, despite their size, the Russian armies were stretched over such a long front that it might be possible to storm the Vistula in the right spot before Russian reinforcements could be brought up. Conrad suggested a point between Warsaw and Ivangorod held by the left of the Third Army, now under Radko-Dmitriev, to reach which additional forces from Warsaw would be involved in a week's hard march.

The plan adopted was virtually the grand-duke's in reverse, aimed at tempting the Russians to attack Mackensen's Seventeenth Corps (deployed midway between Lodz and Warsaw) while the German troops released when the Austrians took over at Ivangorod delivered the blow across the Vistula. Unfortunately, Conrad was not content to hold his line before Ivangorod, but opened up his own defences to entice the Russians and subsequently failed to close them. The Russians simultaneously achieved the impossible and force-marched troops to Ruszki's threatened left. Thus, while the Germans were being held at one point other Russian forces were threatening their right. On 27 October Ludendorff retired "according to plan".

The Russians claimed a great victory, but Ruszki's armies of the North West Front could not pursue the Germans because of lack of adequate intelligence as to their location, while warning the enemy of their own approach by continuing indiscreet use of radio. The heavy mud combined with an absence of roads and bridges (methodically destroyed by the German engineers) increased Russian difficulties.

The Austrian First Army under Dankl, which had taken over the defence of Ivangorod, was left in a most unenviable position by the German withdrawal, and Austria's anger at her ally's behaviour was understandable. Not only had they suffered badly during and since the August-September campaign, but munitions were running low and cholera had broken out. Chased by the Russian Fourth and Ninth Armies, Dankl retreated first from Ivangorod to Cracow, then to the marshy regions of the Nida. In a memorandum to Conrad he advocated a massive retreat by the Austrian and German armies which would so extend the Russians in pursuit that stretched lines and supply difficulties would force them to halt. Such a negative course would have been unthinkable to Conrad who wanted the Germans to take the pressure off the First Army by striking at the Russian Fourth under Evert. The Germans refused, since attacking one Russian army would inevitably involve contact with the next in line, Plehve's Fifth, which could turn their flank. Instead, they suggested bringing Dankl under the command of the Ninth Army, withdrawing his army southward to give their own forces breathing space, and were extremely annoyed when the Austrians not only refused their proposals for uniting the armies, but Conrad announced that the First Army would retreat in parallel with the German Ninth, meaning that both could now expect to be harried by the Russians. As it happened, Dankl's army collapsed on 6 November and its remnants made for Cracow, forcing the other Austrian armies to pull back in line and leaving the fortress of Przemsyl besieged once more. Conrad's last hope rested in the enclave of nearly 100,000 men thus formed in enemy-held territory and he told the commander, Kusmannek von Burgneustadten, that he expected him to hold out until relieved and to tie down considerable Russian forces by an active defence, orders which Kusmannek faithfully endeavoured to obey.

At Cracow Dankl began to re-form his army alongside the Austrian Fourth Army which had also retreated there. The defence line gradually strengthened but was still vulnerable to a determined Russian assault, which was what Ivanov, South West Front commander, wanted. He asked to retain the Fourth and Ninth Armies in order to bring the struggle against Austria to a successful conclusion, but Stavka was concentrating on the attack on Silesia, conscious of the undertaking to the French that not one man would be diverted to the Austrian front until this had been completed. In the end a compromise was reached whereby Ivanov retained only the Ninth Army, which weakened the invasion force without giving the South West the necessary strength.

The plan formulated by the strategists at Baranovichi involved the Fourth Army advancing on the German industrial centres in the Beuthen (now Bytom)-Gleiwitz-Katowice triangle (pinning down the German Ninth Army), while the Fifth Army under Plehve and the Second (now under Samsonov's successor, Scheidemann) outflanked the enemy supposedly concentrating round Kalisz, Mielen and Czestochova after its retreat.

Because progress was impeded by the terrain, weather, lack of railways and obstacles put up by the retreating German armies, nearly a fortnight elapsed before the armies began to take up their positions and orders for the advance could be issued on 14 November.

Even if the original Russian assessments of the main enemy force's location had been correct, this would still have given them time to reinforce and regroup.

Chapter 8

Onset Of Winter

By now the Germans were badly shaken. Their attempt to succour
the Austrians had inflicted losses on the Russians which would
have crippled any other army, but had not improved their own
position anywhere along the front. The gamble of taking troops
from the north to add weight to the blow at the Russian centre
had failed to the extent that they were back in East Prussia, while
the German lines had been pulled back to the River Angerapp. The
threat to Silesia was probably greater than before their intervention, and a major Russian onslaught could come at any time. In
Galicia, the position of the Austro-Hungarian armies looked
singularly unpropitious, with Przemysl cut off once more. In this
black situation Ludendorff went to Berlin to beg Falkenhayn for
reinforcements. The mood of the capital contrasted sharply with
his own and he felt that he was in another world — "People did
not seem to realise the seriousness of our position in the war."
Neither, apparently, did Falkenhayn, for the reinforcements were
refused on the grounds that they could only be made available at
the cost of the Western Front where a battle was developing in
the Ypres salient.

However, a reshuffle of commands took place at Breslau, when
Hindenburg (still with Ludendorff as chief-of-staff) became "Ober-
befehlshaber des Deutschen Streitkrafte im Osten" — a title soon
shortened to "Oberost". This command comprised the Ninth
Army, now under Mackensen, and the Eighth under Prince
Leopold of Bavaria. It was decided that even without reinforcements an attack must be launched if Silesia was to be protected,
and once again the Russian radios showed how this might be done.
Taking full advantage of their carelessness, an attack on their
flank by way of Thorn was planned.

With this objective, the movement which culminated in Tannenberg was repeated. The defence of Silesia was entrusted to
Woyrsch's Detachment of Landwehr and a Guards' corps under

von Gallwitz, while the bulk of the Ninth Army was entrained from Czestochowa to Thorn. In five days, by 10 November, a quarter of a million men were transferred without Russian knowledge. They realised the high risk they ran in leaving Silesia covered by such a small force, but believed that if the Russians attempted to exploit this situation they would expose their own flank to the troops moving down from the north. However, there was considerable nervousness in the frontier areas, and an awareness of imminent Russian invasion. Sixty thousand young men were evacuated to Central Germany, pithead coal was moved and plans made for blowing up the mines. Recognising the likely outcome of these measures, thousands of civilians began to leave while the railways were still operating.

At this critical moment, the Austrians offered to extend their own lines to assist in defending Silesia, and units of Böhm-Ermolli's Second Army accordingly began to assemble. On 11 November the German attacks began. The Russians, drawn up to attack the van of the German armies they believed to be facing due west, were completely taken by surprise when the blow came from the north-east. The army on the extreme left wing was Rennenkampf's First. He had outposted one of his finest corps, the Fifth Siberian, on the right bank of the Vistula north of Wroclawek, just where the Germans would hit its flank. The next corps — the Sixth Siberian — was on the opposite bank, hence if its assistance were needed, it had to cross the river before beginning to traverse the Fifth's line. However, the Fifth managed to escape up-river to Plotsk, whereupon Mackensen wheeled to march down on Scheidemann's Second Army rather than extend his lines in pursuit.

Neither Stavka nor the Front commanders realised what was happening, and remained convinced that the bulk of the Germans were ahead. The advance was to proceed, therefore, and the reinforcement of the First Army by one Second Army corps was all that Ruszki would permit. By moving forward, the Second and Fifth Armies were of course opening up the gap between themselves and the stricken First. Two and a half Russian corps — including the one detached from Second Army — were about to face the onslaught of five German corps, with help receding.

On the 14th, Mackensen's forces struck the Russians at Kutno, south east of Wroclawek and by the early hours of the 16th

German cavalry under von Richthofen entered the town[1]. The Russians fell back hurriedly. The Fifth Siberian had meanwhile been enveloped with the loss of 15,000 prisoners, a gaping hole had been torn in the Russian line and the defenders of Kutno pulled back to Lovicz without attempting to make this good. The Russian commanders still did not appreciate the situation. The Second Army was regrouped to meet the flank threat from the north, but mistakenly believing the greater threat lay on the left, allowed the endangered right to be weakened.

As realisation dawned, however, Ruszki responded boldly and subtly. He swung the armies advancing westward until they faced due north and simultaneously built up a defensive line before Lodz. This was entrusted to the Second Army, already in position, and to the Fifth Army which had to be brought up.

His plan to let the Germans pour in behind the city, whereupon the First Army would come round behind the attackers, required rapid manoeuvring from the Fifth and First Armies. The aged Plehve, commander of the Fifth, covered seventy miles in two and a half days, personally encouraging his columns as they went. At the same time, Evert's Fourth was ordered to advance immediately on Silesia to reduce the pressure at Lodz. Since the Russian command was unaware that this sector of the front had been taken over by other forces and that the Ninth Army had been freed from its defensive responsibilities, his action could not affect the outcome.

The main struggle became a race, therefore, with Mackensen determined not to let the Second Army escape the "new Tannenberg" he had planned for it. By 18 November, he had 250,000 men round Lodz and did not expect it to hold out. Then exhausted troops from Plehve's Fifth began dropping into place in the defensive line next to Scheidemann, their effective strength halved by the loss of stragglers during the rigorous march. For the Russians, everything depended on Rennenkampf moving down in time from the north with his First Army.

Falkenhayn's promise of reinforcements from the Western Front after the Ypres battles had increased German confidence, but the campaign went badly and these troops could not be spared. Further entreaties on 20 November led to four additional divisions being sent on the 24th, despite the fact that since the end of October 5 cavalry divisions, 47 Landwehr and Landsturm battalions, 4 corps of infantry, 44,000 reserves and considerable munitions had already been sent east. Falkenhayn was already considering a separate peace in the east, even if this had to be made at the expense of Austria—Hungary.[2]

On Conrad's sector of the front, fierce fighting had broken out against Evert's Fourth Army round Cracow and before Silesia with some local successes for Austria but no serious threat developing against the Russians. Both armies had sustained enormous losses and were not fit for anything beyond cautious, defensive probes — the Russian artillery being reduced to fifty rounds per gun. Reinforcements were said to be coming from Radko-Dmitriev's Third Army, but delayed by Dmitriev's need to contain Przemsyl as well as other demands on his surplus manpower from Brusilov further south.

The Austrians were also short of artillery and ammunition and their losses had been made good by half a million ill-trained and often resentful conscripts. Some troops managed to push forward a few kilometres here and there, but the arrival of Selivanov's Eleventh Army to take over the investment of Przemsyl in mid-November enabled Radko-Dmitriev to begin moving up to "bastion Evert". The Austrians were forced back on Cracow which would certainly have fallen had the Russians been able to deploy sufficient strength in time.

At Lodz, meanwhile, both Germans and Russians had a heady sense of a decisive battle about to be joined, and the grand-duke had moved his advanced headquarters to Skierniewice, east of Lodz, maintaining contact with Baranovichi by Hughes' apparatus, a form of tape-machine.

Winter had set in when, on 19 November, the German pre-attack bombardments commenced. As the infantry advanced across the snow with every expectation of an easy victory, they encountered the firmly entrenched men of the Second and Fifth Armies; by the next day, however, they were gradually pushing the Russians back and there was still no sign of Rennenkampf who had run into the screening forces left by Mackensen and insisted that they were impeding him.

The defenders of Lodz badly needed men to hold the line, and troops at Warsaw and Novogeorgevsk (intended for Tenth Army) were diverted to Skierniewice and sent to threaten the German rear. Some 14,000 men were even sent up the line without rifles.

Enemy radio-monitors heard appeals from Scheidemann begging Rennenkampf to hurry, but the First Army was still too far away to pick up the messages. Mackensen, elated despite the unexpected length of the struggle, decided to press his attacks vigorously despite the threat which would develop in his rear if Rennenkampf arrived in time. His troops behind Lodz included a group under Scheffer, made up of the Twenty-fifth Reserve Corps, Richthofen's cavalry and a Guard Division under Litzmann. By the 21st, some of these units were in the Lodz suburbs and Mackensen's artillery was only a mile from the city centre.

On 22 November Scheffer sent some of his troops forward for what was expected to be the final stage of the battle, but they ran into fresh Russian forces from Warsaw and Novogeorgevsk, and as fighting flared up all along the line Scheidemann telegraphed North West Front headquarters that he was surrounded. Ruszki tersely telegraphed back: "You have surrounded them; demand their surrender." And so it was, to the equal astonishment of both sides.

At this critical moment, Rennenkampf finally began to move. Troops on the flank of Scheffer's group glimpsed advancing Russian infantry and promptly pulled back, leaving Scheffer isolated. Now the battle was indeed beginning to resemble Tannenberg, but with the Germans as victims. "We could see already", General Gourko wrote later, "how the German transports several times changed direction to diametrically opposed points, searching for an exit from the ever-narrowing circle of Russian troops." Eighteen trains were ordered up to take away an anticipated 26,000 prisoners, and news of a great victory even reached Petrograd.

However, Scheffer's group was not yet finished. Seeing that the bulk of the Russian troops were chasing the flank group which had earlier pulled back, and assuming this to be the main enemy force, Scheffer decided to make a break for it without any idea of the opposition. He was across the River Miazga by the 23rd and was saved by Litzmann's Guards who had taken Brzeziny the previous day. With Brzeziny in German hands, he fought his way to this refuge helped by the confusion reigning among the Russians. He lost about half his men in the process, but captured 16,000 prisoners and sixty-four guns.

However, in the Cracow area where Conrad's forces were still in danger, this German epic was of little significance. Conrad had withdrawn three divisions from his Fourth Army and diverted them to strike the Russians on their southern flank. This was merely a temporary measure, however, like most of the solutions adopted by Conrad in order to avoid disaster in one area at the cost of another where the threat was less imminent. Similarly, he had robbed his Carpathian lines to meet the needs north of the Vistula. The addition of Böhm—Ermolli's Second Army to the Silesian defence left the eleven divisions of the Third Army, under Boroevic, holding a line from the Beskidy—Zachodnie range of mountains in the west to the southern end of the Carpathians. Although Brusilov's Eighth was the only army left in the region, it rightly believed itself equal to the Austrians.

Throughout November, while the battle elsewhere pursued its vacillating course, Brusilov's troops pushed Boroevic from the Beskids to the Carpathians and then out of the mountain passes. This was nothing less than mass suicide, for the defenders had only to group themselves on either side of the defile to take the attackers in enfilade. Each assault degenerated into a confusion of tightly packed fighting men, the way becoming so heavily blocked by Russian dead that second-wave troops had to climb over them to reach the enemy. With high trajectory howitzers, mountain guns, or trained mountain troops, the Russians might have been able to storm, or at worst infiltrate, the enemy positions, but they had none of these. The Russians were predominantly plainsmen with no experience or taste for this kind of warfare, while the defenders possessed some mountain artillery as well as specially trained Tyrolean troops.

Nevertheless, by 29 November, units of the Eighth Army stood west of the Carpathians and the main Austrian defensive barrier, and were able to begin utilising their infantry and cavalry on the wide flat expanses. Boroević planned to stand at Eperjes, but did not expect to hold it The Slav units of the Austro—Hungarian armies were surrendering in thousands and their rifles were actually making up Russian deficiencies; one of the munitions factories went over to making cartridges to fit them.

Urgent preparations were now put in hand for the defence of Budapest.

The fighting at Lodz was prolonged until 6 December, when the Russians were finally compelled to abandon the city. The eighteen trains assembled to take away the prisoners of Scheffer's army steamed away empty, and in Petrograd as in the army, high hopes gave way to angry disappointment. Pavel Rennenkampf, the swashbuckling cavalry commander of the Manchurian campaign, had had his last chance. His reputation had suffered a tremendous blow in East Prussia, where he was now called "General Rennen ohne-Kampf" (Ran without fighting) and he subsequently lost his army command and later left the service. His place at the head of the First Army was taken by General Litvinov.

A conference of the two Front commanders and the grand-duke, held at Siedlce on 29/30 November, was symptomatic of declining Russian confidence. Ruszki, with losses of up to 75 per cent, wanted to disengage from the Germans and withdraw his line almost to the Vistula. Ivanov, on the other hand, wanted to leave his armies in position. "The way to Berlin", he declared, "lies through Austria—Hungary." He was supported by Radko-Dmitriev, the Third Army commander, who reported that the Austrian forces facing him were highly demoralised, and the thousands of prisoners taken in the recent battle bore witness to this. The grand-duke reluctantly consented to Ruszki's withdrawal and Ivanov's planned attack and, from now on, the brunt of the fighting would be on the Austro—Hungarian front, with the front against Germany largely fending for itself.

Incredibly enough, this decision was not made with the objective of exploiting Brusilov's gains in the Carpathians to the full. Instead, at Ivanov's prompting, it was decided that the strategic point for a decisive battle was at Cracow, despite the fact that the Russians had been defeated here by Austrian forces under Roth. Brusilov was accordingly told by Ivanov that he must abandon the gains which had opened up the way to the capital of Hungary at such enormous cost, and dispatch all strength to the Cracow region.

On 19 December, Paléologue rounded on Goremykin, the prime minister, in Sazonov's presence for Russia's "inadequate military support in our common cause". This accusation offended the Russians all the more because of their own growing register of grievances against their allies, not least of these being the feeling in the pro-German and anti-war party that both the British and French parliamentary democrats were trying to topple the Russian régime, which was so unpopular with these two countries.

Sir George Buchanan, the British ambassador, was very disturbed by the growing and overt anti-British feeling at this time, and in a speech at the Petrograd English Club he spoke of his country's sacrifices, the effort of the British Empire, and the fact that the Royal Navy was in the Baltic helping to keep the German navy at bay.[3]

This, however, did not improve results from Allied efforts and the grand-duke had been "much upset that Joffre would not take the offensive" when Russian assaults on Prussia (made at the behest of the French) ran into trouble. In early December, the Russians claimed to have identified troops from the west opposite them, and the grand-duke telegraphed hinting that if nothing was done to hold down enemy forces on that front more successfully, he would have to go over to trench warfare. A bitter Poincaré commented in his diary: "Why is Russia with its great numerical superiority so impotent and how can the grand-duke contemplate standing on the defensive?" Joffre, in reply, telegraphed that only three divisions were unaccounted for on the western front and that these might have gone to Russia.[4] Nevertheless, a week later he announced his intention of mounting "some little local attacks" to prevent the Germans "drawing forces from our front and sending them eastwards". Never less than optimistic, he privately confided to Poincaré that he would be "quite satisfied if at certain points he could push the Germans back 20 or 30 kilometres".

In the centre of the Polish salient another battle was being fought. The day after the fall of Lodz, Mackensen's forces began to line up for the next stage of the offensive, the capture of Warsaw, and the next few days saw them pushing the defenders back on the city. The Germans were within thirty miles of Warsaw when the full violence of the icy Russian winter brought the campaigning season to an end. It was impossible to dig trenches in the frozen ground and the advantage passed to those already established in defensive positions.

The onset of winter in 1914 must have been eagerly welcomed by the grand-duke; notwithstanding the order for offensive action promulgated from the conference of Siedlce, after five months the army of the largest country in the world was coming to the end of its resources, and commanders such as Brusilov must have been aware of this despite the fact that it was officially kept from them. Losses had been astronomical. Divisions which had started the war with 30,000 men were reduced to 15,000; in the Eighth Army no division had more than 6,000 and some were reduced to as few as 3,000 men; the shortage of rifles was such that 800,000 men in the depots could not fight for lack of them.

Finally, the onset of winter raised untold problems. Men fighting in snow and in frozen trenches were still wearing summer uniform because no fur-coats or sweaters had arrived.[5] Death from frostbite became as great a hazard as death in battle. Troops were ordered "to keep their feet warm and drink constant hot tea", but since the tea had to be brought up under enemy fire this alone led to more casualties. The shortage of boots had reached crisis proportions and, since Russian troops were never supplied with socks, the men had only their foot-rags. In despair, the grand-duke turned for help to Mikhail Rodzianko, the Duma president. He undertook to bring together all parties involved and jointly to seek ways of improvement; he did not, however, reckon with tchinovnik bureaucracy. Maklakov, the Interior Minister, was convinced the conference was a political manoeuvre on the part of those seeking a parliamentary government and wrote to Rodzianko saying that the necessary permission to hold it had been withheld by the Council of Ministers. Rodzianko later discovered that the matter had never been raised at the Council, and the supply of clothing did not begin to increase until early 1915.

The continuing ammunition shortage was more serious still. Like the army's other deficiencies, this had been the subject of long and inconclusive correspondence between Stavka and the War Ministry in Petrograd. Because of shortages, the casualty rate rose to between 50 and 60 per cent. and by mid-November Yanushkevich — begging Sukhomlinov to expedite shell output — even suggested hat the mere appearance of shells without — explosive charges would hearten the troops. On 6 December he wrote again reporting that cartridges were now also in short supply; wherever an officer was killed, soldiers, hungry, cold, bootless and with no ammunition were surrendering en masse. The letter closed: "Be merciful and give us instructions for everything possible to be ordered. Horse-shoes, cartridges, rifles. Nothing will be in excess."

On 10 December there was yet another appeal: "Both commanders-in-chief [at the Fronts] have sent telegrams that make my hair stand on end. Cartridges are disappearing. In Germany, articles have already appeared that 'we are at our last gasp', as we are almost not [sic] replying to their firing; that on the evidence of our soldiers [prisoners] our numbers are shrinking without being replaced, and that the artillery has been forbidden to shoot." Sukhomlinov was apparently left completely unmoved by these appeals. On 18 December, the western Allies were stunned to hear for the first time of the lack of rifles and shells, especially in view of the confident answer given to Joffre's inquiry of 23 September on this topic. Munitions were so short that there was little hope of a renewal of military activity before mid-April 1915.

On the home front too, shortages of essential commodities were already causing a rise in the cost of living. At the same time the censored newspapers could not entirely mask the reality of defeats (or victories which turned to ashes at the last moment), endless casualties and crowded hospitals in that first bitingly cold winter. At Tsarskoe Selo the tsar and tsarina hid behind a curtain of austere isolation. "There were", says Meriel Buchanan, "no balls, no music . . . the men we danced with last year had lost their lives in East Prussia or were fighting in the Carpathians."

Yet, although this was how the situation had crystallised at the end of 1914, the Russians had delivered the first serious setback to the Germans. On 2 September 1914, Matthias Erzberger, leader of the Catholic Centre Party in the Reichstag and right-hand-man of chancellor Bethmann Hollweg, presented a memorandum on his country's war aims. Germany would take advantage of victory to seize control of the European continent "for all the time", and one of the preconditions for this desirable state of affairs would be the breaking up of the "Russian colossus".[6]

In contrast, only three months later, even Falkenhayn had

ceased to talk of victory in the east, and was satisfying himself with the contemplation of "a good peace".

Chapter 9

A Cry For Help From the Grand-Duke

The lengthening calendar of grievances nursed by each side of the Triple Entente was composed of many separate issues. The French, for example, though now becoming aware of his difficulties, were impatient of the grand-duke's failure to loose his hordes against a numerically inferior enemy, while the Russians took the enforced stalemate of trench warfare in the west for a deliberate policy of inactivity.

On the Russian side, the most bitter resentment of all was reserved for Britain and the Royal Navy for the sequence of blunders culminating in Turkey's declaration for the Central Powers and, ipso facto, the severing of Russia's only direct link with its allies — the sea-lanes. This seemed to them to far outweigh minor naval activity in the Baltic. Britain's claim to be equally affected, since she was now forced to defend the Suez Canal against a Turkish incursion, scarcely seemed to compare with the magnitude of their own problems.

Since the beginning of the nineteenth century, especially after the Russo-Turkish War of 1877, the Sublime Porte's continental neighbours had become predatory relatives round the bed of "the sick man of Europe", carrying off any scrap of the Ottoman Empire its grasp had become too faltering to retain. First Greece, then Serbia, Bulgaria, Montenegro and Rumania had procured their independence. Bosnia and Herzegovina had been seized by Austria; Cyprus by Britain; Crete by Greece. Russia was ever-watchful for a greater opportunity: since St Basil had brought Christianity from Constantine's capital to the Steppes, Russia periodically restated her ambition to gain control of the Dardanelles Straits — the only route from the Black Sea to the Mediterranean — and to raise the cross of Christ once more on the Santa Sophia, even though Kuropatkin, the prudent Minister of War, had pointed out that retaining what was taken might put too great a strain on Russia's capacity.

Making Turkey an ally did not occur to anyone, even after 1908 when the Young Turk Party, under the Germanophile Enver Pasha, deposed the tyrannical Abdul Hamid and replaced him by his more liberal brother who ruled as Mehmet V, and revived Pan-Turanian dreams of a union of the ethnically-related peoples of Caucasia and Azerbaijan. The country's resurgence of spirit was nowhere under-estimated so greatly as in Britain, Turkey's long-standing ally. When the Turkish government made approaches for a treaty in 1911, Winston Churchill (then First Lord of the Admiralty) visited the country and delivered a homily on the benefits of maintaining good relations with Britain and the risks involved in falling foul of her. Their proposal for a treaty was rejected, and not even Germany considered it worthwhile to pursue the opportunity spurned by Britain.

Both countries had closer links with Turkey than the rest of the continent. Since 1822 Germany had been responsible for army organisation and training in Turkey, and this association was so strengthened under the Young Turk government that by 1913 a German military mission headed by General Liman von Sanders had virtually taken over the entire military administration of the country. Another German officer, Field Marshal von Goltz, was vice-president of the Superior Military Council through which the Minister of War delegated his functions.

At about this time, Britain had accepted an invitation to put the navy in order. This action was looked at askance in some Russian quarters since the Triple Entente was unlikely to benefit from an increase in Turkey's naval resources or fighting efficiency. However, it was preferable for this to be done by a friendly state rather than a hostile one. In 1912 the Germans had offered to sell two of their capital ships, the "Göben" and "Moltke", to the Turks, intending to devote the money raised to acquiring newer and better-armed vessels for themselves. To their chagrin, the offer was declined in favour of the purchase of two dreadnoughts from Britain, the "Sultan Osman" and the "Reshadieh", though the cost of some £10 million so exceeded imperial revenues that a popular subscription had to be raised.

As war became increasingly likely, Germany and Austria both awakened to Turkey's strategic importance astride the Dardanelles; if the straits were blocked the Russian Black Sea ports would be useless and her highly efficient fleet there, reformed and

modernised as a result of the "Potemkin" mutiny in 1906, either
made harmless or highly vulnerable to the Turkish shore batteries
if a break-out were attempted. Russia and France were also alive
to the situation and Turkey, therefore, suddenly found herself
with suitors on all sides. She was in no hurry to decide who to
favour until Britain precipitated matters. In late July the Turkish
crew of the "Reshadieh" which was about to be commissioned,
arrived in the Tyne to sail her home. The British Admiralty was
worried about the future of the two dreadnoughts for, if they
were handed over and Turkey came out on the side of the Triple
Alliance, their naval forces would have been augmented by two
capital ships. This could be avoided by seizing the vessels and thus
increasing the Allied navies, but repercussions on delicately
balanced Allied-Turkish relations might be highly unpleasant. No
one considered using the ships as a bargaining base for Turkey's
neutrality and on 28 July (the day Austria declared war on Serbia)
the ships were seized without warning or mention of restitution.

Britain's only expression of regret was a telegram from the
British Foreign Minister, Sir Edward Grey, in which he said he was
sure the government would understand why the two vessels had
been seized because of Britain's "own needs in the present crisis".
In view of the Turkish population's contribution to the dreadnoughts' purchase, ripples of fury over the incident were widespread. Six days later, to the ecstatic joy of Wilhelm II, the
Sublime Porte approached Germany in great secrecy for a treaty.
A draft had already been prepared and a copy was now telegraphed to Constantinople, where the Turks first hesitated to sign.
Their excuse was that several Cabinet ministers, assuring the treaty
was a draft, were highly critical of the fact that it both placed the
country's destiny completely in German hands. But actually
the Turks wanted to see the outcome of the first battles (which,
despite some disasters, appeared to be going in the Entente's
favour) before declaring war. Rifat Pasha, Turkish ambassador in
Vienna, telegraphed home: "Russians have taken Lemberg, they
dominate the road to Vienna . . . The only sane course for Turkey
consists in obtaining advantages from the Entente by pursuing a
strict neutrality."

Because of the secrecy surrounding the Turco-German Treaty,
the Russo-French manoeuvrings to preserve Turkey's neutrality
continued, the Russians abandoning their crusading mission to

Constantinople to the extent of combining with their allies to offer guarantees of "territorial integrity and political independence of Turkey — even in the event of Russian victory".

"The most we should ask," Foreign Minister Sazonov told Paléologue "is that a new régime should be drawn up for the Narrows, a régime which shall apply equally to all the states on the Black Sea, Russia, Bulgaria and Rumania."

At that time the British, French and German navies were all represented in the Mediterranean. France's main task was to guard the seaways from North Africa to her own Mediterranean ports at Marseilles and Toulon, along which transports were bringing colonial troops to the front. The principal threat came from the "Göben" (23,000 tons) and the "Breslau" (4,500 tons), vessels of the German Mediterranean fleet under Admiral Wilhelm Souchon. Both were faster than any of the 16 battleships, 6 cruisers and 24 destroyers of the French fleet. Because of this, the instructions to Admiral Sir Berkeley Milne — Souchon's British adversary — in the period before 4 August were to shadow the German ships and, should war be declared, "cover and if possible bring them to action". The Royal Naval forces involved were slower and heavier, comprising three 18,000 ton battle cruisers, for armoured cruisers, four light cruisers and some destroyers.

In late July Souchon sailed from the Austrian Adriatic port of Pola, where the "Göben" had been undergoing repairs; although these were not complete, it was essential he should be ready for action if war came, and he sailed full steam ahead towards the toe of Italy, arriving on 1 August. Although Italy was the third partner in the Triple Alliance, his request to call at Brindisi to fuel was refused on the grounds of neutrality. He accordingly sailed on toward the French sea-lanes, arranging a rendezvous with a German merchant ship in order to requisition coal from her, as was his right under German naval law. On 3 August he continued towards the Algerian ports of Bône and Philippeville, which he bombarded, but the German admiralty had bigger fish in view and had lost interest in French transports. Souchon was ordered to change course and make for Constantinople, but on the 4th encountered two British ships, the cruisers "Indomitable" and "Indefatigable". Since Britain was not yet at war, these vessels could only veer round and follow, but Souchon managed to shake them off and kept another rendezvous to take on coal in the

Straits of Messina. Again he was seen but no action was possible. This time the Italians invoked their neutrality, whereby the British ships were prevented from entering the straits, and the Germans were required to leave territorial waters within twelve hours. Both the Germans and Italians assumed that the interregnum would be used by the British to bring up overwhelming forces, but neither Sir Berkeley Milne nor, apparently, anyone else had considered the possibility that the "Göben" and "Breslau" were making for the Dardanelles; anxious to safeguard Alexandria and Port Said, Milne had taken the greater proportion of his forces to Malta, where Sicily lay between him and his quarry. Furthermore, Austria was now at war with Britain, and her small fleet could constitute a superior force if combined with German naval strength. The sole vessel lying in wait for "Göben" and "Breslau" therefore, was the light cruiser "Gloucester", whose commander could only signal position and course to the rest of the fleet, and pursue.

By the 8th and 9th the German ships were approaching the straits and though Souchon believed himself in imminent danger of attack, the Royal Navy was far behind. By the 10th he stood under the Turkish guns as every diplomatic endeavour was exerted by the Germans to let them through and by the British and French to keep them out until their own ships arrived. The Turks only submitted to the German demands when a virtual ultimatum was issued and it was agreed that, should the British follow them into the straits, they would be fired on. By the time the Royal Navy arrived, the German ships were sailing down towards the Sea of Marmara and their pursuers were warned to advance at their peril. Thus the supposedly invincible navy of the world's greatest sea-power had remained helpless while the vital interests of an ally were irretrievably damaged.

However, forcing the Turks into compromising their neutrality was only the first stage in German strategy. The "Göben" and "Breslau" were offered as substitutes for the vessels Britain had sequestrated: in practice they were given Turkish names but remained under Berlin admiralty orders. The embarrassed Turks were still in no hurry to declare war. By the end of September, Germany, with some 4,000 soldiers and sailors in Constantinople alone, decided matters must be brought to a climax: the renamed "Göben" and "Breslau", flying the crescent flag, sailed through the Bosphorus into the Black Sea on 28 October and bombarded

Odessa, Sebastopol and Feodozia.

The Turks' first inclination was to repudiate this deceit practised in their name and they sent a note to the Russian ambassador suggesting that "the happening on the Black Sea should be adjusted in a friendly spirit or by arbitration". However, the Allies demanded they prove their professed neutrality by expelling all the German forces in the country — an order which Djavid Bey, the Turkish Finance Minister, confessed his government was unable to give, much less enforce.

On 30 November Russia was compelled to declare war, and four days later Britain and France followed suit.

Thus, by first seizing the two Turkish ships on the Tyne, then by failing to keep the "Göben" and "Breslau" out of the Sea of Marmara, they had forced Russia to face a third enemy. Her armies were now opposed by a total of 153 divisions, against 141 opposing the combined French, Belgian and British armies in the west.

Infinitely more disastrous, Russia no longer had access to the Mediterranean. The only ports available for the importation of badly-needed munitions and the export of grain to pay for them were Archangel and Murmansk in the Arctic and Vladivostok in the Pacific, none equipped for handling large cargoes, all thousands of miles from the front and served by totally inadequate railway lines. Russia could only be reached by passing through Norway and Sweden, then across the Gulf of Bosnia to Finland, and the German fleet was present in overwhelming force in the Baltic. Even telegrams from France and Britain had to be re-routed.

In Russia, unfavourable comparisons were inevitably drawn between the British navy and their own, whose actions — though not affecting the final outcome — had on the whole been vigorously pursued by bold commanders like Kolchak, Essen and Eberhard whose large-scale mining operations had mainly forestalled German offensive efforts.

Yet there was no unanimous dismay at this menacing situation. Among Russians "mesmerised" by the "Byzantine mirage", as Paléologue put it, Turkey's belligerence seemed a God-sent way to realising the "age-old dreams" she had recently been prepared to renounce unconditionally, and the Foreign Minister commented that soon after the start of the war he had "strongly felt the pressure of public opinion urging" that the international situation should be used to satisfy Russian aspirations. There was now talk of Constantinople becoming a new southern capital of Russia, of the abolition of Turkish power and of uniting the Aegean and Black Seas.

With the more extreme members of the predominantly right-wing Duma adding their weight to the other pressures, negotiations with France and Britain began immediately, the Russians convinced that Britain was favourably disposed to their demands. This assumption was based on a remark reputedly made by King George V to the Russian ambassador, saying "Constantinople is yours", though the British Foreign Office gave a different reading of it.[1] By 11 November, Britain had conceded through ambassador Sir George Buchanan that "the question of the straits and Constantinople must be solved in the manner Russia desires". An ardent Sazonov told him: "Russia will never forget the proof of friendship England has given her today, never," and he was happy to agree to Britain's reciprocal demand that part of Persia, including Ispahan, should be incorporated into the British zone of that country. In consideration of the likely effect on such neutrals as Greece, Rumania and Bulgaria, this was to be kept secret.

On 21 November the tsar summoned Paléologue to Tsarkoe Selo where they discussed war aims. These had been concisely stated to Paléologue on 20 August by Sazonov, who declared: "My formula is a simple one. We must destroy German militarism." It was also agreed that there must be sweeping political changes in Germany to avoid any revival of Kaiserism (thus acquiescing in the kind of danger Witte had envisaged: the creation of more republican democracies in Europe). Other provisions were that France, Britain and Belgium should take over Germany's colonies, Bohemia should be given sovereign independence and Belgium enlarged.

In the new situation created by Turkey's hostility, the tsar felt that these aims did not go far enough. While agreeing the prime objective to be "the destruction of German militarism", he also wanted the Turks expelled from Europe, Thrace annexed and Constantinople neutralised under international status. France should retain her interests in Syria and Palestine; Serbia should have Bosnia and Herzegovina restored and also gain part of Dalmatia and North Albania. Greece should get South Albania, except for Vallona which was to go to Italy. Bulgaria would probably gain Macedonia from Serbia; Russia would acquire Austria's Polish territories and part of East Prussia; France would not only recover Alsace-Lorraine but would gain the Rhine provinces, while Belgium would get Aix-la-Chapelle. France and England would share the German colonies; Schleswig would return to Denmark and the State of Hanover would be revived.

Thus Europe was parcelled out as though the end of the war were in sight, before Turkey had fired a single shot. The shooting, however, was soon to begin, though even here the Russians allowed themselves to be restricted. The British commander-in-chief, Sir John French, was concerned that troops should not be diverted to this new theatre of operations, but Sazonov quickly reassured him that not one man would be deflected from the German front: "Before all things, we must beat Germany whose defeat will involve the ruin of Turkey." The task of holding up any Turkish incursion would thus fall to the Russian Caucasian Army, made up of two army corps, the First Caucasian and the Second Turkestan, with a strength of about 100,000 men. They were commanded by General Myshlaievsky, a military historian rather than an experienced field-commander, but his chief-of-staff was General Nicholas Yudenich, an excellent soldier who had instituted his own training schemes geared to fighting in the local conditions. He now faced a very considerable test.

The Porte's armies were personally commanded by the Young Turk leader, Enver Pasha, thirty-three years old, dark, handsome and arrogant. Having developed a vast plan to humiliate Russia and annexe her "Turanian" lands in the Caucasus, he had three army corps deployed along her front in this area, the Ninth, Tenth and Eleventh, consolidated as the Third Army and totalling some 150,000 men against 100,000 Russians. Like the whole Turkish army, these troops were variable in quality; the best of the "askers" came of Anatolian peasant stock, and and although their bravery and natural warrior instinct was combined with a tendency to desert in large numbers when things proved too unpleasant, they were nevertheless asked to endure far greater hardship and deprivation than almost any other troops.

Enver's ambitious plan called for a frontal attack by the Ninth

Corps, pushing the Russians towards Sarikamis, while the Tenth and Eleventh Corps, concentrating along a line from Trabzon on the coast, made their way through the high mountain passes, wheeling round to encircle the Russian defences after by-passing them. His German advisers gave this a mixed reception. One group felt that the offensive was too ambitious to be carried out in winter before the Turkish armies – destitute of everything from warm clothes to field kitchens – had been adequately prepared for it. The majority believed that even if the operation were unsuccessful it would help to divide Russian efforts and, if successful, might open new possibilities for the future on the eastern battlefront.

The dilemma was resolved by the Russians themselves when Yudenich and Myshlaievsky decided to take the initiative against Turkey. A few days after the declaration of war the First Caucasian Army Corps, under Bergmann, crossed the border and marched on the town of Koprikoy encountering negligible resistance. The Turks were ready, and forces from the Ninth and Eleventh Corps mounted a speedy counter-attack which – but for the arrival of reinforcements – would have threatened the Russians with encirclement. Even so, they were compelled to pull back and the situation was only stabilised after fierce engagements which cost the Russians some 40 per cent of their men. The Turkish troops were highly encouraged and Enver decided to attempt his great offensive movement on 22 December.

On paper, the two Turkish armies were timed to advance simultaneously, but the troops marching in single file through the narrow mountain passes were impeded by heavy snow and blizzards; in thin uniforms and with inadequate rations, casualties from frostbite were heavy and units lost contact with one another. The Tenth Corps thus found itself too far forward, with a widening gap between itself and its sister-corps.

As usual, the Russians had only a confused idea what was happening, and after first wildly underestimating the opposition, they then overestimated it, causing Myshlaievsky to order a general retreat beginning on the night of 25/26 December.

Meanwhile Yudenich, who had assumed command of the Second Turkestan Corps (i.e. half the Russian Caucasian Army), decided to resist at Sarikamis. On the 26th, when his defensive dispositions were far from complete, superior Turkish forces from the Ninth Corps began advancing on him from Bardiz. Skirmishes between the Turks and some Cossack patrols led the Ninth Corps commander to believe the Russians were present in greater numbers than they actually were, and he therefore broke off battle and bivouacked. With a night temperature 20° below freezing and gale-force winds, hundreds of "askers" were frozen to death while many others deserted, halving the Turkish strength in less than twelve hours.

Hafiz Hakki, commander of the Tenth Corps still well ahead of the other two, had the idea of taking Ardahan — deep inside Russia — on his own, but was ordered back by Enver in order to take the Russian defence at Sarikamis from the rear. This involved crossing the Allahuekber massif by way of a high pass between the central and southernmost peaks, and though this was achieved in just over thirty-six hours, it cost more than 30 per cent of the troops. The 26th saw Enver anxiously awaiting the arrival of this unit in order to continue the assault on Sarikamis with all strength.

On hearing that the Turkish corps were approaching his rear, Myshlaievsky again wished to order a general retreat, and it took all Yudenich's persuasion to obtain a deferment of this order. By the 27th it was the Russians instead of Enver who were being reinforced.

On the 28th the Tenth Corps arrived, but were so exhausted by their exertions that Enver had to give them a day's rest. The following morning, however, having suffered further losses through exposure and desertion, the Turkish armies began taking up position. The Russians at Sarikamis were apparently surrounded; their only exit road — that leading to Kars — was straddled by detachments of the Tenth Corps.

The anxious grand-duke, now back at Baranovichi, was getting only pessimistic reports. Moreover, the two Russian corps commanders were still at odds: Yudenich opted for standing at Sarikamis but Bergmann pressed Myshlaievsky to execute his order to retreat.

Myshlaievsky himself was pleading for reinforcements, but the grand-duke — remembering his undertaking to restrict the forces engaged against Turkey in the area — refused his request, deciding to ask the other Allies for help. As Britain was most concerned about the threat the Turks might pose to Egypt and the Suez Canal, he turned to her. What he had in mind was a distraction, perhaps some sort of British naval threat, for while he did not personally share dreams of a re-Christianised Constantinople, he would be playing into the hands of his court enemies if he encouraged another power, even an ally, to Middle Eastern adventures.

The Russian appeal, dispatched by Sir George Buchanan on 2 January 1915, reached London at a moment of psychological uncertainty. The war which was to be "all over by Christmas" showed no sign of ending; the war of movement had atrophied in the trench-lines, and the so-called "race to the sea" in which each army tried to outflank the other had extended these from Switzerland to the Channel; while the failure of Falkenhayn's Ypres offensive had shown them to be virtually impregnable to frontal attack. At the same time, the Russian steamroller had not so much ground to a halt as failed to grind at all. Leading military, naval and political figures were all urging the necessity of discovering new theatres where the war of movement could be restored and Lloyd George submitted a lengthy memorandum to the War Council on the day the grand-duke' telegram was dispatched suggesting that the French and British either combine forces with the Serbians in a mass move against Austria, or attack through Syria against the Turks.

As early as 6 September, the First Lord of the Admiralty Winston Churchill, had suggested that the landing of a sufficiently large army at the Gallipoli peninsula would secure the Dardanelles. Since the troops in this case would have been Russian, and they were fully extended elsewhere, the proposal was allowed to lapse though the secretary of the War Council, Lieutenant-Colonel Maurice Hankey, was appointed head of a Dardanelles' Commission set up to examine the possibilities. A report appeared on 21 December, its arrival on Churchill's desk coinciding with a letter from Kitchener, the War Minister, suggesting naval action to prevent the Turks from sending more men to the Caucasus. Had the grand-duke been considering this particular locality and type of enterprise, he could have utilised the Russian Black Sea Fleet which, with 5 pre-dreadnought type battleships, 3 cruisers, 17 destroyers and 4 submarines, was immeasurably larger than the

Turkish Fleet even when the "Göben" and "Breslau" were added. Although currently bottled up in the Black Sea, it was a highly formidable force despite the disadvantage that its ships, being coal-burning, had a shorter range than the oil-burning ships of the Royal Navy. It was commanded by the experienced and resourceful Vice-Admiral A. A. Eberhard, whose exploits included mining the entrance to the Bosphorus, sinking Turkish troop transports destined for Enver's Caucasian campaign and twice engaging the "Göben" and "Breslau". The grand-duke would not have considered storming the Straits without enlisting his co-operation.

Another plan was advanced by Lord Fisher, the First Sea Lord, who wanted to build 600 craft of all types and use them to transport a Russian force to the Pomeranian coast. He objected to the plan for the Dardanelles as a purely naval concept, pointing out that so far bombardment from the sea had only succeeded in stirring the Turks into improving the poor condition of their short batteries.[2] The operation could only succeed if mounted as a joint naval and army assault, and even then the essence of success would be "celerity". The army opposed a combined operation, however; they had no troops to spare for such excursions and therefore the whole thing must be left to the navy (currently under-employed, in their opinion) which at long last would have a positive role in the war.

Despite Fisher's Napoleonic exhortation to celerity, the debate dragged on after the crisis leading to the grand-duke's telegram had passed.

Yudenich, who besides being commander of the Second Turkestan Corps, was also chief-of-staff to the Caucasian Army, assumed the leadership of the First Caucasian Corps himself. He felt sure that the Turks were now in straitened circumstances because they were less acclimatised and inadequately equipped for a winter war. A suicidal attack on Sarikamis by the Eleventh Corps on 1 January resulted in heavy losses for both sides, and the Tenth Corps was meanwhile threatened with encirclement by the Russian reinforcements and had to withdraw. In this it was more fortunate than the Eleventh Corps which, forced to surrender when surrounded on 2 January, was reduced to a thousand men.

Discouraged, Enver began to pull his straggling troops back

through the mountain passes. The army of 95,000 which reached
the Russians had suffered 75,000 casualties, some 30,000 of which
caused by exposure. A subsidiary column which had invaded
north-western Persia was also forced back, harassed both by the
Cossacks at its heels and mountain robbers pillaging their supplies.
The return to metropolitan Turkey of the mauled and bedraggled
remnant of the Third Army signalled an outbreak of furious wrath
upon the Turkish Armenians through whose land it had man-
oeuvred. Since the Turkish occupation of Armenia began in the
16th century, its Christian inhabitants had been treated with even
greater cruelty than most of the subject races, and in 1896 the
world had been shocked by accounts of appalling massacres and
atrocities. Now the whole pattern was to be repeated on an
infinitely vaster scale, and in contravention of an international
agreement signed only in February 1914. The Turks claimed in
justification that the Armenians had largely caused their defeat by
actively assisting the Russians, but this did not hide the evidence
that the extermination of the Armenians had formed an essential
part of the Young Turks' policy from the outset. This was no
spontaneous outburst of primitive vengeance, but a planned
campaign whose execution merely awaited an excuse and such a
screen from world opinion as the war now afforded. In an active
campaign of genocide maintained until the end of 1915, perhaps
as many as 500,000 died and many more − particularly young
women − were carried off into virtual slavery.[3] The secret was
kept until the middle of 1915 even from the Germans, who then
promptly protested. The Turks, mindful of Louvain and Brussels,
declared that "they did not consider their allies competent to
instruct them in humanity".

As the invaders pulled back, the grand-duke sent immediate word
to London that the help he had sought from them was now
unnecessary. It was too late, for at its meeting on 13 January the
British War Council had authorised preparations "for a naval
expedition in February to bombard and take the Gallipoli peninsula with Constantinople as its objective."

Chapter 10

The Jackals Close In

Since its inception in November 1914, the headquarters of Oberost had been a palace at Posen (Poznan), where each evening the twenty or so senior officers dined together in one of its halls. The ends of the table were occupied respectively by the commander and his chief-of-staff, but any resemblance to dinner party hosts was dispelled by the stern masculinity of their countenances. Once the meal was over, the group would linger to smoke cigars and talk, and Ludendorff wrote of this as his one relaxation through the day, before leaving to continue working in his office until the early hours. But in those first days of January 1915 there could have been little to cheer either his colleagues or himself.

German newspapers had applauded the victories of Mackensen's Ninth Army which had won Lodz and half Russian Poland, and Hindenburg and Ludendorff found themselves hailed as Germany's up and coming men. As Hindenburg admits, however, they had secured only a temporary reprieve, and while Brusilov in Galicia might have withdrawn behind the Carpathians, there was little confidence among the Austrian commanders that he could be prevented from penetrating again. Reports on the state of the Austrian armies reaching the Germans through their liaison officers were consistently pessimistic.

The defeat of the Turkish Third Army came as a further blow, for while the Russians would feel disinclined to reduce the guard on their southern marches, they would certainly feel it inessential, for the immediate future, to increase the number of troops there. In addition, the enemies which Austria's heedless policies had made for her in the past were making it clear that they did not intend to be left profitless by her present embarrassment. As the price of continued non-intervention, Italy was demanding Trentino, Istria, Dalmatia and Albania, and Rumania the provinces of Transylvania and Bukovina. The behaviour of Bulgaria,

Turkey's traiditional enemy, was also unpredictable; Tsar Ferdinand saw Constantinople as the seat of a new Byzantine Empire, where in this case he would reign as "basileus". All these countries had forces to be reckoned with, in the case of Italy an army 2 million strong.

On 5 January, the commander-in-chief of the Austro-Hungarian army, Archduke Frederick, had written gloomily to the Emperor: "It is certain that an attack by Italy or Rumania or even only one of these two states would place the Monarchy in a militarily untenable position." This view was echoed by the politicians. The only way to silence the whining of these jackals, as the archduke pointed out, was by demonstrating with a resounding victory that the Hapsburg empire remained a force to be reckoned with. Thus — at a time when both sides might have been prepared to consider more reasonable counsels — the issues were hardened by those neutrals who, proclaiming their dedication to peace, were showing they had a vested interest in the continuance of war.

To further confuse the complicated situation, Serbia, the country where a military success seemed easiest to attain, was also the place where a campaign would be least prudent. A victory here would bring the Austrian armies close to the borders, thus provoking Italy to an alarmed, defensive response.

In any case, Conrad felt his most urgent problems lay in the Carpathian mountain passes; there was also Przemysl fortress where Kusmannek's army of 100,000 men was still besieged, and which had become invested with as much emotional significance as the French were later to attach to the fortresses of Verdun. The notion that "he who has Przemysl has Galicia" had become so fixed in the Austrian mind that, as the Austrian Official History stated, its "relinquishment except under the utmost duress, would have undermined the spirit of army and people." The effort expended on its retention was quite disporportionate to its intrinsic military value. As to the manner of its relief, Conrad's mind constantly returned to the great theme of the double-headed assault in which Austrians and Germans would meet in triumph midway across the salient of Russian Poland. This would not only save the fortress, but the gaining of so vast a territory would also deter any would-be aggressor. His one problem, however, was that he was desperately short of the men needed for his part in such an enterprise.

On New Year's Day, 1915, he and Ludendorff went to Berlin to meet the German commander-in-chief, where he argued that his deficiencies should be made good from his ally's resources. Falkenhayn, remembering von Schlieffen's aphorism that "the fate of Austria will be decided not on the Bug, but on the Seine", was as implacably opposed as ever to what seemed a policy of throwing good money after bad in supporting a dangerously weakening ally, when a definite verdict could only be obtained in the west. For, as Hindenburg explains, "in the west was that enemy [France] whose chauvinistic agitation against us had not left us in peace even in times of peace. In the west, too, was now that other enemy [Britain] who every German was convinced was the motive force working for the destruction of Germany." This apart, soldiers like Falkenhayn — responsible for overall strategy — were still terrified that what had happened to Napoleon's forces would happen to their own.

The argument became so intense that the Kaiser was called upon to arbitrate. Oberost, the leading counsel for the "easterners" propounded Conrad's plan and added that once it had succeeded in its purpose of "striking Russia to the ground", a revitalised Austria would, with Turkish co-operation, be free to sweep through the Balkans. Here the Kaiser saw a "way round" for Germany, and he was supported by Chancellor Bethmann-Hollweg, Foreign Minister Jagow and others. In addition to their pressure, Falkenhayn also had to contend with the much-publicised achievements of the Hindenburg-Ludendorff partnership. All he could offer were arguments based on strategic technicalities which, because they only half-understood them, the politicians found unimpressive. Hollweg even suggested dismissing Falkenhayn in favour of the Oberost "double act".

The Kaiser succumbed to the seductive picture presented to him. On 8 January, two and a half infantry and one cavalry division were handed over to Conrad which, when augmented by Austro-Hungarian units, constituted the nucleus of a new formation, "The German South Army", commanded by the German General von Linsingen and with a German staff. In mid-January it started to take its place in the line on the right of Boroević's Third, and at the same time Oberost received four corps from army reserve which formed a Tenth Army under General von Eichhorn.

Falkenhayn perceived the threat posed by the Oberost commanders to his own position too late, and tried to reimpose his rule by dividing the opposition, making Ludendorff chief-of-staff of Linsingen's army. However, Hindenburg successfully appealed to the Kaiser to revoke this decision.[1] The commander-in-chief was further chagrined because the decision to support the eastern front involved his being compelled to send four reserve corps, made up of conscripts of the 1914 class, which he had personally earmarked for France. He only handed these over when Hollweg renewed his demand for dismissal.

Having acquired extra, if insufficient, troops, detailed plans were drawn up and on 12 January the dining room at Posen was honoured by a visit from the commander-in-chief himself. Hoffmann, as operations chief, explained the proposals: at one end of the front Conrad would use his enlarged forces for an offensive in a north-westerly direction, taking the pressure off the Carpathian line and, with luck, relieving Przemysl. The Germans would attack in a south-easterly direction, out of East Prussia towards Bialystok. The Russian armies would, in Churchill's phrase, be grabbed in the pincers of some giant crab.

Falkenhayn disliked this plan on sight, mainly because the Austro-German forces, inadequate for such grandiose operations, were heavily out-numbered by the Russians; the offensive troops would include the inexperienced 1914 conscripts who would be expected to behave like veterans; and there would be no reserves available.

Further, a 370 mile-long front lay between the two enemy flanks and the need to make the attacking force as large as possible involved the line here being thinly stretched. There was, he felt, little chance of co-ordinating two such widely spaced movements, and weakening the central front carried considerable inherent dangers. He was also worried about the weather, with ice likely to continue into March, followed by thaw and floods. Even now, Falkenhayn as chief commanding officer, was prevented from making any changes while the chancellor was lobbying for his dismissal and the Kaiser himself had given the eastern front commanders his imperial blessing. Active preparation was therefore allowed to proceed.

Brusilov had said that the initial Russian Plans "A" and "G" represented the entire product of her High Command's strategic creativity, and certainly seemed at a total loss after the march on Silesia had twice been thwarted. Winter weather and the ammunition shortage were additional problems.

On 5 January, the grand-duke asked the French if he should go on the defensive in order to let them have all available resources, or assume the offensive in which case he urgently needed some of the ammunition destined for the French Army. This hint for material assistance was reinforced by the tsar who, in a message to the French president, reasserted his determination to "fight to the finish", but insisted that shortage of ammunition precluded an advance before April. Poincaré paraphrased the French answer as "we can give nothing because we have not sufficient even for ourselves", illustrating the different scale of values on the respective fronts. When the grand-duke begged Joffre several weeks later to be as active as possible in preventing the Germans from continuing to move large forces, the French commander-in-chief claimed he was unable to meet this request because to do so would involve his supplies falling below 400 per gun. This compares with the 100 per gun (see p. 68, Forward – To Berlin) regarded by the grand-duke as the essential minimum.

The Russian army's stagnation was mainly caused by dissension splitting their command. The disagreement between the two Front commanders Ivanov and Ruszki, which had first arisen at the Siedlce staff conference in November, had increased as each demanded priority of resources for his own sector. Stavka merely stood by, either from inertia or because alternative men of talent were lacking, though replacement of one or both commanders was the only permanent solution.

Ivanov, who with his long, forked white beard looked like a Father Christmas who had absentmindedly donned the gold epaulettes of a Russian general, was an officer of "mouzhik" stock who had worked his way up to a professorship at the Nicholas Academy and so despised luxury and soft-living that he slept on a broken down camp bed in a billet which had neither carpet nor curtains. Brusilov, who has scarcely a good word for any of his colleagues nevertheless describes him as narrow-minded, vacillating, finicky and "deficient in intelligence though not in self-esteem".

Ruszki, on the other hand, was a former guards' officer with an executive flair for delegation, idolised by his staff. Brusilov's comments are unlikely to be unbiased in view of the fact that he considered Ruszki had cheated him of recognition at Lemberg, but Knox, on what subsequently seemed flimsy evidence, admired his clarity of mind. He claimed priority for his own front on the grounds that he was facing the Germans, while the South West Front faced only the inferior Austro-Hungarians.

At Stavka, opinion generally favoured the Ivanov thesis that "the way to Berlin lies through Austria-Hungary", one strong argument being that Vienna was 400 kilometres nearer. But in mid-January Danilov, as operations chief, wrote a memorandum urging that East Prussia be conquered because of the flank-threat it represented. In consequence, Ivanov was now ordered to go on the defensive, as Ruszki had been in late November. Since he was then planning an offensive which he did not propose to abandon, he quietly continued making plans and drawing supplies. Although rank disobedience, this was the only course open to him since – with Przemysl held in balance – if he did not attack, Conrad would have to do so.

Stavka aimed to launch the new East Prussian offensive on 23 February. This was the earliest practical date because of the need to stockpile ammunition, a task now more complicated by a crisis in rolling stock in addition to the existing shortage of railway lines.

Nevertheless, Plehve was detached from the Fifth Army and sent north to form a new Twelfth Army, which was to be positioned from the Narev line across the East Prussian salient, severing it from West Prussia and Germany proper. Everything was done to give the Twelfth overwhelming strength, and Stavka even parted with two of its own reserve corps. The long delay in beginning the assault was the more dangerous because of the Russians' notorious inability to keep their movements secret, and to cover this their Tenth Army under Sievers was ordered to keep the enemy engaged. Sievers' main forces were concentrating along a line running southwards from east of Gumbinnen to Johannisburg (Pisz), in front of the Masurian Lakes; its right, along the River Memel, was only lightly held as Sievers believed that the Germans would not risk extending their lines in the north while the south was in danger. Had the Russian commander been the agent of some colossal German sabotage conspiracy he would hardly have offered up his army more skilfully to what was to come.

For their part in the coming combined offensive, the Germans envisaged a pincer movement by their Eighth on the right, and the newly constituted Tenth Army under von Eichhorn on the left, coming through Sievers' flanks to envelop him. Their Tenth would therefore strike just where he had weakened his line. Falkenhayn had expressed concern about the centre of the German line facing Prussia, and the Seventy-sixth Reserve Division (under von Gallwitz) and Mackensen's Ninth Army, north and south of the Vistula respectively, were to maintain an active defence here. It was hoped that Mackensen might also be able to re-liquefy the battle lines east of Lodz between the rivers Bzura and Ravka, and the Germans had a secret weapon which they hoped would make this possible.

Mackensen concentrated some 600 guns, including a number of 15 cm. heavy howitzers, along a seven-mile front. Over 100,000 hand-picked troops of the "Death Divisions" had been massed ready to exploit the openings about to be torn through the Russian lines. On 3 January, the artillery opened fire. Russian officers advancing during a lull noticed, above the usual smell of burnt explosive, an odour of formalin, strongest near the centre of the explosions, but no one attached particular significance to this.

Germany, the least affected of the belligerents by the shell shortage, suffered only from a shortage of steel. This had led to their using cast iron which, because of the thickness needed to compensate for the materials' frangibility under stress, so reduced the size of the explosive charge that it failed to fragment the casing. Experiments aimed at improving this led to the idea of filling the cavity with an irritant gas. At first a combination of gas and bullets was used in shrapnel shells;[2] when this failed it was mixed with TNT in the vain hope that this would spread the gas. Mackensen's heavy howitzers had been firing shells of this type while Hindenburg, Ludendorff, Hoffmann and a group of German chemists watched from a strategic point. The experience was another bitter disappointment for, as Hoffmann said, "the chief effect of the gas was destroyed by the intense cold". The liquid gas in the shells failed to vapourise and, where it did, the mystified Russians stood their ground choking and weeping. In fact, the unprecedented rain of high explosive endured by the Russian troops as usual without reply from their own guns, should have neutralised the defences, but such was their determination that they only gradually fell back before the German infantry.

When the Germans pursued, they fell victims to the trap the Russians had prepared; behind the first trenchlines machine and field-guns now opened fire. The assault lasted for seven days, during which the Russians drove the attackers back to their starting points.

The Russians claimed a victory, but the Germans had succeeded in their primary objective of diverting attention from the line further north and making it appear that any attack would come in the centre. They therefore reinforced their front at this point, and when captured German army orders pointed unmistakably toward an augmentation of strength in East Prussia — site of their own projected offensive — the Russians did nothing beyond withdrawing their siege artillery some miles.

To prevent the Russians from transferring troops from one part of the front to another, the Austrian and German attacks in the south and north respectively were roughly to be co-ordinated, but the Austrian offensive in the Carpathians was timed to move first. It began on 23 January and lasted three days, and, apart from the recapture of the Uszok Pass, achieved nothing before the cold, lack of ammunition and chaotic communications brought it to an end.

However, those who took part experienced the agony of waging war in such altitudes. Because of the Austrian shortage of troops, men were kept in the line far beyond the normal limits of endurance and only admitted to hospital when half-dead. Bootless, in stinking rags, their bodies covered with lice, they were tired enough to fall asleep standing upright, and were exposed to frequent Russian harassment. Whole companies vanished overnight in raging blizzards, to be discovered later as piles of frozen, blackened corpses. Under these appalling conditions, they were expected to advance against an infinitely stronger, better equipped and acclimatised enemy and attempts to persuade Conrad to stop such operations only resulted in the dismissal of the protesters. The only success came from an army group under von Pflanzer-

Baltin, at the extreme southern end of the Austrian line. He advanced steadily through three-foot deep snowdrifts on the Russians in Bukovina, pushing them toward the River Dniestr.

At the end of the month, Ivanov launched the offensive for which he had secretly been preparing. Within days, Boroević's Third Army was retreating in disorder, having lost more than 100,000 men since 23 January. A fortnight later, Brusilov's Eighth Army was moving on the passes once more. Despite his insubordination, Stavka was sufficiently pleased with Ivanov's results to send him the experienced Thirteenth Finnish Corps from Ruszki's front, which further weakened the defences on the right flank of Sievers' Tenth Army.

In the northern sector the German advance began on 7 February with the Eighth Army, which took Sievers so completely by surprise that it was two days before he realised what was happening. The weather and consequent state of the terrain put the heaviest brake on German movement; the troops marched through blinding snowstorms, roads and railways were covered by deep drifts and the ground was so hard and slippery it was as much as ten or twelve straining horses could do to drag a single gun. Nonetheless, as their armies gained momentum they were able to use their artillery to full effect, while the Russians constantly ran out of ammunition.

The Eighth Army's right wing, pushing round the Masurian Lakes, took Johannisburg while other units crossed the River Pisa and advanced on Rajgorod where they met with some resistance. Meanwhile, the centre was pursuing Russian forces in the direction of Lyck (Elk). All these movements converged on the fortress town of Augustow to capture the Russian forces there; then in the second phase Eichhorn's Tenth Army began advancing on 8 February and two days later reached the Insterburg – Kovno Road, wheeling to take up a position north of Augustow. There had been some delay to the Eighth's centre caused by the Third Siberian Corps' obstinate defence at Lyck, so the town was not taken until 14 February when the Siberians evaded the German attempts to surround them.

The Russians were now mainly confined to an area between Suwalki and Augustow where there had been much heavy fighting the previous autumn.

Since the Eighth Army began operations a day before the

Tenth, and this came in the wake of Mackensen's attack south of the Vistula and the diversionary tactics by Gallwitz's Seventy-sixth Reserve Division north of the river, Ruszki concluded that the enemy thrust would develop on his left. He therefore moved troops from the right to protect the flank of the armies massing along the Narev and, once again, made the Germans' task easier. By 15 February, the Tenth Army had reached the town of Suwalki. Some 70,000 troops of Sievers' army, mostly from the Twentieth Corps under Bulgakov, were concentrated in the area round Augustow with the Germans on both flanks and at their rear.

Now Plehve's Twelfth was at last ordered to abandon its East Prussian offensive and rush to the assistance of the Tenth, while the First Army was sent to face Gallwitz.

By 21 February, the Twentieth Corps and Bulgakov were completely ensnared in the forest. Eichhorn, in command of the entire sector for this battle, including the Eighth Army formations already there, rearranged his troops to guard against a Russian counter-attack from the Narev direction. The Eighth was ordered to move on Bialystok and then against the fortress of Osowiec, but everything depended on the quick subjugation of the troops in the Augustow forest. Here any similarity to Tannenberg ended. This time the Russians did not disintegrate into frightened and disorganised groups so intent on survival that they flung themselves against the enemy's cordon. Under Bulgakov, himself severely wounded, they held out and kept German troops and artillery tied down.

The German attack on Osowiec went ahead, but failed for lack of strength, and the Russians brought up sufficient reinforcements to enable them to hold the line.

In Augustov the Twentieth Corps made two unsuccessful attempts to break out, on the 19th and 20th. They subsequently regrouped, and with no food, ammunition running low and their communications with Ruszki at Godno cut off, they still held out, eventually being pushed back on the 21st after a heavy bombardment from eleven artillery batteries. Trying to escape to the south, they ran into other enemy formations and were forced to surrender.

The Germans captured about 100,000 prisoners, including 9 generals, also 300 guns and 170 machine guns. The Tenth Army was broken, and Sievers became another Russian general who the Germans had outwitted, discredited and destroyed in battle.

However, the problems caused by the strained relations between the South West and North West commanders were solved, for after the battle Ruszki was retired and his place taken by Alexeiev, Ivanov's chief-of-staff. Alexeiev tried to organise a counter-attack across the Nieman with the new formations which had been collected, but the raw, half-trained troops attacked over open ground in closed formation and were cut down by machine-gun fire. In all 80,000 fell to no avail, though further attacks on Osowiec by the Eighth Army were beaten off.

By the end of February, Hindenburg and Ludendorff had to call off their offensive. The Winter Battle of the Masurian Lakes, as it was later called, was over and the Russians could regard the Polish salient as saved. The Germans had once more inflicted enormous casualties and made territorial gains which were widely publicised at home. Yet these gains were meaningless. With the Russians in strong defensive positions, liable to attack, they were untenable and had to be abandoned. Moreover, Austria was still in danger and a new, ominous threat was looming in the Mediterranean.

While yet another great battle had raged along their front, it seemed to the Russians that their allies had been incapable of giving effective aid. On 16 February, claiming it was prompted by the need to help Russia, Joffre had launched an offensive in the Reims-Soissons area, which was being steadily pressurised by the Germans. On 12 March, after a month of heavy but fruitless fighting, Grand Quartier Général produced a communiqué claiming that it had helped to secure "the brilliant British and Russian victories . . ." by pinning down large forces on the front. Even Poincaré dismissed this apologia, considering French losses — 25,000 — exorbitant for a mere "pinning down" operation. The sceptical Russians were unimpressed, and Paléologue recorded that the Russian public displayed an open francophobia, aggravated by the discovery that the Germans were transferring troops from west to east with impunity, and also sending newly-raised divisions to the Russian rather than the France-Flanders front. By 17 March, according to the estimates of Russian intelligence, there were forty-seven or forty-eight German corps in Russia, whose army was also in confrontation with the Austrians and Turks, compared with approximately the same number facing the combined forces of France and Britain.

However, the Russians were not entirely accurate regarding the facts of Allied assistance. The War Council in London, which on 13 January had decided to send a naval force to the Dardanelles, had on 9 February approved the plan put forward by Lloyd-George (Minister of Munitions) to send forces via Salonica to stiffen Serbia's resistance. If joined by the neutral Balkan states such as Rumania, Bulgaria, and particularly Greece, whose premier leaned towards the Entente, it would be possible to strike the Central Powers in the rear by way of the Danube. Kitchener, whose presence dominated not only the War Office but also the General Staff, had earlier refused troops for the Dardanelles but was now able to provide a division of regulars – the Twenty-ninth – for Salonica, in conjunction with a French division. Since this operation bore none of the political complications of that against the Turks, the grand-duke was also able to promise a corps of his best troops. There were therefore two separate operations in hand at this time, one naval and one military, both intended to affect the Eastern Front.

The first began on 19 February when eight British and four French battleships, concentrated in the Dardanelles approaches, bombarded the Turkish forts guarding them with inconclusive results. Bad weather intervened, but following a resumption on the 25th, the long-range guns guarding the approaches were systematically destroyed at a total cost of 160 rounds of ammunition. The minesweepers moved up, and by the 26th, three battleships entered the Straits. More remarkable still, naval landing parties were put ashore and destroyed the remaining guns with little serious opposition from the Turks.

The reputation of the Royal Navy, tarnished by the "Göben" and "Breslau" affair, was so far redeemed that toasts to it were drunk in Russian messes. By 2 March, the outer defences had been destroyed and the minesweepers could move forward once more. When Churchill telegraphed Admiral Carden, the British naval commander, and asked how many "fine days" were needed for the navy to get through, he was told: "Fourteen."

The naval operations also had a striking effect in the Balkans. Bulgaria now seemed likely to move against Turkey while Rumania and Italy appeared to be preparing to declare for the Entente, and on 1 March Venizelos, the Greek premier, offered an army corps to be sent to Gallipoli.

The closing days of February found Conrad still desperate to relieve Przemysl where supplies, according to a commisariat report, would run out by 18 March. On the 27th another agonising offensive was launched in the Carpathians. Bohm-Ermölli's Second Army was wedged between the threadbare Third and Linsingen's German South Army, and a group from it under the bombastic Hungarian general, Tersztyanski, was to assail the Russians from behind the Uszok and Lupkow Passes. However, the Russians simply pulled back until the attackers had outrun their supply lines. Even the successes of Linsingen's army and Pflanzer-Baltin's forces on the right, which pushed the Russians across the Dniestr, could not affect the issue: they were too far away.

The fortress had so far cost the Austrians three abortive offensives, but the Russians could now concentrate all their efforts on its investment. Although a fortified city, Przemysl was something of a contradiction for it was surrounded by peaceful gardens and neat farms and had a civil population of some 50,000 people. Its defences were in the form of concentric rings, according to principles adduced by the Belgian engineer Henri Brialmont. Nineteen permanent forts and twenty-three lesser ones with batteries and fieldworks stood sentinel along its thirty-mile perimeter, and a further ring was formed by the city ramparts themselves. As well as 7.5 cm and 15 cm guns in cupola mountings, there were four 30.5 cm Skoda howitzers.

The Russians had no comparable artillery, and certainly nothing capable of breaching the defensive walls, but they had tried aerial bombing and undermining in their efforts to do so.

Kusmannek, on the Austrian side, had made various attempts to reach his compatriots, and in a successful sortie on 9/10 December 1914, a force from Przemysl under General Arpad von Tamasy succeeded in joining hands with the advance guard of the Third Army under Krautmann. This had lasted only until the Russians separately defeated both Tamasy's and Krautmann's forces, and Conrad's later offensives of 23 January and 27 February had come nowhere near this success. Przemysl had extended its lease of life beyond the supply limit set by the Austrian commissaries by slaughtering army horses. This provided meat and saved fodder, but sacrificed the mobility needed to break through enemy lines.

In a night attack on 13/14 March, the Russians made their first major advance, gaining one of the heights overlooking the fortress. Kusmannek was unable to muster his forces quickly enough to counter-attack before they had consolidated and emplaced their artillery. He now knew that his rations would give out by 24 March and decided that rather than capitulate he would try to fight his way back to his own lines. Preparatory movements began on the night of 18 March, but half-starved men collapsed in the cold and sleet and every sort of delay dogged departure. The Russians had discovered the plan via decoded Austrian radio messages, and when Kusammek finally set out he was met by artillery fire and an infantry strike from the south. The Twenty-third Honved (Territorial) Infantry Division, the first to be hit, suffered 68 per cent casualties, and the troops behind moved back into the fortress's cover. Their ordeal continued, and during the next two days they were hard put to repulse three determined Russian attempts to storm the ramparts.

Yet within the city an eerie gaiety persisted, amid which Kusmannek called his officers together on 21 March. There were only three days' rations left, scurvy had broken out among both garrison and civil populations, and they decided there was no alternative but surrender. Everything possible was then destroyed, culminating in an enormous explosion which was heard and seen by Tersztyanski's troops fifty miles away. Far from being depressed, they broke into cheering, convinced that now their country would have to seek peace.

At sunrise on 22 March, white flags began to appear along the battlements and, at nine o'clock that morning, the Russians entered the city. When the news was received at Stavka, the tearful grand-duke told the tsar, then visiting his troops at the front. Later that day a "Te Deum" was sung in the wooden headquarters' church according to custom.

By the 23rd, paroled Austrian officer prisoners of war and their Russian captors were mixing in the cafés, laughing, joking and discussing the battle. A Russian general wrote: "With the fall of Przemysl the last vestige of Austrian prestige had evaporated, and even the small unfriendly faction that secretly disliked our occupation abandoned all hope."

The Russians were now free to add Selivanov's troops to their other forces, and on 19 March Stavka, won over to Ivanov's case, gave its backing to another Carpathian offensive.[3] Late that month, Brusilov struck Tersztyanski's forces in the Lupkow and Uszok passes and other troops then began attacking the Dukla Pass. Everywhere the Austrians were pushed back, crisis succeeded crisis along the front, and preparations were made for a retreat to the fortified line from Vienna to Budapest. Arrangements were made for the government to move to Slazburg, and a car stood by to rush the emperor to safety if need arose.

Chapter 11

The Tsar Visits His New Dominions

Russia had lived in the shadow of revolution for decades. People spoke of its inevitability, discussed with as little passion as they would the latest play or novel whence and how it would come, and what régime would emerge not only in the conclaves of the prescribed political parties, of disaffected workers or exiles living abroad, but in the salons of Petrograd and Moscow. The shadow had grown vaster and more tenebrous since the events of 1905 and 1906, yet year succeeded year and it did not descend.

In exile in Switzerland, a small man with a neat beard had ceased to believe in its imminence. Ivan Vladimir Ulyanov, now known as Lenin, told his sister Anna in 1912, "I don't know whether I shall live to see the next rising of the tide," and in 1914 he wrote to a friend in the same strain.

Neither repressive despotism nor governmental incompetence — nor the capricious Russian amalgam of both — automatically bring about revolution, though they may create the desire for it. History abounds with examples of incompetent and despotic régimes which have survived. What provides the essential opening is the shattering of those bonds which give the rulers their cohesion. Then the leadership, both potential and actual, is broken into a myriad of groupings from which one successful strain will appear, more dynamic or ruthless than the rest.

"For the success of the Russian revolution war is essential, without war our revolutionaries can do nothing," Piotr Arkadyevich Stolypin, chairman of the Council of Ministers from 1906 until his assassination in 1911, had told Sazonov. No doubt he had in mind the revolution of 1905 following the Russo-Japanese War; also the French Revolution of 1789 succeeding France's eclipse by Britain in the Seven Years' War, and the establishment of the Commune after the Franco-Prussian War of 1870.

Yet these, a contemporary optimist could have pointed out, were all defeats, and greatly though the Russian army had suffered

114

and would continue to suffer,[1] it was undefeated and indeed on the threshold of stupendous victories. Brusilov's Eighth Army was back in the Carpathian passes, though in battles with the ferocious Magyar defenders operations were hampered and made bloodier by the shell shortage. It had been decreed that officers who fired more than three shells daily would be court-martialled and each separate hill of the deep Carthian range had to be taken by bayonet charge. An offensive planned by the South West Front in the spring would, however, carry this battle to a satisfactory conclusion on the plains where the infantry and cavalry could once more come into their own.

For all the present difficulties in the matter of supplies, there was some sign of impending improvement. Kitchener had invited a Russian delegation to London so that supply requirements and methods could be discussed. The Russian armaments factories were gradually being put on a war footing, and would shortly produce the first heavy guns; French experts had arrived to help organise production.

The enemy had reached an impasse: "We are stuck fast on the whole front," Hoffmann admitted in his diary on 5 April. Meanwhile, powerful allies were at last making their way towards the besieged Black Sea, and the ancient dream of Constantinople was within sight. At Odessa and other points along that coast, a huge Russian army was being concentrated to descend on the Bosphorus and capture the Turkish capital.

Many Russians believed that their government's periodic renewal of the pledge to fly the Russian flag over Constantinople was one of those self-deceptive shibboleths adopted by failing régimes. Yet, despite the toasts in the officers' messes, the Russians had been torn in two by an emotional conflict over the Allied Dardanelles expedition, as summed up by Sazonov: "I was very much in sympathy with the idea of French and English troops driving a wedge between Turkey and the Central Powers, but I intensely disliked the thought that the Straits and Constantinople might be taken by our allies and not by Russian forces." To prevent it, he threw his weight behind an all-out effort in Salonica, for which the Russians had insisted forces were not available, and when told that the Gallipoli expedition was to go ahead, commented: "I had difficulty in concealing how painfully the news affected me."

On 9 February, a new session of the Duma opened, and one of the questions raised was that of Russia's position in relation to the Dardanelles. In Russian eyes, King George V's declaration had been unequivocal, but in view of British governmental hedging and since other powers with aspirations in the area were likely to become involved, they now sought public acknowledgment of the paramountcy of Russian claims. This was exactly what the British and French wanted to avoid on account of the reaction in Greece, Rumania and Bulgaria. On 3 March the tsar told Paléologue: "I could not admit my right to impose on my people the terrible sacrifices of this war if I did not reward them with the realisation of their time-honoured ambition ... The city of Constantinople and Southern Thrace must be incorporated into my empire." Obviously this far exceeded the terms to which the British government had agreed on 11 November in conceding that "the question of the Straits and Constantinople should be settled in conformity with Russian desires."

The effect of this on Balkan neutrals would be bad enough, but a worse blow was to come. The Greeks, having offered their army corps for Gallipoli, were now negotiating as to its precise role in the assault. Moreover King Constantine – hitherto favouring a pro-German neutrality – had come out on the Entente side. Greece too had Byzantine ambitions, and Russia meant to ensure these were not realised at her expense. On 3 March, whilst Paléologue was with the tsar, Sazonov was telling Buchanan that "the Russian government could not consent to Greece participating in operations in the Dardanelles". Simultaneously, in Athens, the Russian minister there was endeavouring to exclude the Greeks, insisting that on no account would King Constantine be allowed to enter Constantinople with his troops.

The following day the French were told by Russia that Greek co-operation in the Dardanelles could only be accepted if the country supported the entire war effort, including active support for Serbia. In the current inflammable political situation in the Balkans, the Russians knew this was totally unthinkable: it was highly probable that once Greece was engaged on two fronts, Bulgaria (defeated enemy of the Second Balkan War) might sieze the chance to repossess her lost territory. Greece took the hint. Prime minister Venizelos continued to urge the Entente case, but he and his Cabinet were forced to resign when Constantine refused to agree. Henceforward the dichotomy between royalists and Venizelists diminished the country's potential usefulness as an ally.

To keep the Alliance intact, the west was forced to agree to the Russians' proposed annexation of Constantinople, and this fact was made public on 12 March. History has delivered its verdict on the Russian action as encapsulated by Liddell Hart: "She preferred to choke rather than disgorge a morsel of her ambition", and Churchill has written of her "failing, reeling backward under the German hammer". However, events are viewed differently in their own time. The Turkish invasion which had originally prompted the grand-duke's request for help to his allies, had been defeated and far from reeling back, the Russians had held their own despite the cost and seemed poised for a second great victory in Galicia.

The Allied and Russian press in April 1915 openly suggested that the eastern campaign was as good as over and the enemy defeated. As far back as 1 January, Paléologue, on his own initiative, had suggested to Sazonov that Austria be detached from the "Teutonic Alliance" by an offer of peace. He pointed out that Franz Joszef was known to regret the war, and his armies had not only been beaten by the Russians in Galicia, but also by the Serbs at the Battle of Valievo. Rumania threatened to join the Entente and Italy was wavering in that direction. Paléologue privately suggested to the Russian Foreign Minister that if Galicia were ceded to Russia and Bosnia-Herzegovina to Serbia, this might be an adequate return for making peace with Austria-Hungary.

Hearing of this, Poincaré reacted with predictable dismay, being still beset by the idea that with the southern enemy defeated, Russia would lose interest in the northern force. When Count Witte gave an interview to the Petrograd newspaper "Novoe Vremlia" in the previous November, he had suggested that the victory over Austria and the repulsing of the German offensive against Warsaw provided a useful opening for a negotiated peace. Shortly afterwards, Prince Yusopov (husband of the tsar's niece) while visiting Paris had spoken with chilling candour of German influence in Russia; they controlled commerce, he said, and the Moscow police was in their pay. Poincaré insisted, therefore, that his ambassador see Sazonov again and make it clear that he spoke purely in a private capacity, without government sanction.

Paléologue, nearer to Russian realities, was dismayed at France's failure to appreciate the immediate and irreparable loss to Germany which the defection of Austria would involve.

In any case, Poincaré's anxieties were groundless, for his faithful ally had no intention of failing the Alliance at this early stage. On 28 March, the Austrians made a tentative peace approach themselves when a letter from Prince Gottfried von Hohenlohe, Austro-Hungarian ambassador in Berlin, found its way to the tsar. This hinted at the mutual benefits which would flow from peace, but the tsar told Sazonov that he did not propose to dignify it with a reply.

Yet the undoubted achievements which had brought Austria to this point entitled Russia to feel she had outrivalled her confederates. Sazonov at that time suggested to France and Britain that Italy's entry into the war should be prevented, since a fourth partner in the Entente might affect the division of spoils after peace.

Peace seemed already to have descended along some parts of the Galician front. To the right of Brusilov's army, fighting to clear the Carpathians, was Radko-Dmitriev's Third Army. Dmitriev was a Bulgarian, trained in Russia when the two countries were allies, who had remained after they quarrelled to rise to army command. He was a personal friend of Brusilov and noted for his energy and boldness.

In early March he suggested to Ivanov that the Third Army should be augmented with three infantry corps which, in conjunction with his six cavalry divisions, he would employ to invade Hungary in the direction of Budapest. This suggestion had been refused.

His army, which had taken part in much of the fighting round Przemysl and Cracow, held a line some 150 miles long facing Auffenberg's Fourth Army east of the Dunajec. Because of the length of front, he was defending positions consisting of two or at most three trench-lines with some 300,000 men. Furthermore, far from getting the reinforcements he repeatedly requested, he was constantly called upon to supply troops for the Carpathians where, it was felt, the real battle was raging.

Now — with his part of the front quiescent — the local inhabitants had begun returning to their homes in the way of peasants throughout the history of warfare, and were grazing their sheep on the no-man's land which in places was as much as 2,000 yards wide. Russian soldiers, mostly country boys, would call them and make jokes.

The battle on this sector of the front had, in any case, been comparatively chivalrous. An informal truce had enabled both sides to draw water from the Dunajec, and after the great battles Austrian officer-prisoners were invited to dine in Russian messes; Russian soldiers visited enemy wounded in hospital, bringing gifts, and in one case had given their own rations to feed injured and hungry men abandoned in a church by retreating comrades.

In 1915, Easter fell on the same day in both Catholic and Orthodox calendars, and on Easter Sunday the Russians raised a great banner over their trenches proclaiming "Christ is Arisen." On this day, the most important of the Russian liturgical calendar, soldiers were each given ten eggs and eight buns. They crossed the lines to share these with their opponents, while Officers took gifts of sweets, cakes and wine to their Austrian and German counterparts. Such fraternal interchanges continued throughout the war, and came so naturally to the Russians that for the most part commanders made only half-hearted attempts to stop them.

A few days after the fall of Przemysl, the tsar travelled from Baranovichi to the site of the battle. The disapproving tsarina wrote: "Our Friend [Rasputin] would have found it better had you gone after the war to the conquered country", but she was furious anyway to learn that "Nicholasha" (the family name for the grand-duke) was to accompany him and would share in or perhaps attract greater acclaim. Her modest husband remonstrated that the commander-in-chief's presence was proper and necessary, while the grand-duke felt his own presence would help to impart a military rather than political complexion to the visit. It was precisely because the various speeches and responses would entail a commitment to political attitudes which was premature in a province not yet positively in Russian hands that Brusilov found "this tour more than untimely". Rodzianko, president of the Duma, who also visited Galicia at the time shared this view and was sufficiently indiscreet to express it to the tsar.

From Petrograd, Paléologue spoke of the army's "coldness and indifference" towards the visit. Tortured by shyness, the man who regarded the "noble Russian peasant" as the mystical source of his country's salvation was completely tongue-tied when face to face with the tsar. Polish views about his presence were never canvassed, hardly surprising when the attitude prevailing in government circles was contained in the words "conquered country" in the tsarina's letter. The tsar, who had failed to ratify the promises made by the grand-duke on the grounds that the Polish question could not be discussed in wartime, was treating the Galician Poles as his liege-subjects. The Poles had in any case ceased to believe in the promises after the appointment of a Russian governor: Lieutenant-General Count J. Bobrinski, a mediocre ex-Hussars officer who had rejoined the army when war broke out. Equally ignorant of Galicia and of administration, he had successfully stamped out all pro-Russian sympathies amongst the Poles — no small achievement for these initially extended even to the clergy of the province.

Most of the 3,750,000 Galicians were members of the Uniate religious sect, affiliated to the Roman Catholic Church. Bobrinski, who claimed to recognise only three religions in Eastern Europe — Orthodox, Catholic and Jewish — began a campaign of persecution in direct contravention of the declaration on religious freedom in the grand-duke's manifesto. The highly active Orthodox archbishop of Lemberg was given a free rein in proselytising his beliefs, while the Uniate metropolitan, Count Szeptycki, was put under house arrest. Monks were expelled; church property confiscated; vernacular missals destroyed and Uniate priests replaced by Orthodox. Children were carried off to Kiev and Kharkov to be brought up to Orthodoxy, newspapers banned, Galician officials replaced by Russians, and schools and universities closed. The western Allies were aghast at the whole performance, from Bobrinski's behaviour to the tsar's triumphal tour.

The royal progress continued with visits to the troops along the Carpathians: to Zloczow, where the tsar heard about the fighting along the Zlota Lipa; to Krosno, where he inspected Irmanov's Muslim Third Caucasian Corps which had distinguished itself in battles round Warsaw and Ivangorod the previous October. At the Eighth Army headquarters at Sambor the tsar presented Brusilov (who said the tsar detested him) and his leading officers with the

Cross of St George. At Lemberg the grand-duke was given a victory sword wrought in gold and diamonds "Pour la libération de Galicie". After visiting Prezemysl, he left at the end of April and went to see troops gathered at Odessa and Sebastopol for the invasion of the Bosphorus and Constantinople. A vast plan was being prepared whereby an army of 130,000 men was to be landed on the European side of the Bosphorus while thousands of tons of burning oil would be carried down to Constantinople by the current to set the harbour and city alight.

Towards the end of April it was observed that the sheep normally put out to graze between the Russian and Austrian lines were absent, but little significance was attached to this and Dmietriev even suggested a visit by a British war correspondent in early May.[2]

On 1 May an artillery bombardment was launched on Dmitriev's positions between the towns of Gorlice and Tarnow, following the usual German pattern of first firing on the rear to destroy communications. The shells landed among Dmitriev's limited artillery, which had been left so long that the enemy gunners knew their positions by heart. Thus every shell accurately took its toll and the Russians had nothing with which to reply.

In the early hours of 2 May, the bombardment was intensified. During four hours, 1500 guns of all calibres fired 700,000 rounds into the Third Army's line in the greatest barrage so far of the war. Dmitriev's guns were obliterated and his defensive positions shattered, whilst German officers casually and openly watched. At one o'clock that morning waves of German and Austrian shock-troops who had dug in close to the Russian lines overnight, advanced with fixed bayonets.

There was no opposition. The few surviving Russian troops were half-crazy and incapable of resistance. The German Official History describes the scene: "Here and there loam-grey figures jumped up and ran back, weaponless, in grey fur caps and fluttering, unbuttoned great coats, until there was not one remaining . . ."

Dmitriev tried to fight a rearguard action. Just before the attack, Ivanov had sent Irmanov's Third Caucasian Corps, recently admired by the tsar, to the Third Army's front. Tired from the long march and arriving in disparate groups because of the distance, they were thrown pell-mell into the battle. Nevertheless, by the end of the day Dmitriev's line was destroyed, the second trenchline had been carried and the Germans were through into open country. Three days later Gorlice itself fell and a ten-mile gap was opened. However, by nightfall on 2 May — the day on which the troops of the German Twelfth Army "swept the unwieldy enemy before them in the exuberant joy of the attack", when the Third Caucasians strove to hold the advance and Brusilov's forces in the Carpathians looked uneasily towards their right, it was not only the Third Army defences which had been cracked. Cracked, too, was the already crumbling cement holding Russian society together.

The multi-millionaire metallurgist, Putilov, the brain behind Russia's greatest industrial enterprise, told Paléologue: "The days of tsarism are numbered ... Revolution is inevitable ... The educated class is only a tiny minority and will be swept away ... There will be ten years of anarchy."

He spoke from experience, for agitation against the deplorable conditions in his factories had led to the protest march of 9 January, 1905, in which over 120 people were shot down.

Chapter 12

Falkenhayn Ascendant

Erich von Falkenhayn was a tall, slim man whose youthful features were belied by his bristly white hair and moustache. German war correspondents described his mien as "keen-eyed" and "intellectual".

In the late March of 1915, he might have been forgiven for feeling triumphant at having been proved right, not only against his now-acknowledged rivals at Oberost, but against foremost German opinion. However, he was too austere a man for such feeling, which in any case would have been tempered by knowledge of the seriousness of the "Teutonic Alliance's" position which looked bad enough before the Austro-German offensive in January and February against which he had inveighed, but had taken a turn for the worse during its abortive execution. Russia, as Hoffmann has pointed out, could be strangled if she could neither find an outlet for her exports nor import the war materials badly needed to make up the deficit of her own pitiable production; but this necessitated her outlet via the Black Sea remaining closed, and it now looked as if this might be reopened by the Anglo-French Dardanelles initiative.

Turkey's attempts to hold this off were endangered by diminishing ammunition supplies and these would cease altogether if Constantinople — centre of most of the munitions factories — was to fall. At the same time, Britain was not only drawing on her dominions and colonies for manpower, but at home was recruiting and training substantial new volunteer armies which would soon swell her active forces in the west.

Italy's declaration on the Central Powers was expected daily and would probably be followed by that of Rumania. The one new ally Germany could hope for was Bulgaria, but this again depended on whether the Entente or the Central Powers could offer her the more attractive pickings. "The moment had come", Falkenhayn wrote with the characteristic economy of statement, "when decisive actions in the east could be delayed no longer."

The form such action took was necessarily governed by the nature of the problems confronting him and his resources for solving them. He had just taken into army reserve some fourteen divisions formed by the regrouping of the German armies. As a "westerner" he felt they were most needed where they could parry the coming onslaught of the British armies; on the other hand, Turkey needed immediate aid, and to bring this to her necessitated defeating still-resisting Serbia whose armies barred the only available route, and who would be further helped by the Entente's Salonica expedition once it began in earnest. Italy and Rumania also had to be kept at bay, and Conrad had already requested seven German divisions for this purpose. Before forces could be freed for these two tasks, the immediate menace of the Russians must be removed.

The grand strategy he formulated amounted to a great circular tour. German forces were to go to Russia and there deal a crippling blow; then they would journey to Serbia and, by subjugating her, make the Salonica venture pointless. By late summer they would be back in France and Flanders, waiting to resist any possible attacks there. A critic might have questioned the realism of a commander who believed that war could remain static long enough to enable all this to be achieved — even within his own time limit — but would also have commended the coolness with which he set about its preparation and execution. History acknowledges how far he succeeded.

The Russian line could be divided roughly into three sectors (this was later tacitly acknowledged in the Russian command structure). Firstly there was the southern area, starting near Czernowitz, running mainly parallel with the Carpathians to the Dukla Pass and enclosing much of Galicia. Bending to form a central area running up to Przasnysz, it then followed the southern border of East Prussia from Przasnysz to Suwalki. Thus, the central area encompassed most of the Polish salient. At Suwalki it turned at right angles to meander up to the Baltic Sea, forming the northern sector containing the Baltic states of the Russian Empire.

The first question confronting Falkenhayn was, therefore, where along this attenuated line could the Austro-German forces strike most effectively? Predictably, the commanders of the two national armies involved each had his own clear idea. On the

German side, Hindenburg and Ludendorff wanted to strike out in the north, from East Prussia towards the Baltic states, making immediately for Dvinsk (Daugavpits) and Vilna (Vilnius). Both were nerve-ganglia for the Russian army and their loss would further jeopardise the Russians' tenuous and erratic communications. Hindenberg and Ludendorff also expatiated on "opening the road to Petrograd", notwithstanding that the city lay some four hundred miles to the north east! Falkenhayn was unconvinced and could not see this plan achieving the substantial success he sought within the allotted time, a view supported by von François, the general who had been instrumental in bringing about the victory of Tannenberg.

For the Austrians, Conrad offered an alternative. He pointed out that their advances in the Carpathians had greatly lengthened the Russian lines, and since they needed a victory here without weakening themselves in the north after the winter battles, it was most likely that they had thinned out their centre. If, he forecast confidently, Falkenhayn were to throw all his available strength at the right point, the Russian defences would be torn apart. Falkenhayn agreed, but Hindenburg and Ludendorff remained so adamant about the merits of their Dvinsk-Vilna attack that it was finally necessary to seek the Kaiser's casting vote. Both plans were presented to him without naming their authors, though Falkenhayn explained his own preference for Conrad's. Wilhelm agreed, and the decision was conveyed to a furious Hindenburg and Ludendorff, who, as a sop, were told there would be a special role for them — this can hardly have soothed them.

During the Masurian winter-battle, Oberost had moved to Lötzen, near the East Prussian frontier, and discussions there must have centred on the fact that Falkenhayn, having opted for an offensive on the front they regarded as their own preserve and on the scale for which they had been agitating over past months, had made it abundantly clear he intended to run it himself. They were to be mere subordinates.

The point chosen for the main attack was a twenty-five mile sector running from just north-west of the Lupkow Pass, between the towns of Gorlice and Tarnow. A success here would mean that the attackers, swinging south once they were through the Russian line, would threaten the rear of Brusilov's army in the Carpathian passes. Falkenhayn even suggested that the Eighth Army be allowed to break through so that it would be cut off after the enveloping move, but Austrian nerves were unequal to the prospect of rampaging Russian hordes with Vienna and Budapest lying before them, and they settled for a conventional defence of the area.

To Falkenhayn's mind, there were three essential prerequisites to success: total surprise, overwhelming numbers and crushing technical superiority. In achieving the first, he kept his plans from even the Austro-Hungarian instigators until mid-April, though on the 9th his staff were drawing up schedules for moving some eight German divisions quickly and inconspicuously to Cracow, the nearest concentration point. At the same time, commanders along the whole of the remaining front were ordered to mount diversionary attacks to keep the Russians guessing. Finally, in late April, the civilian population near the front line was evacuated as a precaution against espionage (hence the absence of sheep in no-man's land).

As far as numerical superiority went, he believed that the Russians were relatively weak at the chosen point and that the combination of the troops he was sending with those already there would ensure that they were outnumbered. Although the actual margin was small,[1] Falkenhayn judged it to be increased by technical superiority. Assembled along the front were 250 heavy guns, including several of the 17-inch siege howitzers used to obliterate the Belgian forts, as well as about 700 field pieces. Approximately 3 million rounds of ammunition had been dumped at convenient points. At the same time, a technique was being developed enabling infantry to follow up the artillery barrage so quickly as to prevent the defenders re-forming.[2] To facilitate the speedy movement of the advancing armies, and ensure that the guns were kept close behind them, teams of army engineers were to build roads and railways and repair those destroyed in the Russian retreat.

There remained the question of command. The new German divisions would be responsible for the attack, in conjunction with the Austrian Fourth and Third Armies on either side. The German forces were constituted into a new Eleventh Army commanded by Mackensen (commander of the Ninth Army which had invested Lodz the previous November). His chief-of-staff was General Hans von Seeckt, the blue-eyed, monocled archetype of the Prussian

officer with his ramrod back and high uniform collar, who had
been commissioned in a Prussian footguard regiment at the age of
nineteen. He had been appointed to the General Staff while still in
his twenties, and earlier in the year had been responsible for the
breakthrough at Soissons which had forced Joffre into taking the
offensive in Champagne. He was largely responsible for the
development of new methods of employing artillery in close
support of infantry.

Falkenhayn hoped to get an agreement from Conrad that in
return for German help he would put his Third and Fourth Armies
under Falkenhayn's direct command, so that they would act only
in collaboration with German Eleventh Army Command; the
Austrian commander would also ensure the quiescence of the
Serbian front and — in the event of her declaring war — hold Italy.
On 13 April Conrad formally wrote giving his agreement. "The
operations proposed by Your Excellency", he said, "coincide with
those I have so long desired, but which were hitherto impossible
owing to lack of sufficient forces . . ." In the evening of 14 April
he arrived in Berlin to discuss details, and promised that the
Italians would "break their teeth on the Isonzo" if they ventured
an attack. With sufficient German troops and other assistance now
reaching him, Conrad was able to reinforce his line in the
Carpathians so as to secure it against a Russian breakthrough.

On 15 April, troop movements eastward began, and by the 21st
the build-up at the front had started. By the time it was completed
there had been a dramatic shift in the balance of forces between
Western and Eastern Fronts: formerly the French and British had
faced the preponderant weight of the enemy, now Russia was
doing so. In France there were some 48 German infantry divisions
and 2 of cavalry; in the east were 27 German and 25 Austrian
corps plus 20 divisions of cavalry.

Yet for all Falkenhayn's secrecy the attack did not come
without warning. From about 21 April the French and British
noted that a number of divisions were missing from their front and
warned Stavka that they might have gone east. Reports of massing
German and Austrian forces also came from other sources, notably
the local spy-network which the Russians had built up among
sympathetic Slavs. Rumour travelled as far as Petrograd, where
Paléologue heard of a German "sledge-hammer blow" being
prepared in Galicia.

On 27 April came definite intimation of the presence of large numbers of German troops in the south, where hitherto the defenders had been predominantly Austro-Hungarian.

Ivanov was busy preparing for the attack which was to carry him through the Carpathians in May, and except for the movement of Radko-Dmitriev's only reserve – the Third Caucasian Corps – from Krosno to Gorlice, ignored everything else. At the same time, Dmitriev also asked for other reinforcements from South West Front and for additional artillery and shells as he had only three medium batteries along his whole line. These requests were turned down.

Russian attention was diverted by events in the north. Hindenburg and Ludendorff had been given three cavalry divisions as part of the reinforcements they demanded, and the armies in East Prussia and Poland were regrouped with Oberost's area of command extended to include the region south of Lodz where Woyrsch's Landswehr detachment was holding the line.

They were also given details of their "special assignment" in the context of the whole battle, which involved a threefold attack: the Ninth Army in the bend of the Vistula, south of Warsaw, using gas; Eichhorn's Tenth Army north of the Masurian Lakes at Suwalki; the three cavalry divisions allocated to them were then to sweep through Kurland (a strip of Baltic littoral, north of Lithuania now incorporated into Soviet Latvia) and East Lithuania.

The first moves were made toward the end of April with the gas attack by the Ninth Army. That the Germans regarded this as a failure does not mitigate the sufferings of those who experienced it. A Russian communiqué stated "the troops had time to take the necessary measures"; this meant urinating on their handkerchiefs and clasping them over mouth and nose, but the device was completely ineffective and 1,000 men died in the attack. Nevertheless, they held their line and when the Germans repeated the gassing the wind had veered and their own men were overcome.

Combined with the cavalry attack in the north opening on 27 April, these measures proved so successful in preventing the Russians from drawing troops from their northern flank to reinforce their southern front that they were extended. Another

German army was formed under General Otto von Below, former Eighth Army corps commander; this was called the Army of the Niemen after the river running through its area of operations.

However, this was not the end of Falkenhayn's diversionary activities. At five o'clock on the afternoon of 22 April, a tremendous artillery bombardment began along the Western Front at the Ypres salient. Front-line troops were fascinated by a creeping mist carried towards them by the slight breeze, and shortly afterwards British officers, whose troops held part of the line, saw Algerians of the French army running to the rear, choking and pointing to their throats. As the afternoon wore into evening the French seventy-fives which had been returning the German fire suddenly stopped. The retreat of the Algerians — soldiers of great courage — left a breach in the line four miles wide where nothing remained but the dead and dying. Poison gas had been used successfully for the first time on the Western Front.

The Germans advanced two miles but, instead of turning about and taking the British and Canadian defenders in the rear, the infantry attack which followed the Ypres gas-cloud was half-hearted in the extreme. It only achieved a flattening of the sharpest point of the salient, from which the British withdrew to re-form their lines, having lost nearly 60,000 men as against 30,000 German losses.

Why was it, the Allied commanders wondered, that the Germans failed to exploit the opening they had made so easily? The answer was that they had no reserves with which to do so: these had all gone to the east.

Falkenhayn who, in order to be near the centre of operations, had moved his headquarters from Mezières in the Ardennes to Pless, fifteen miles west of Cracow, could not insure against all risks — there was still the possibility of a sudden sweep by Italy or Rumania or the two together, which Conrad might find himself unable to contain. There was also the danger in the Mediterranean, and the fear that Turkey might fail before help could reach her, but here he was granted a respite.

Through February and early March the naval bombardment

which had destroyed the Turkish forts in the Dardanelles was continued, though more sporadically than formerly, as the battleships' advance was slowed by the difficulties of mine-sweeping.

The Straits make a double bend some ten miles from their entrance at Cape Helles, and the stretch of water between the bends is justly termed the Narrows, since in part it is under two miles wide. The first sharp corner is marked on the Asiatic shore by the town of Chanaq, where the naval squadron had now arrived. Before facing the uncertainties of the Narrows, the British commander, Carden, hesitated and on the 17th he fell sick. His place was taken by Admiral de Robeck who decided to press the attack on the 18th.

Ten days earlier, however, a Turkish boat had evaded naval patrols and laid a string of mines in Eren Keui Bay, near the entrance of the Straits. Some mines were found but it was assumed they were strays, perhaps floated into the current from higher up.

By early afternoon on the 18th the Narrows' forts had all been silenced and minesweepers went forward while the capital ships moved back outside the Straits. As the French ships were pulling back through Eren Keui Bay, the "Bouvet" exploded and within minutes heeled over and sank with the loss of almost the entire crew. Later that afternoon, the Royal Navy ships "Inflexible" and "Irresistible" both struck mines, and the "Ocean" struck one while going to their aid.

After weeks of unimpeded movement in and out of those waters, the whole episode was extremely unnerving and a most ominous start to de Robeck's command. Since it was not thought possible that the Turks could have laid a new minefield, the only explanation was a submarine (which the Turks were not thought to possess) or – more sinister – some secret weapon on the shore. The Admiralty telegraphed that five ships were coming out as replacements, but de Robeck had changed his mind about the feasibility of a purely naval operation and won the Sea Lords over to his opinion: the army must help them out.

To the incredulous relief of the Turks and their German advisers, the naval action was called off. Enver Pasha realised that this was simply a prelude to preparations for troop landings and, with Liman von Sanders, began his own planning. He was left to perfect them for over a month while the enemy forces, including

those destined for Salonica, were assembled. This period of preparation was far too brief for such an operation, and the plans made by the army commander, Ian Hamilton, could hardly be more than temporisations which, in the event, hazarded the whole enterprise by their improvised and niggardly nature. Nevertheless, Falkenhayn was afforded a breathing space in which he moved his troops into position.

On 25 April, the landings on Gallipoli Peninsula began. Where naval demolition gangs had moved freely six weeks earlier, now the Turkish army was assembled in strength.

Five days later, Mackensen's Eleventh Army was in battle positions behind the Austrian Fourth Army as it faced Radko-Dmitriev's Third.

It was still doubtful whether the Turks would hold on — initial reports from Gallipoli were far from encouraging — but when the Third Army's front had been breached a week later, there was a feeling that the first step toward helping them had been success-fully negotiated. Now was the time to take advantage of the opportunities provided.

In fact, after the successful attack of 2 May, it had taken time for Mackensen's Eleventh Army to roll its gigantic battering-ram of guns forward, but by the 7th they had taken up new positions and the pattern was repeated. Despite a call from Ivanov to hold a new line on the Wisloka at all costs, Radko-Dmitriev was forced back again with such losses that his twenty divisions were now reduced to the equivalent of five. The same day, the Eleventh Army began crossing the river at Jaslo and Frysztak. Next day they forced another passage at Rymanov, and Mackensen's chief-of-staff, von Seeckt, declared: "The tactical and strategical breakthrough has fully succeeded."

Dmitriev was threatened at the centre and also on both wings as the Austrian Fourth and Third Armies moved up beside the Germans. Higher up the Wisloka, at the point where it swings eastward almost at right angles, an attempt was made to hold another river line. The tenacious Russians held the line for three days, sacrificing themselves to meet attack after attack until Dmitriev was forced to retire, his forces having "shed all their blood". Only then did the full magnitude of events penetrate to the South West Front. It was now clear that there would be no break-through in the Carpathians and no debouching onto the Plains of Hungary; instead, the enemy — wheeling southward — was already threatening to cut into the Eighth Army's rear.

From Stavka, the grand-duke begged the western Allies to launch a diversionary offensive, and urged that Italy (the desirability of whose commitment the Russians had earlier questioned) should be hastened on to the field despite the higher price she was now asking. In return, they were prepared to accede to all her former demands and also cede her Cisalpine Tyrol, Trieste, Gorizia, Gradisca, the Istrian Islands, part of Asiatic Turkey, Eritrea, Somaliland and Libya, as well as those parts of Dalmatia which the Russians had hitherto wanted to claim for themselves.

Meanwhile, the disasters which had befallen the Third Army were spreading into the southern sector and moving up the central one, as the armies on the wings sought to keep contact with Dmitriev's disintegrating line.

On 11 May, the armies in the Carpathians began to move back. Brusilov conducted the withdrawal with customary skill, moving his equipment and supplies along designated roads kept clear for the purpose, and fighting strenuous rearguard actions as he went to hold the enemy at bay. The recall of his army had not come a moment too soon, and even so the Twenty-fourth corps were almost enveloped. The commander of one of its divisions — the brave but insubordinate Lavr Kornilov — was actually taken prisoner but escaped disguised as an Austrian officer and carrying forged papers.

As the Russians drew clear of the Carpathians, Böhm-Ermolli's Austrian Second Army began to advance while, at the other extremity of Dmitriev's line, the First Army started moving forward. Evert, the Russian Fourth Army commander, tried to reorganise his forces and counter-attack here where the odds were less heavily weighed against him, but was unable to progress although the Austrians had to fight desperately to hold on to their gains.

Woyrsch's Landwehr detachment on the left of the First Army took Kielce, over sixty miles from the main axis of the attack, and threatened Radom, forty miles further north.

The Russians were retiring along a line of over 300 miles and the names of obscure little towns and river banks suddenly assumed world prominence as delaying actions were fought. By 15

May, the Eleventh Army had advanced over fifty-five miles in a fortnight, and inflicted at least 100,000 casualties on the defenders; the Russians were not only exhausted but in many places short of food because supplies could not locate them. An attempted offensive by the Third Caucasian Corps, which had been fighting almost continuously since its move to Gorlice and whose numbers were down from 40,000 to 8,000, inflicted heavy casualties on the Austrian First Army and took 6,000 prisoners and 9 guns; but the only significant result was to halve its own numbers and reduce ammunition to 1 round of shell per gun and 75 cartridges per rifle.

Two days after this further disaster, Radko-Dmitriev was relieved of his command and replaced by Lesh the commander of the Twelfth Corps, Eighth Army, regarded as a capable leader, "strong, cool and daring". Reporting Dmitriev's supercession to the tsarina, the tsar said that before the battle he had failed to prepare fortified positions in the rear as ordered, but the real cause of his downfall was the constant dissension between himself and his superior commanders at South West Front and Stavka. Both refused his request for a quick withdrawal to the San which he believed could have saved his depleted and exhausted armies, a view shared by Ivanov's own chief-of-staff, Dragomirov. Forced to fight delaying actions to retain as much conquered territory as possible, he had seen his army cut down to a "harmless mob", suffering appalling losses for which the reinforcements of 2—4,000 a day could not compensate.

Figures issued in June showed that Russia's war losses now stood at 3,800,000, of which 412,000 had fallen in the May battles. Fifteen divisions of reinforcements sent to the South West Front during the month had evaporated. With such losses they found themselves outnumbered along almost the entire fighting line, with 100 weak infantry divisions facing 65 German and 45½ Austrian divisions. To make good the total estimated deficiency of approximately ½ million men, drafts being sent up the line included the very young, the old, men half-trained or so totally untrained as to be unable to load and fire a rifle. Often they were back at the first aid stations in a day or two, being unable to take the most elementary precautions of self-preservation in battle. Of the best of them the grand-duke complained to the tsar that their "training was beneath criticism". Commanders like Brusilov often had to train men near the front itself.

By general admission, the prime cause of the gigantic losses was the artillery and shell shortage. The brunt of the fighting fell on the hapless and frequently totally inexperienced infantry repeatedly exposed to enemy savaging. In one instance a Russian corps commander had two guns to answer a German heavy battery of forty-two. General Zuiev, the Thirty-ninth Corps commander, told the War Minister: "The Germans expend metal, we expend life. They go forward . . . we only beat them off with heavy losses and our blood, and are retreating."

Shell became a luxury. "When, after a silence of three days, our six-inch howitzer battery received fifty shells the fact was communicated by telephone to every regiment and company, and the men heard it with delighted relief," wrote General A. I. Deniken. Knox commented: "It is cruel to see our batteries standing idle and helpless."

Infantry officers would beg artillerymen to fire "just one or two shots", but they could only refuse, for they had orders to keep their empty limbers a secret, and to say they were conserving their ammunition for a critical moment. Many of the drafted men could not be used because of the deficit of 150,000 rifles; only 40,000 poor-quality weapons had been scraped together for the reinforcements, including obsolete Mexican models. One army commander was told by Stavka that some infantry companies were to be armed with long-handled axes, while replacement troops were informed that their only hope of acquiring a weapon was to take it from a fallen comrade; entire companies were sent to the forward trenches for this purpose.

The railway system, too disorganised to carry such munitions as there were to the front, also hindered attempts to reinforce the lines. Lack of railway line parallel with the fighting front meant that troops had to be conveyed far into the rear before they could be re-entrained for their destinations.

"Exasperation" was the word common to all the soldiers' letters home. Pares was told by one man: "This is not war, sir, this is slaughter." Countless families were bereaved and, in one village known to Knox, twenty-four out of twenty-six men called up had been killed. A peasant told Pares: "Getting empty in the villages", with a kind of cheery objectivity, and admitted three of his brothers had died at the front and that he was looking after their families.

The horrors of war, spreading throughout the country, soon had their repercussions. The Opolchenie or national militia was split into two divisions according to age, the Second Ban consisting of men of thirty-five and over who regarded themselves as free of active military commitments. The Second Ban had only twice been called to the colours: in 1812 and in the Crimean War in 1854. In June 1915 it was proposed to call upon them once more to fill the gaps in the ranks. Added to all the other burdens, the prospect of being consigned to speedy execution in the trenches was too much, and in Moscow rioting broke out. This took a directly political turn when crowds outside the Kremlin demanded that Sukhomlinov, Maklakov and Shcheglovitov be dismissed; that the tsarina be sent to a convent for the duration; that the tsar should abdicate and the grand-duke be crowned in his stead. The disturbances lasted three days, and when shots were fired on the rioters they rounded on the police shouting: "You have no ammunition to fight Germans, but you have plenty to shoot down Russians."

In the field, voluntary surrenders to the enemy became increasingly common, encouraged by the Germans who had run a ceaseless campaign from the beginning of the war. Wine and cigarettes were displayed in front of German positions as an inducement. To try to combat the wave of surrenders, it was decreed that the families of men who gave themselves up would receive no allowances, and that after the war they themselves would be sent to Siberia.

This was not, however, the only means of escaping from the battlefield. Men reported "sick" at the least excuse and desertions increased, with bands of runaway soldiers breaking into shops — especially Jewish ones — and terrorising villages so that army units had to be diverted to hunting them down.

As the officers maintained, the surest way to keep up morale would have been by providing adequate artillery.

The horrors of the struggle which drove men to these lengths continued unabated. In late May, Mackensen's Eleventh Army surged forward upon a Russian line re-formed on the San. After the usual artillery barrage, Prussian Guards crossed the river and the defenders wavered and broke, although the desperate search for reinforcements involved bringing up even the Fifth Caucasian Corps, then training at Odessa. The fortress of Przemysl was thus ripe to fall back into German hands. The Russians at first seemed mindful to hold it to the last as Kusmannek had done and built up the armouries and stores. Then they decided otherwise and a useless delaying action, costing thousands of lives, was fought as stores were hurriedly reloaded on trains.

On 25 May, the Italians declared war. The Austrians were with difficulty made to honour their promises to use only those forces already in the area to "break the enemy's teeth on the Isonzo", though in fact elements of the Third Army were sent to the southern front.

Despite von Seeckt's announcement of a breakthrough, the Russian line was still intact, if bent, and would have to be pushed still further back before Falkenhayn dare disengage his forces. He therefore had to make more gaps in his Western Front, and two divisions were moved east in late May to combine with the Austrian Second and Fourth Armies into a single entity: the Army Group Mackensen — giving the Germans the "unity of command" for which they had clamoured.

On 3 June, orders were given to recommence the offensive in the south with the object of capturing Lemberg. As an augury of success, Przemysl fell that day.

Coincidentally with the advance of the Army Group Mackensen, the Austrian Fourth and Seventh Armies were to press toward the Dniestr. On 12 June these movements began, and once more the list of place names streaked across the world's headlines: the Lubaszovka crossed, Sienawa occupied, and so on.

By 17 June, the defenders were being forced back on Lemberg. On 22 June, the city surrendered. Halicz, too, taken by Brusilov in the first month of the war, was also recaptured. In all these places where their departure had been welcomed, the Austrians found themselves greeted with a real relief.

Chapter 13

Changes In Petrograd

The one positive effect arising from the remorseless defeats at the front and their accompanying carnage was the stimulation in the Russian public of an overwhelming desire to throw itself into the struggle to redress matters. However, there was no means of canalising this enormous fund of patriotic goodwill, for the government — suspicious of any form of association — had either stifled or emasculated almost all the national organisations. The tolerated few (as well as those not officially tolerated) were thoroughly infiltrated by the Okhrana. In this way, tsarist Russia denied itself not only the means to combine its citizens' endeavours, but also the talents of many able men and women. This was no accident but the deliberate policy of a government which accepted as axiomatic the thesis that ability and opposition to the régime were synonymous. It had been made plain at the outbreak of war that the emergency was to provide an excuse to break up such bodies as existed in the name of internal security.

Kerenski cites a secret police directive, published on 16 December 1914, which contains instructions on the insinuation of agents into left-wing parties, to argue against any coalition in the interests of victory. Throughout the war, the pro-German group in the Cabinet and court were anxious to stifle all expressions of patriotism as inimical to what they considered the true interests of the nation. Patriotic demonstrations were broken up and their leaders arrested, while those protesting against the war and its hardships proceeded unhindered.

This persecution of all patriotic elements extended even to the Duma. After a one-day session on 8 August in which it threw itself on the government's side, the Minister of the Interior, Nicholas Maklakov (joint-author of the anti-Allied memorandum to the tsar), suggested that it should not reconvene for more than a year.

Various subterfuges had been adopted to evade all these prohibitions. The All-Russian Union of Zemstvos (rural councils)

137

and of the Towns (Zemgor),[1] over which the liberal Prince Lvov presided, had formed a relief organisation to provide hospital trains, ambulances, canteens and other amenities for the troops, thus helping to make up some of the leeway in these respects. At the same time, the meetings to organise these matters provided cover for political discussion.

While unwavering in persecution of all who seemed likely to threaten autocracy's complete dominance, the government had remained oblivious to problems such as the shortage of supplies as manifested both in the scandalous lack of army equipment and munitions and the dearth of essential commodities on the home front. By this time virtually everything was short and there was a rampant black market. In cities like Petrograd and Moscow the cost of living had risen by 40 per cent up to 1915 with no commensurate rise in wages. Bread had increased from three kopeks to five, and long queues waited in snow and ice at the bakers. Tea had risen from 160 to 180 kopeks. Meat and sugar had disappeared from the tables of the poor, and even officers' wives often had to eke out their existence with food saved out of army rations and sent home.

The whole situation had been brought about by a number of interrelating factors. When the 1914 reserves had been called up, an enormous number whose contributions to the economy was negligible, were exempted whereas other groups had been called up willy-nilly. In this way the "mouzhik" smallholders, who usually operated as a single family unit, could claim exemption for sons or fathers, but the large estates, which were the most productive, were deprived of the greater proportion of their labour. The initial effects were beneficial, for there was vast rural unemployment remaining both from the emancipation of the serfs sixty years earlier and the various ill-considered and poorly executed measures of land distribution since that time. This particularly afflicted the small-holders, many of whom had lived only slightly above subsistence level in peacetime but now found a thriving demand for their produce. However, farming on this scale was not sufficient to meet a need increased by demands from the army, where many men ate better than in civilian life, and where rations had actually increased since the outbreak of war.[2] In any case, by 1915, scarcity of consumer goods meant there was nothing on which the "mouzhiks" could spend their newly-earned money (Kerenski blamed the prohibition on vodka among other things) while rouble inflation destroyed the incentive to save. There seemed no point in producing beyond family needs.

At the same time, Russia had made little provision for preserving excess food. There were no refrigerators in government possession, and the number in private hands was totally inadequate. Not only was there a shortage of tinplate for canning purposes, but there were only fifteen canning factories in the whole country.

Nevertheless, there was no basic food shortage. Wheat and rye could no longer be exported and so were available for home consumption, and there was no shortage of other produce which could not have been made tolerable by properly organised distribution. No attempt was made to ration goods, however, until shortages became so acute that hoarding made organisation virtually impossible. The movement of supplies was hindered by the very size of the country, the chronic shortage of usable ports — especially in the Black Sea — combined with the dearth of rail line and rolling stock. The only ports now available were Archangel, icebound for half the year and 2,000 miles from the front; Murmansk, open all year round but initially with no rail connection, and Vladivostok on the Pacific, 8,000 miles from the front. As a result, exports dropped 98 per cent and imports 95 per cent. During the entire war, an average of 1,250 ships a year arrived in Russia compared with 2,200 a week in Britain. The enormous call on these few remaining ports created such abnormal situations as a need to convey twelve submarines and destroyers for the Baltic and Black Sea Fleets (built in Canada) across the Pacific to Vladivostok, where they were dismantled, packed in crates and carried by rail for re-assembly at their destinations. Thus, as Kerenski says, the nation suffered "even more than Germany from the isolation imposed on her by the war".

In June, 1915, the grand-duke admitted to the French military attaché at Stavka that many of Russia's problems sprang not so much from the distance as from the corruption and incompetence which they cloaked. To move goods, railway officials at all levels had to be bribed. Private manufacturers accepted this situation and simply added these sums to their final prices, but since the government was unwilling to subscribe to such practices, its freight received the lowest priority. Cattle in open cars would be left to starve or freeze to death while at the ports, imported goods, including vital war materials, rotted. At Archangel, Rodzianko saw supplies from America, Britain and France piled "mountain-high" because they could not be moved to the interior or the front. No equipment existed for handling cargoes of this size and, once the warehouses were full, packing cases had to be left in the open sinking slowly into the mud from the weight. The railways from Archangel had been changed from narrow to standard gauge in an effort so speed up movement, but they were still inadequate and it was reckoned that at least 25 per cent of goods failed to reach their destinations.

All these matters were coming to light in the spring of 1915 because, among other reasons, the members of the Zemgor Red Cross and the Duma were visiting the front where they could experience first-hand and report back various abuses. Consequently, an angry and increasingly vocal public demand rose for the dismissal and punishment of those responsible. In fact, the government was by no means complacent before this outcry and the state procurator's department was busy preparing cases. That so few actually reached the courts was due less to lack of diligence than to the peculiarly Russian attitude to law breaking. From a long experience of the legal system's arbitrary injustice, when its processes ultimately came down to individuals, they were seen less as a means of social retribution than as a personal disaster like illness or other visitations of fate, evoking pity rather than wrath. In consequence, extenuating circumstances could always be found!

There was, of course, considerable dissatisfaction and anger but for various reasons this was not yet being expressed in an organised political way. The first was that the upsurge of patriotic fervour in 1914 took by surprise those who, like the Bolsheviks, were capable of turning distress into a political weapon. Finding themselves in a hostile atmosphere, says the Soviet historian M. N. Pokrovsky, they took "the only course open to them — they slowly but surely recruited allies. This painstaking work resulted in the gradual correction and elimination of this subjective failing manifested by the party ranks at the beginning of the war. As it recovered and became ideoligically firm, this party stratum began a relentless struggle against the patriotic feelings of the Revolutionary masses." But in early 1915 their efforts had not begun to bear fruit.

Secondly, members of the proscibed parties who (particularly since 1905) had been assiduously kept out of the armed forces, had to be drafted when it became necessary to replace vast losses by using all available manpower.

Thirdly, the threat to withdraw exemptions was not only levelled at potential agitators but quickly executed at the least sign of activity on their part. Thus, the problem of political malcontents had been adroitly "exported" to the armed forces from where it was reported early in 1915 that even the Petrovski and Volhynian Regiments of Guards were "contaminated" by "Socialist" propaganda. Fourthly, the average Russian who still had confidence in the Duma as the vehicle for the redress of grievances preferred to leave matters in its hands.

When out of session the Duma was personified by its president, Mikhail Rodzianko, whose office permitted him direct access to the tsar. Portly and self-important, both characteristics detested by the tsar, he was also courageous, loyal and, if anything, over-zealous. His disagreement with Maklakov (Minister of the Interior) the previous autumn had led to a permanent coolness between the two men and each wearied the tsar by bearing stories about each other. Since the tsar tended to find Maklakov more congenial, Rodzianko inclined to damage himself in the royal eyes by this practice.

Laudably, the Duma president was less concerned at the time with punishing the culpable than with taking more positive steps towards solving the problem. Early in 1915 he had suggested to the grand-duke that "Special Defence Council" be set up to perform a similar function to that of the Ministries of Munitions in Britain and France. The grand-duke heartily approved, but after 1 May the crisis at the front occupied all his attention and he told Rodzianko that, at present, implementation was impossible. Subsequent reconsideration, however, led to a deputation consisting of Rodzianko, the head of the Department of Industry and the industrialist Putilov attending on the tsar and the commander-in-chief at Stavka. To the tsar, their proposals appeared to offer a united step towards recovery and he supported them so enthusiastically that outline plans were drawn up on the spot.

At a further audience on 12 June, not only were these plans advanced further, but Rodzianko took the opportunity to press for the dismissal of those members of the Council of Ministers like

Sukhomlinov, Maklakov, Shcheglovitov and Sabler who were a burden on the war effort or were known for their pro-German views. Only a few days earlier, the Moscow rioters had specifically mentioned three of these names, so it was not difficult to persuade Nicholas that their dismissal would facilitate reconciliation with his people.

However, the four discredited ministers sealed their own fate. In mid-June, plans for the Special Council were sufficiently advanced to be put before the Council of Ministers. Since the tsar was in favour, Goremykin expected unquestioning approval, but as Maklakov was dedicated to the system of autocracy and the Special Council represented a dilution of the royal prerogatives, he voted against it. Shcheglovitov and Sabler, while critical, did not go to this length.

The tsar saw the Interior Minister's action less as high-minded adherence to principle than as a simple flouting of his will, and on 16 June he was dismissed. A few days later, Shcheglovitov and Sabler followed him into the wilderness. Maklakov's place was taken by the liberal Prince Shcherbatov, who immediately — with royal approval — set about re-forming his department, seeking to limit and define police powers. The Justice Minister, Shcheglovitov, was succeeded by A. A. Khvostov, admittedly Goremykin's nominee but also held in high esteem as a scrupulous and gifted lawyer; Sabler's place was taken by Samarin, scion of one of Russia's oldest and most respected tchinovnik families. Now only Sukhomlinov remained, and it seemed that Rodzianko had succeeded; the changes were welcomed not only in Russia but in France and Britain as making the tsarist régime more palatable to their electorates' fastidious tastes.

Events now began moving towards the departure of the fourth member of the group. On 10 March — though not made public until nearly a month later — Colonel Miassoiedev appointed by Sukhomlinov to keep watch on the general staff, fulfilled Guchkov's expectations when he was found guilty of spying for the Germans and was hanged. The revelation of Sukhomlinov's association with the Colonel was a further nail in his coffin, but he survived a little longer until Guchkov rained down a further tattoo of hammer blows.

Like Rodzianko, Prince Lvov favoured the idea of enlisting the support of Russian industry in the war effort and, on 18 June, called a conference in Moscow to establish what came to be called the Central War Industries Committee, with members from all sections of industry, including the workers. The main speaker was Guchkov who, having lived at the front, took advantage of that special knowledge to launch upon a public denunciation of Sukhomlinov as the man principally responsible for the sufferings of the Russian soldiers.

Yet the final blow was delayed until Sukhomlinov's letter answering Joffre's inquiry about Russian shell and artillery supplies with an assurance that "there was nothing to worry about" was shown by Paléologue to Sazonov, and by Sazonov to the tsar. On 25 June, with every manifestation of deep reluctance, Nicholas summoned the War Minister and dismissed him. Even now he was allowed to go on living in his flat at Tsarskoe Selo, and continued to move in court circles, finding in his sovereign a ready listener to his ingenuous and dangerous advice.

Sukhomlinov was succeeded by General Polivanov, one of the "Young Turk" officers whom the grand-duke had wanted to take to Baranovichi at the beginning of the war. A vigorous, if brusque soldier, with a record of professionalism from his first action against the Turks in 1877, in which he was wounded, he had held a succession of important posts in the military administration and already shown his willingness to co-operate with the Duma; on his first visit to the Tauride Palace he was loudly cheered as he climbed the tribune to address them. That same month, when the House met in secret session, it was decided to call to account all those to blame for the army's equipment failure.

The new Ministry consisted almost entirely of men sharing Polivanov's attitude to the elective assembly. The one exception was Ivan Logginovich Goremykin, who went on conducting affairs of state like a devoted family retainer. This exception notwithstanding, the tsar's changes in his government had not only put more capable men in office but shown a readiness to meet his peoples' wishes. The new era was greeted, therefore, with unanimous satisfaction in every quarter but one. To compromise with constitutionalism, democracy and parliamentarianism was strictly counter to the empress's views. Even shyer and more tongue-tied than her husband, she was, says Meriel Buchanan,[3] "cold, aloof, restrained and formal in manner, with no love of gaiety or fun, no sense of humour and no imagination to see things from any standpoint but her own." Detesting what she regarded as the immorality of the Russian court, she had isolated herself in her own world of make-believe where the devout and heroic Russian peasantry — personified for her by Rasputin — lived in a world of idyllic saintliness, justly and benevolently ruled by her husband.

Because of the military situation, the tsar had taken to spending most of his time at Stavka, anxiously watching the progress of the critical battles. In her letters to him, his consort expressed her opinions with growing bluntness about the liberals now in the Council of Ministers or others who were exercising influence that she and — she assured him — "Our Friend" (Rasputin) regarded as baneful. Guchkov, Rodzianko, Polivanov and Samarin, the last of whom had soon shown that he proposed to wield his purely religious portfolio without reference to the staretz — all came in for bitter vituperation.

The tsar accepted this advice with an affectionate toleration and often ignored it. However, as a man regarded by history as weak, and who above all loved his wife and family — finding in them some relief from a burden he neither desired nor enjoyed — he could hardly be expected to risk his domestic serenity for the continuance of a policy whose success was yet to be proved.

The main problem confronting the new Council of Ministers revolved round the single question of supply. With regard to the military aspect, Polivanov applied himself to its solution with promptitude and address. As far as manpower was concerned, he set out to build up a reserve, ultimately to number 2 million, all having four, five or six months' training. He steered the Bill constituting "The Special Council for the Co-ordination of Measures of National Defence" through the Duma. The Council, presided over by Rodzianko as it was now concerned with other than purely military matters, consisted of four members of the Council of State, four members of the Duma, representatives of the ministries directly involved — War, the Navy, Transport and Finance — and of trade, industry and the banks. It had been decided to extend activities to fuel and food, and there were finally four separate committees regulating munitions, food, fuel and transport; later a fifth, responsible for refugees, was added.

To equip the armies, Polivanov did all he could to encourage indigenous industry. In March a party of French technical instructors sent at Paléologue's request had arrived, but they were hampered by the positive hostility of Sukhomlinov's minions, and made little progress. Nor were their efforts made easier when on 12 April the largest of Russia's few explosive factories, the Okhta factory on the Neva east of Petrograd — which made propellants, cartridges, fuses and grenades — was totally destroyed in an explosion thought to be the work of saboteurs. In any event, the French mission was forced to the conclusion that "it would be impossible to form new factories, as there was already a want of trained personnel". This was the industrial legacy of a mobilisation policy which ignored civil needs. At the beginning of the war thousands of skilled men were taken into the army, and large numbers were killed in the first campaigns. Later this policy was so totally reversed that the War Industries Committee managed to keep 2½ million able-bodied men from army service, which worked out at 16 per cent of all men called up.

The shortage of labour in 1915, however, forced Polivanov to look abroad for equipment, though with the foreign trade deficit resulting from her inability to export her agricultural produce, Russia had to seek increased credits with her allies. In fact, purchasing abroad on a large scale had already begun, and in mid-May Kitchener, in whom the Russians had great confidence, had been personally appointed by the grand-duke as his agent with carte blanche to procure shells, rifles and ammunition. The grand-duke told him: "It is against the law of Russia to give such powers to a foreign general, but since it is a question now whether Russia should be victorious or defeated we will spit on those laws . . ."

With a world in arms, however, the Russians found themselves trawling in waters already well-fished. Everywhere factories were working to their fullest capacity, especially among the belligerents. Consequent delays in delivery dates meant that 2 million shells and 1 million fuses ordered from Britain, plus 5 million shells from Canada, had not arrived in time for the crucial summer battles. The infuriated Russians thought the British and Canadian firms were enriching themselves at their expense, and when the great demands made upon these industries were explained to them, they pointed to their own achievements in output. Their puny and backward industry had increased its output by about 1,500 per cent, from 35,000 shells a month in August 1914 to 550,000 in April 1915, while the infinitely larger and better organised industries of manufacturing countries like Britain could achieve only a rise of 1,900 per cent.

At the same time, foreign purchases were not always enhanced by the Russian urge to improve upon them. For example, two Austin armoured cars, thought to be inadequately protected, were sent to the Pulilov works to have extra thick plate fitted, but the work was so badly done that bullets penetrated the joints killing the drivers. After the first gas attacks the Russians had asked Britain and France for help. Hundreds of thousands of gas-masks were despatched to Petrograd, but the consignment was held up because, on inspection, the Russian chemists believed they could produce something better. The improved gas-mask was never invented and soldiers were asphyxiated because there were only ever enough for the front-line troops.

The chemists of a nation which had done some of the fundamental research on synthetic copolymers, and produced such giants as Mendeleiev who first enunciated the periodic law of atomic weights, were unable to cope when asked to urgently develop a new explosive for cartridges and shells because of the shortage of existing ones. After a long delay, enquiries at the laboratories revealed that the scientists were following up another discovery and had forgotten all about it!

Such failures apart, however, there was now a feeling that the War Ministry and other government departments were in more capable hands and that the defeats in the field had been perhaps more than counter-balanced by the promise of a future of solid and united achievement. To realise this it was necessary to stabilise the military front and, in late July, Polivanov could only tell the Duma "There is no ray of light in the situation in the theatre of war."

Chapter 14

The Great Retreat

Like a forest fire which reaches its limit in one direction only to flare up in another, by early July the battle in the south was beginning to smoulder out after two months of almost continuous German offensive and Russian retreat. There, at last, the front was becoming stabilised. Brusilov had drawn his army back so that the right wing ran down to the Sereth, while further north the Russians were trying to consolidate a line running through Opole. In a few places they had even been able to counter-attack, making surprise night sorties in which the bayonet could be effectively employed. On 1 July an attack by Evert's Fourth Army so threatened Mackensen's left flank that hurried measures had to be taken to retrieve the situation.

However, the crucial area of the battle, which continued to slide in a northerly direction throughout, was what remained of the central sector of the Polish salient after the Germans had thrust beyond Lodz in November and December 1914. The area still in Russian hands was mainly east of Warsaw, and it was here that, from the German viewpoint, the greatest potentialities seemed to lie. The two armies on the flanks were closer to one another than when Falkenhayn first criticised the idea of combined Austro-German attacks in January, while at the centre Woyrsch was applying significant pressure.

Mackensen was ordered to advance from the base of the salient up toward the Bug, making for the centre rear of the Russian armies. To match this, Oberost put forward a variation of their Dvinsk-Vilna plan, proposing a movement on Vilna alone by way of Kovno, but it found little favour with Falkenhayn who would have preferred an advance from the southern border of East Prussia which afforded a shorter route toward a junction with Mackensen. Having made this clear, there was further disagreement over its implementation.

German forces thrusting into Poland from the northern marches were confronted by a broad belt of marshland, running roughly from Osowiec to Grodno. Of the two possible routes, Hindenburg preferred the more easterly which cut deepest into "the very heart of the Russian army". Falkenhayn feared, however, that if the Russians drew them eastwards in pursuit, his armies would be led toward the marshlands such as those of the Pripet – bordering Russia proper – and in which, it was said, whole armies could be lost. Moreover, the Russians' superior knowledge of the terrain would favour them, and at best it would degenerate into the kind of long, arduous campaign he had to avoid if his troops were to return to the Western Front in time for the expected Franco-British initiative in late September. For this reason he did not wish to go further east than Brest-Litovsk. Hindenburg and Ludendorff countered this by saying that such a movement would involve frontal assaults on the Russian fortresses lying along the rivers Narev and Vistula.

On 2 July, a conference was called by the Kaiser at which all these possibilities were assessed. Ludendorff was instructed to use Gallwitz's Twelfth Army to break through the Russian Narev positions, advancing on both sides of Przasnysz – west of the Osowiec-Grodno lines – to take the weight off Mackensen's attack. The Twelfth Army advance began on 13 July with south-easterly thrusts from the top of the salient; on the 14th, Przasnysz fell, but "incessant frontal actions" (seemingly to justify Hindenburg's and Ludendorff's qualms) prevented the Narev being reached until the 17th; Roshan and Pultusk along its banks did not fall until the 23rd.

On the 15th and 16th, Mackensen's forces, supplemented by two further infantry divisions taken from the Western Front, began their upward north-easterly drive. Simultaneously, "to clear the way" for the attack on Vilna so favoured by Ludendorff and Hindenburg, the Niemen Army began a separate offensive in this direction following the usual pincer form: one army moved on Kovno while another advanced between Shavli and Schadow in the centre of the Russians' northern line. The fall of Shavli on 20 July brought an unexpected bonus for the Germans for it was the centre of the tanning industry, and £400,000 worth of abandoned hides were found; for the rest of the war the German army was shod with Russian leather.

The drive of Mackensen and Gallwitz round both Russian wings in Poland, the pressure on the centre and the movement eastward from East Prussia, inevitably led Stavka to reappraise their overall position in Poland.

As Alexeiev, the able North West Front commander, struggled to keep his armies intact, the grand-duke decided to abandon not only the Vistula region but all Russian Poland. Many commanders, including Golovin, felt that if his decision had been taken weeks ago the army would not have been exposed to slaughter and destruction in a futile effort to retain what had become, by any considered military standard, untenable.

However, knowing that there were no more prepared positions on which to retire, Alexeiev had been reluctant to abandon the defence line offered by the system of fortresses running in two chains across the Polish plains, although many were obsolete. What was more, while the Armed Forces Commission of the Duma had seen the wisdom of strategic withdrawal from Poland, the idea of such a drastic step was completely repugnant to the Council of Ministers. The chief-of-staff South West Front, Dragomirov, who had talked of the advisability of retreat on Kiev, capital of the Ukraine, was described by the tsar as having lost his nerve, although many supported his view at the time.

All strategical arguments were now purely academic. Gallwitz's and Mackensen's moves which threatened the double envelopment of the fortresses could involve their being cut off with the troops they contained. However, it was even more imperative for the tired and decimated Russian forces to get beyond enemy reach in order to rest and regroup; at the same time holding a line shortened in proportion to their reduced numbers. Orders were given accordingly.

The fighting men and the Polish population had plumbed the depths of misery during that hot, agonising summer of retreat. The decision to withdraw still further only increased the number and size of the areas involved.

To the hollow-eyed troops in their ragged, sweat-soiled uniforms, retreat meant long, dispirited marches in worn-out boots on painful feet, accompanied by perpetual hunger and thirst and relieved only by brief halts or occasional ferocious delaying actions with no hope of victory, in which men died or were hideously wounded. At other times, discipline – already precarious – was threatened by the discovery that the enemy was closing in; the one desire was to escape and men would throw away full cartridge bandoliers or even precious rifles to lighten their load, later claiming they were broken.

To the civil population retreat meant such suffering that even observers were left with a permanent memory of horror. In the eleventh-hour hustle of preparation for war, it was discovered that no provision had been made for legally delineating the rights and duties of commanders within the fighting zones. The French method had been to divide the country into two as between the Zone of the Armies, where the commander-in-chief had far-reaching and unassailable powers, and the Zone of the Interior. The arrangement was much criticised during the war, particularly when Joffre used his prerogatives to prevent any surveillance by the civil and properly elected representatives of the people, and kept them in ignorance both of his own intentions and the current war situation.

The Russians went still further and the Statute of Field Administration, presented for the tsar's signature on 29 July 1914, gave the army command total authority, overriding the Municipal Dumas and the Zemstvos, not only in the operational areas but also in a large and geographically undefined region in the rear. Thus Finland, Poland, the Caucasus, the Baltic Provinces, Archangel and Vladivostok came under army control, and Petrograd itself was within the military command of the Sixth Army. Commanders did not even require the sanction of the Council of Ministers for their actions, hence the grand-duke's ability to publish his manifesto on Polish autonomy without prior consultation.

The powers so obtained were exercised without restraint by chief-of-staff Yanushkevich, who took every opportunity to flout the wishes and defy the authority of civil government. Like the tsar, he was a blind Jew-hater, so his wrath first turned in this direction, especially when it was found that the enemy – unprejudiced in this respect – was recruiting alienated Russian Jews as spies.

Since the time of Catherine the Great, a committed anti-semite, Russian Jews had been restricted within the Pale of Settlement, comprising mainly the eastern provinces of Russian Poland, where they were confined to the shtetls and ghettoes. Catherine was also responsible for the doctrine that anything not expressly permitted to a Jew was forbidden and, among other things, had squeezed them out of agriculture — their traditional pursuit.

There were a ¼ million Jews fighting in the ranks of the Russian Army and, according to Knox, units such as the Polish ones with a substantial Jewish element often conducted themselves better than some Russian urban units. In the Duma a Jewish deputy from Kovno, Friedmann, pointed out that countless young Jews had voluntarily enlisted without waiting for the draft. Many were entitled to commissions by virtue of their education, but despite the desperate shortage of officers these were not awarded.[1]

In October 1914, hundreds of thousands of Jews were driven from their homes in Lidz, Kielce, Petrokov, Ivangorod, Skiernievice, Suwalki, Grodno and Bialystok. Shops, homes and synagogues were looted and every day, according to Paléologue, Jews were hanged in the army zone on trumped-up charges. In one case known to Knox, a Jew was executed for allegedly helping a German officer to escape by carrying him through the lines in a sack!

In March 1915, the Jews of Lithuania were forced to leave the frontier zone without any of their possessions. Violence and pillage raged unchecked and fleeing Jews were driven across the snows by platoons of whip-brandishing Cossacks. Altogether 600,000 were driven from Lithuania, Poland and Kurland, and this figure later rose to 800,000.

Even with the armies in retreat, there was fresh agitation. The reactionary paper "Volga" urged its readers: "People of Russia! Look round and see your real enemy. The Jew! No pardon for the Jews!" These events were not without repercussions, and the Western Allies had diplomatically pointed out that United States anger against these Jewish policies was being freely exploited by Germany. Although Sazonov had talked to Paléologue of ameliorative laws whereby the Galician Jews would become subjects of the tsar, an unnamed Russian statesman, to whom the latter spoke, responded: "What? Re-open the Jewish question in wartime? It's impossible. We'd have the whole country against us."

With the extension of the retreat, the mass uprooting of the Jews was to include the Gentile populations of those areas in the armies' wake. Entire regions were completely evacuated – the human inhabitants moved; the animals destroyed when they could not be moved; crops were burnt; factories dismantled and their machinery loaded on rail trucks where in many cases it remained to the end of the war.

None of this wholesale destruction took cognisance of the fact that a war being waged on such an enormous scale encompassed land and populations of previously inconceivable size; not only was the suffering multiplied, but the entire body-politic of Russia damaged. In Poland the aim was nothing less than the complete evacuation of the country, though no preparations were made for such an exodus or for the reception of the refugees. The few who tried to stay had their cattle and food confiscated on the premise that they must be pro-German, but even so some prudently preferred to hide in the countryside until the Germans occupied the area.

"Only those who have actually seen the flight of the Russian people can in any way conceive of the horror which attended it," wrote General Gourko. The roads from the towns were choked with refugees stretching in lines twenty miles long. "We saw," says Knox, "the most pathetic sights . . ." and describes families with all their worldly belongings on carts or carried in bundles on their backs. Every time the troops halted, the refugees did the same, setting up gipsy encampments and jamming the roads. When the troops resumed their march, so did the people, though they had no idea where they were going and some had been on the road for a month. Attempts were made to feed them at mobile centres organised by the Red Cross or the civil authorities. The ordinary soldiers showed "real kindness", and army purchasing officers paid fair prices for cattle they bought, but individuals and the existing organisations were powerless to help such numbers. Thousands died, especially children, not only from starvation and exposure but also from the cholera, typhoid and typhus which broke out among the fugitives.

All this misery was crowned by a heedless and often inefficient "scorched earth" policy. Knox saw military gendarmes burning straw, but leaving crops standing. The loss of 4 million head of cattle in the retreat affected the meat situation for the rest of the war. In the Council of Ministers, the Minister of Agriculture presented a memorandum warning "Curses, diseases, grief and poverty are spreading all over Russia. The great migration organised by Headquarters is leading Russia to revolution, to perdition, to the edge of an abyss . . ."

Four years later, many of those refugees were still living in dugouts, and a decade later scores of wooden crosses along the roadside marked their passing and commemorated those who had fallen.

This wholesale movement of population assisted rather than impeded the enemy. There were fewer mouths to feed, and the battlefield had been conveniently cleared of obstacles to their advance, although they had not taken full advantage of this. In the centre, Woyrsch's detachment had broken through at Sienno, and by 21 July forced the Russians back on Ivangorod fortress, but Mackensen's advance had run into trouble when its left wing (Austrian Fourth Army) was fiercely counter-attacked at Krasnik and had to be supported by the Eleventh on its right which was already under heavy pressure.

In order to rescue the Fourth Army, Falkenhayn proposed that Woyrsch should advance below Ivangorod, but Conrad (nominally in command) wanted the attack to be made above the fortress to draw the enemy further from the Fourth, and Mackensen had promised to secure the Austrian army in the meantime. On 29 July, therefore, Woyrsch crossed the Vistula, while Mackensen broke through the Russian lines which began to withdraw from the Bug to the Narev towards Brest-Litovsk.

On 4 August, Ostrolenka — connected by rail to Warsaw — fell to Gallwitz advancing from the Narev. Warsaw and Ivangorod had to be evacuated, but the grand-duke decided on a stand at Novogeorgevsk fortress, west of Warsaw, which had a garrison of 80,000 and 700 guns. "It had still been possible on 9 August," wrote Falkenhayn, "to retain the hope that the strong Russian forces crowded into the area between Narev-Vistula-Wiepsch and Wlodava would be prevented from escaping eastwards and would be annihilated." The investment of Novogeorgevsk and also of Kovno in the north began on the 9th. Alexeiev, at North West Front, was confident that Kovno would hold out, but it fell on 18 August to a straightforward infantry attack by Eichhorn's Tenth Army. Eichhorn was therefore able to advance within striking distance of the railway line carrying troops out of Warsaw, and Alexeiev was forced to move all available forces to hold this vital link.

On the same day, Mackensen captured Wlodava, which placed him midway between Novogeorgevsk and Brest-Litovsk, the strongest of the Russian forts. On the 19th, Novogeorgevsk fell and Hindenburg and his Kaiser entered in triumph. A delaying action was mounted at Brest-Litovsk, but Mackensen's huge Austrian Skoda siege howitzers were brought up, and by the 25th, Hungarian infantry was fighting its way into the suburbs. The fall of Brest meant a further loss of rail connections and the Russians were forced to fall back twelve miles east on Kobrin; then on Khomsk; then on Pinsk in Russia itself.

They had been cleared from the Polish salient. Even Baranovichi was now behind enemy lines, though Stavka had moved east to Mogilev some time previously.

Already shaken to the marrow by external events, the Russian army now faced internal disruption. The summer-long retirement had given the grand-duke's critics the heaven-sent opportunity for which they had waited and hoped since his appointment. The tsarina's loathing increased as she saw the generalissimo's popularity exceeding that of her husband. As she utterly rejected any evidence of Rasputin's scandalous conduct, however impartial the witness, so she also avidly grasped at any gossip about Grand-Duke Nicholas. Her only close friend was Anna Virubova, described by Paléologue as plain and dull-witted, another sycophantic follower of Rasputin; she fed the tsarina's prejudices by collecting the most unsavoury slanders from Stavka through young aides-de-camp as witless as herself.

The vilification campaign was diligently forwarded by those in court who had a personal score to settle, like Sukhomlinov – or who saw criticism of the army command as an infallible way to advance their own interests. Goremykin, chairman of the Council of Ministers, had seen the dangers of this and in a memorandum to his colleagues, he told them: "Irritation against the grand-duke at Tsarskoe Selo has become of a character which threatens serious consequences."

On 6 August it became clear what "serious consequences"

meant, for Polivanov, the War Minister, burst upon the Council the news (still supposedly secret) that the tsar intended to take over command of the armies. There was an immediate horrified uproar but on 12 August, nevertheless, Polivanov was despatched to Mogilev with the difficult task of informing the grand-duke of his supercession. He treated the news as if the tsar had granted him a favour: "God be praised! The tsar releases me from a task which is wearing me out." His two aides, Yanushkevich and Danilov, were also relieved of their duties. Danilov was demoted to command of the Twenty-fifth Corps, but the grand-duke insisted on taking Yanushkevich with him when he took up his new appointment as viceroy of the Caucasus. For many, the departure of these two was adequate compensation for the upheavals in leadership.

The man chosen to replace Yanushkevich was Alexeiev, the commander of the North West Front, whom the grand-duke had first proposed for the post. Alexeiev was liked and respected throughout the army. Now fifty-seven, he had risen from the ranks but remained simple, unassuming and pious. During his military career he had served in the Nicholas Academy, been quarter-master-general in Manchuria and chief-of-staff of the Kiev Military District from 1908 to 1912. He was well thought of as a strategist, but regarded in some quarters as indecisive, possessing the self-made man's typical inability to delegate. The feeling of many — though not all — Russian commanders was reflected in Brusilov's summary: "I consider that, had he been the chief-of-staff of a real commander-in-chief, he would have been above criticism. But with a commander whose mind he had to make up for him . . . Alexeiev was not the right man."

The truth was, as Cyril Falls has stated, that a giant was needed for Alexeiev's task and the Russian system prohibited the breeding of such a man. Moreover, a giant would have had to tell his master the truth ungarnished by flattery, and this was the certain way to a short career in the tsar's service.

The general horror felt throughout Russia was expressed by Prince Yussupov, senior, when an Order of the Day on 6 September announced the changes: "I feel it is the beginning of the end. It will bring revolution." This feeling was reflected in the reactions of Russia's allies when they heard the news. They knew and trusted the grand-duke and esteemed his soldierly and loyal qualities. He sought to assure the French that nothing was changed, that the new chief-of-staff was "a soldier to the core", but they saw the whole affair as the counsel of despair of a collapsing régime. Poincaré drafted a discreetly worded telegram tactfully expressing his feelings, but refrained from sending it on the advice of his Petrograd ambassador.

For all the lobbying against the grand-duke, it seemed that the tsar's motives were mixed with a characteristic mysticism. It had been hard to restrain him from taking command of the army in 1914, and now that the country was suffering blow upon blow, he felt he could no longer shirk what he considered a personal duty. Paléologue records a typical remark just before he took over: "Perhaps a scapegoat is needed to save Russia. I mean to be the victim. May the will of God be done." In such phrases Meriel Buchanan saw an essential key to the tsar's character; the strong sense of fatalism which atrophied his will to fight back against circumstances.

The tsarina was jubilant. After urging her husband to "get Nicholasha's nomination quicker done", she wrote shortly after the take-over: "You are about to write a glorious page in the history of your reign and Russian history." It was always a source of annoyance to her that the tsar remained on good terms with his uncle.

At Mogilev, Stavka at least attained the dignity of bricks and mortar in place of the Baranovichi railway carriages. The tsar had his personal quarters in one wing of the large, ochre-washed house. If protracted boredom formed any part of his gesture as scapegoat for Russia, this he certainly had. The only amusement in the town was a weekly cinema show at a local theatre. Lack of experience or inclination precluded his participation in the day-to-day military decisions of his headquarters, and when he had neither meetings to attend nor visitors to be entertained, he passed his time in reading the third-rate English and American novels his wife sent him,[2] or writing letters to her about them. Nevertheless, Stavka offered a happy sanctuary in some respects. Nicholas and his spouse had always disapproved of Russian high society, whose affairs and divorces provided others with titillating gossip. They were nauseated by the continuance of this existence during the war, when Petrograd seemed bent only on pleasure and luxury, oblivious of defeats and retreats and of the millions slaughtered on the distant battlefront. In contrast, Army headquarters seemed the haven of robust decency and even nobility, despite the jealousies and intrigues. Nicholas had always looked back on his soldiering days as among the happiest of his life, and enjoyed his protracted visits to Stavka early in the war. Moreover, living at Stavka enabled him to avoid another aspect of his life in the capital which he abhorred. It might be said that there were now two struggles raging in Russia, one physical, the other spiritual. Nicholas, brave enough amid physical dangers, was a coward before spiritual conflict.

At the height of the summer, the forces of liberalism and constitutionalism might have appeared to have the upper hand. The tsar behaved as if won over to their cause, and once the essential preliminaries had been completed, Russia was set to organise herself effectively to meet the external enemy. This new order seemed to be confirmed in August when public pressure was instrumental in the Duma being convened to debate the state of the railways, and the horrors brought about by the Statute of Field Administration. As after the promulgation of the Constitutional Manifesto in 1906, there was a feeling of new freedom in the air; on 19 August the Petrograd "Bourse Gazette" even dared to attack Rasputin.

However, those opposed to change, or seeking its reversal, were merely regrouping their forces while their opponents, lacking the relevant tactical experience, played into their hands. In the Duma the cry was raised for a "government enjoying the confidence of the country" — the argument being that only such a government would be strong enough to rid the nation of the abuses practised by employers and labour. This was clearly understood to constitute a call for deliverance from the moribund leadership of Goremykin — though having realised that his tsar wished for a more liberal administration, he had gone some way toward co-operating in its establishment.

At the same time a "Progressive Bloc" had been formed of the Labour, moderate left and centrist parties in parliament, aiming not only for the realisation of the "Ministry of Confidence", but also the implementation of various civil and political liberties, including an amnesty for political prisoners; restoration of the Finnish constitution; cultural freedom for the non-Russian minorities; abolition of restrictions on the Jews and an end to religious intolerance; removal of the limitation on working class organisations and trade unions. Much of this had been guaranteed under the 1906 constitution, but never put into effect. In addition, the bloc also took up the refugee problem and wanted to restrict the rights of the military to override the civil authorities. The tsarina was furious at these demands, the tsar non-committal but not implacably opposed, though he insisted that satisfaction of most of them must wait the end of the war.

In fact the Progressive Bloc's programme was so moderate that the Council of Ministers objected to very little. Furthermore, individual Council members felt they had co-operated with the Duma and had little to fear from a "Ministry of Confidence". The sole exception was their president, to whom the call for reforms and government changes represented not only a personal threat but defiance of the tsar. Most of his colleagues favoured the Duma being prorogued in such a way as to allow negotiations with the Progressive Bloc to continue afterwards, but Goremykin wanted prorogation to bar the way to further talks, as punishment for the deputies' effrontery.

The majority of the Council might have won the day, they had already upset the tsar. On 21 August, as part of the campaign urging reconsideration of his decision to take command of the armies, they had written not only declaring that his action would "menace Russia, himself and his dynasty with serious consequences", but tactlessly referring to the "irreconcilable differences between themselves and their chairman." The letter ended: "Such a state of things is inadmissible at all times, at the present moment it is fatal. Under such conditions we do not believe we can be of real service to Your Majesty and our country." This last phrase could have been interpreted as resignation en bloc, and this was how Nicholas took it. Its signatories included Piotr Bark, Finance Minister; Krivoshein, Minister of Agriculture; Shcherbatov, Minister of the Interior; Samarin, Procurator of the Holy Synod and Foreign Minister Sazonov, all deemed by the tsar to be in open rebellion against his own appointed President of the Council and hence against himself.

In this state of affairs, Mogilev — 24 hours' rail journey from Petrograd — seemed a refuge first from the wrangling between government and Duma and now between individual members of the government. This proved illusory when Goremykin scurried down there and, on 12 September, took advantage of an acrimonious debate in parliament to obtain authority for immediate prorogation without set time for its recall.

Told of this as a meeting on 14 September, the Council were confused and horrified. At the Tauride Palace all the recent divisive issues were forgotten, and Rodzianko needed all his persuasive powers to accomplish an orderly dispersal of the deputies. When the news became public there were strikes at the Putilov works and in Baltic shipyards, which by the 17th had spread to most factories in Petrograd. However, there were no clashes with the police and — having made their token gesture — the men returned to work on the 20th.

On 29 September, the Cabinet assembled at Stavka and several of the more outspoken members expressed their views. Nicholas scarcely seemed to listen, but told them, according to Paléologue: "I won't have my minister going on strike against my President of the Council. I insist upon everyone respecting my wishes." They were to return and continue work until he released them. He telegraphed his wife: "I told them my opinion sternly, to their faces."

To Nicholas, who bore no grudges, this was the end of the affair, but at Tsarskoe Selo the tsarina and Rasputin were busy looking for new names. The tsar, already cut off from the tide of events at Tsarskoe Selo, had further isolated himself by moving to Mogilev, performing — as Kerenski points out — yet another severance operation. He had rejected parliament's tender of collaboration and broken with the "conservative-liberal majority in the legislative chambers".

However, after his arrival at Stavka Nicholas was able to point to a minor military success in answer to critics of the changeover.

Along the Southern Front, Conrad — ostensibly concerned that the Russians might attempt to retake Lemberg — proposed to secure it by driving eastward from Kovel with his First and Fourth Armies. Actually, the move formed part of a much greater concept he had in mind at this juncture, whereby, after pushing the Russians completely out of Galicia, he would move on to the Ukraine whose cereal riches would ease Austria's blockade. The Germans in the north were to attack simultaneously in order to prevent any transfer from one end of the line to the other.

As it happened, the Russians chose the end of August and early September for attacks of their own. At Tarnopol on the Sereth, on the 26th, Brusilov's forces advanced to take 7,000 prisoners and thirty guns. To meet the new emergency, Austrian troops intended for the next phase of the campaign — against Serbia — had to be sent down to the Sereth and replaced in Serbia by Germans. In return for this, Falkenhayn extracted a promise that the Lemberg attacks would be called off, but the crisis was not over. The Austrian Fourth, advancing from Lutsk toward Dubno and Rovno, was smashed in a Russian counter-attack in mid-September; the Germans again came to their aid, rushing two divisions to check the attacks, and again extracted a payment: that all Austro-Hungarian and German units up to just north of Pinsk should be combined to form a single front as Army Group Linsingen.

Nonetheless, this was no more than a diversion gone awry. The main axis of the battle had shifted northward to the line from the Baltic coast to the confluence of the Niemen and Dubysza rivers, held by Plehve. Here Hindenburg and Ludendorff had endeavoured to execute a flanking movement on Augustow, where Russian forces had earlier been enveloped. Augustow was taken on 26 August; Olita next day; and Grodno on 2 September, while further north a fierce attack was launched to expel the Russians from their winter base at Riga and make it available to the Germans. Despite repeated attacks, the Russians retained a bridgehead at Friederichstadt and attempts to take them in the rear from the Baltic were foiled by the combined action of the Russian fleet and the British submarines.

This battle struck more terror into the heart of Russia than any previous action, for if Plehve's army — the last barrier to an enemy advance deep into their country — were to be enveloped, Petrograd itself would be menaced. Feeling in the capital ran close to panic and all those who could do so fled. The possibility of moving the government to Moscow was actively discussed; but after Plehve's army was reinforced by a Guards unit, the front held together. "The Russians", said Ludendorff ruefully, "always succeeded in escaping."

By 9 September, nevertheless, the German front had been extended east along the river Dvina and von Below's troops were moving on the road and rail centre of Vilna. When the Russians reinforced their centre by injudiciously depleting their wings, the consequent gaps in the lines enabled 40,000 German cavalry to stream through. This could not have happened at a worse moment as Alexeiev had only just moved from North West Front to take up his new post as chief-of-staff to the tsar, leaving the front temporarily leaderless. They were soon threatened by a worse disaster than any since July, with a wedge driven between the two armies and the enemy cutting behind the rear. The Germans took Sventsiany by 12 September and Smorgon by the 14th.

They now hoped to seize one of the Russians' few remaining railheads at Molodechno, the loss of which would severely hamper the armies' escape. German cavalry reached the town but it could not be held by the worn-out infantry who followed. By 25 September, the enemy was pushed back on Vidzy and Smorgon, and the Russian line re-established with thousands of German prisoners taken.

Chapter 15

The Offensive Ends

"If only God would grant that the British and the French began now – it's long overdue", the tsar wrote to his consort shortly after his arrival at Stavka, and at about the time he was reporting on the victory in Tarnopol.

He was expressing in restrained form the deepening Russian bitterness at their allies' apparent unwillingness to take any practical action to relieve their agonies in the smallest degree. One could not, wrote Poincaré, "pay sufficient tribute to the dogged energy with which the Russians fight on, as every fight means for them an appalling hecatomb of the slain." Knox, seeing a Russian officer with a newspaper, asked him how the Allies were doing in the west? "Doing? Oh, they're lost in admiration for the Russian army and its marvellous valour", he replied.

Yet when, in late July, Sazonov begged Paléologue: "For heaven's sake, get your government to give us rifles", they refused the request within a week. Similar appeals were declined by Britain. The Russians, said Lloyd-George (Minister of Munitions) simply could not believe that Britain had not sufficient for her own requirements and when refused would argue that "it was in our interest to help, for they would do the fighting if we would give them the wherewithal to do it."

In both the western countries there was sincere sympathy, not to say anxiety and depression at the Russian disasters. In so far as this constituted self-interest, Paléologue was quick to try to raise his president's spirits by reminding him that "even if obliged to assume the defensive the Russian forces are of great value to us."

In British government circles, sympathy for Russia had been sufficiently intense to alarm the War Office. They were concerned lest the despised civilian members of the War Council be so carried away as to insist Russia be helped at the expense of the generals' own pet schemes. To circumvent this, they proposed recalling Knox, the British officer who so heedlessly persisted in reporting the true facts from the Eastern Front; it took the intervention of Prime Minister Asquith, and the Foreign Secretary Lord Grey, to save him.

However, the Allies had not been totally unresponsive to the Russians' plight. Joffre answered the grand-duke's appeal of 2 May with commendable promptitude, launching an offensive between Lens and Arras within a week. "I consider it essential", he wrote later, "to afford immediate moral and material aid to our Russian allies." Nevertheless, such an offensive had been planned and would have been mounted anyway – if only to prove that there were no French troops to spare for the Dardanelles. In any case, the sporadic attacks into which the British armies were drawn until mid-June had no marked effect on the Germans' eastern drive or the movement of their troops from the western to eastern theatre. They cost the French 102,500 men, nearly double the German casualties, without territorial gain.

Late in June it was suggested through the British War Council that the most direct way to help Russia was through an all-out drive in the Dardanelles, which would require going on the defensive on the Western Front. Notwithstanding opposition from General French, the British commander-in-chief, who had told Joffre that he favoured an enveloping attack on the French front, it was perfectly clear to civilian representatives that, at a conference at Calais in early July, this course had been agreed upon by all parties.

On 7 July, however, the whole topic was reopened at a meeting of the Allied chiefs-of-staff at Chantilly (the French Grand Quartier). Joffre recalled Russia's sacrifices at the beginning of the war and said the time had come for the west to reciprocate. Since "the Arras attack did no good", he proposed to launch fresh attacks "as soon as the ammunition supply had been built up". He did not then mention the scale of operation he had in mind.

In the weeks following the abandonment of the Arras attacks, the Russians – their armies being repulsed by an enemy constantly increasing his numerical superiority by transfers from the western lines – had asked with a "feverish impatience", which Poincaré seemed to find surprising, when the French would resume activity. By the third week of August an answer to this question was beginning to emerge – to the consternation of the War Council.

At its meeting on the 21st, a nervous but excited Kitchener told them that he had agreed to an offensive in France greater in magnitude "than anything before conceived." Among the reasons he offered for this complete reversal of intention was the deteriorating situation in Russia. The attack was to be a joint Anglo-French initiative, and the place chosen for the British effort was a six-mile stretch of line on the right of La Bassée Canal at Loos. The French assault would open later in the Champagne area. Joffre seriously believed that a breakthrough on these two sectors would enable an offensive to be launched along the entire British and French front, leading to a German retreat beyond the Meuse and possibly ending the war. Apparently he had so won the British commanders over to this optimistic scheme that they were blinded to the inherent difficulties of their own part of it.

The terrain round La Bassée was some of the most heavily defended of the front and was too flat to afford cover to attackers. To compensate for other disadvantages, resources of artillery which the British army still lacked were needed, and batteries had to be rationed to 90 rounds for heavy guns and 150 for the field-guns — hardly generous by Eastern Front standards and utterly inadequate for destroying the deep defences of the Germans.

It might be supposed that in accepting the idea of an offensive under such handicaps, and in direct opposition to earlier agreements, Kitchener was influenced by the same motives as those proclaimed by the French — namely the urgent need to aid Russia at whatever cost. This was not so. He was already convinced that the Russians were defeated beyond Allied salvation weeks before, and was haunted by the certainty that the Germans were about to transfer "immense forces" to the Western Front. At that time, the appointment of a supreme commander of the Entente armies was being discussed, for which post Kitchener believed himself eminently qualified. Rather than argue the demerits of the plan, which were as clear to him as to anyone else, he had acquiesced to ensure that the French, if not supporting his candidature, would at least feel less inclined to oppose it.

On 21 September, the British First and Fourth Corps began their advance. A gas attack preceding the infantry assault went awry poisoning their own troops and, at the only point where objectives were achieved, they had to be abandoned from lack of flank support. Reserves could not be brought up because they had too far to come in the time.

At the end of the battle the British had taken the village of Loos at the cost of 60,392 men, many of these from Britain's New Armies taking the field for the first time. The other outcome was the dismissal of Sir John French as British commander-in-chief, and his replacement by Sir Douglas Haig.

The French offensive in Champagne and Artois began on 25 September in an atmosphere of great optimism. In Champagne, the cavalry stood by for the breakthrough, and buses were parked behind the lines ready to bring up support troops. Gas was effectively used in large quantities, and the French were better supplied with guns and shells than their allies. The first waves advanced three-quarters of a mile, but despite the threat of a German retreat at one point, Falkenhayn — now back from the east — was able to restore the situation. This was essential for his own survival since he had kept the area short of reserves, being certain until shortly before the assaults began that the French were in no condition to attack, and thereby giving them a three-to-one superiority. For the first time, however, the Germans had their defence organised in depth, and the offensive was held at the second line. By 28 September stalemate had been reached.

In Artois a determined assault took the crest of Vimy Ridge before bad weather brought the operation to an end.

The French took 18,000 prisoners in Champagne and inflicted 120,000 casualties there and in the Artois. They lost 191,000 men, while the British had inflicted only 20,000 casualties for a loss of 60,000 men. As further proof of the superiority of defence over attack, it had taken the Germans only 6⅓ divisions to rupture an offensive mounted by 20 British and French divisions. The forces which Falkenhayn had cautiously brought back from the east during the campaign might just as well have remained where they were for all the good they did.

However, the most serious effect of this abortive offensive was to starve the Dardanelles of men, with the result that after the first landing on 25 April progress had been checked even by the comparatively weak and confused Turkish forces present there. Although the Allied forces could have surprised and out-manoeuvred the enemy, despite their meagre numbers, their inability to conceal their intentions constantly allowed the Turks to reinforce in greater strength. Here, as in France, attacks resulted only in long casualty lists and no gains. Landings at other points along the Gallipoli peninsula briefly re-introduced the element of surprise but were too small to be effective, and in Britain hopes were turning sour. The British army commander, Ian Hamilton, was replaced by Sir Charles Monro, who promptly declared complete evacuation to be the only answer, and this was begun. At this point, Wemyss, the naval commander who had followed de Robeck, proposed a new scheme for forcing the Straits by naval action alone. It was too late: all anyone cared about was getting the troops safely home, and the need to reopen the Russian door to the Mediterranean was forgotten.

Additionally galling, and further proof of Allied impotence, was the fact that this particular failure was against an enemy whom the Russians were defeating on both land and sea. Between May and July, a number of operations had taken the Russian army deep into Armenia and Urmia, inside the Persian border, where the inhabitants warmly welcomed them. This opened the way either to a southern movement bringing them into contact with the British army in Mesopotamia (Iraq), or a westward movement encircling the Turkish forces at the fortress of Erzerum, regarded by its defenders as impregnable.

On the Black Sea, the Russian navy under Kolchak had attacked the Turks so effectively that, despite the acquisition of the "Göben" and "Breslau", they lost their supremacy and Russian transports were able to move freely. Unless the corridor from the Black Sea were opened up, however, this was a victory with little more than defensive value.

Throughout Russia, feeling about their allies' apparent overall failure was expressed with increasing fervour. Pavel Lebedev, quarter-master general to Fourth Army Commander Evert, told Knox that history "would despise England and France for having sat like rabbits month after month." He pointed out that Russia alone of the Allies could easily make peace, but if Britain was compelled to do so, she would be finished as a great power.

It could be argued that much of the Russian contempt arose from a lack of understanding, for trench warfare was hardly known on the Eastern Front, and the casualties suffered by the western Allies – with their smaller manpower resources – were indicative of their sincere desire to help the Russians. However, faced by such paltry results, it was difficult to persuade them that an all-out effort had been made or that their own disastrous situation had been uppermost in the minds of the Allied General Staffs in their strategic planning.

Nonetheless, in August the French were again asking Russia, whose forces were still retreating before the Germans, when they would be able to go back on the offensive. Polivanov, the new War Minister, gave the improbable answer: "in December." Even more improbably, they were as good as their word.

That December two further events occurred. On the 4th Paul Doumer, a future president, arrived in Petrograd and told Paléologue that he intended to demand supply-troops from the Russians to bring the French armies up to strength. Paléologue pointed to the depleted condition of the Russian armies and the difficulties of conveying men to the west. However, on 18 December serious talks began with the object of sending 400,000 men to France in batches of 40,000 a month; indeed the first 40,000 men did arrive, and took their places in the western lines.

The same month Knox met Wilson, chief of the British Imperial General Staff, who told him that the Anglo-French armies would not be able to break through in the west until the Russians had drawn off thirty divisions — "When," he demanded, "could this be done?" Knox indicates that he gave the most courteous answer of which he was, in the circumstances, capable.

Meanwhile, along the front after their drive toward Molodechno, the German camapign was nearing its end. "Our offensive is slowly coming to a standstill," wrote Hoffmann in his diary on 26 September. Since the Russian line remained intact, Ludendorff wrote with understandable bitterness of "the great anxiety of those September days" which achieved only "tactical success." He was perhaps over-pessimistic; in terms of losses inflicted, the campaign was in fact a strategic victory.

A month earlier it had been estimated that some corps in the central First Army sector were down to 5,000 men. Along the front as a whole the corps averaged 12,000 men instead of the normal 28,000. Total campaign casualties were 1,410,000, an average of 235,000 a month. This was the highest figure of the war — the overall monthly average being 140,000. After one year of war an entire army had disappeared and there had been no opportunity to produce its successors. "The professional character of our forces disappeared," commented Brusilov. In his view, the army gradually deteriorated into a "badly trained militia", with such losses that the Russians were outnumbered two-to-one along the line.

A generation of officers lay dead upon the battlefield; not only pre-war professionals, but also those who had volunteered in 1914 or later, the young rebels of the universities who had rediscovered patriotism. The educated in Russia could always avoid military service or, if drafted, could at least keep clear of the fighting, so that those who were at the front came from the most idealistic of the middle-class families. From now on, 70 per cent of Russian officers would be drawn from the peasant classes, always insufficient in number and so ill-trained that special tactical schools had to be set up near the front where they could take a six-week crash course.

The great descent on the Bosphorus had been abandoned, and on 3 October Sazonov told Paléologue that their losses made it impossible to send Russian troops to Salonica. "There is a limit to human power . . ." he said, "Our fighting strength is negligible . . ."[1] In terms of actual materiel there were 650,000 rifles, 2,590 machine-guns and 4,000 three-inch field guns in the whole army. Shell was down to 60 rounds of high explosive in many places, and there was an average of 200 rounds per gun, but a high proportion of the batteries had been withdrawn either for lack of shell or because they were worn out.

Both fortress lines were now in enemy hands. The new Russian line ran from just south of Riga, still occupied as a bridgehead, down to Czernowitz in Bukovina. Although the army had not fallen back as far as Kiev, the enemy was well inside Russia and held Pinsk.

"The Russians," said Hoffmann, "had been beaten along the whole front . . ." yet, as he admitted, not so decisively "as to compel them to sue for peace." This was not for want of trying, but as Falkenhayn wrote, annihilation of an enemy who gave ground "regardless of sacrifice of territory and population as soon as he is grappled with", and who had the whole of Russia at his disposal, was impossible to achieve. From July onward, the

German GHQ had urged that attempts at rapprochement with the Russians should be made; these culminated in approaches being made to Tsarskoe Selo through contacts in the Berlin court in December 1915, which drew no response from the tsar. Early in 1916, the Russian Madame Vassilichikova returned from Germany with a letter, suggesting the opening of pourparlers, from the German government, but the tsar ordered her to be sent to a convent for the duration.

The German peace offensive, Falkenhayn continued, "resulted, indeed, in such an increase in hostility to Germany that we all thought it better to break off entirely for the time all bridges to the east."

In September, Polivanov had told the French that the Russian armies would be ready to take the offensive by December; this could hardly have been regarded as a serious declaration of intent, yet circumstances conspired to bring it about. With the Russians pushed back, the Austrians and Germans proceeded to the next stage of Falkenhayn's grand strategy: the final subjugation of Serbia. Bulgaria, encouraged by events in the east and realising by mid-August that the Dardanelles expedition was doomed either to outright failure or to becoming another battle of attrition, had come in on the side of the Central Powers on 11 October. Only two days earlier an Austro–German army of nine divisions had occupied Belgrade, the Serbian capital. By December, the Bulgarians – intent on regaining Macedonia which they lost in 1913 – were pushing the Serbian forces back across the mountains into the pocket kingdom of Montenegro. The Allies' anxiety at this defeat was compounded by concern at its effect on Rumania. On the other hand, the perennially inadequate Anglo-French forces in the Mediterranean had been divided in two, and the half concentrating in Salonica was powerless to help the other half in the Straits further south. Russia was again asked to take action which would cause the Austrians to withdraw some of their forces from the Serbian front or, at least, prevent further transfers.

On 23 December, ½ million men from Brusilov's Eighth, Lechitski's Ninth and the Eleventh Army now under Sakharov were thrown into the assault on the South German and the Austrian Seventh Army. The Ninth was to aim at the heights of

Czernowitz to draw the enemy reserves to the south of this sector, while the Seventh Army was to strike for Bessarabia. The Russians bombarded the enemy for thirty-six hours and then attacked. The Austrians, however, had been alerted by their aircraft which had spotted the troop concentrations, and they repulsed repeated Russian attacks, inflicting heavy losses.

On the last day of 1915, after a brief regrouping, another heavy bombardment rained down on the Austrian positions and in the succeeding assault the enemy was driven back about a quarter of a mile along a thousand-yard front at Rarance. This was a small reward for all the effort and bloodshed, though much was made of it in the Russian and Allied press, and it did at least indicate that the Russians could still be reckoned with.

No further infantry attacks were attempted, but an intermittent artillery duel lasted for another two weeks until, in mid-January, Ivanov, reluctant to waste ammunition or risk further lives, decided to let the battle die down.

Chapter 16

The Recovery

Taken as a whole, the year 1915 could be described as one in which massive disasters on the battlefield were in some degree compensated by apparent progress on the home front. On the other hand, if 1916 did not begin with progress on the front, once the guns had fallen silent in Bukovina there was something akin to quiescence. With so little activity there were barely 200 casualties a day, but this was counterpoised by a darkening mood, a subdued but sullen rumble among all classes as it became clear that the previous summer's promises were to prove empty.

There are certain yardsticks which can normally be employed in judging governments, such as the supposition that the most mistaken or evil rulers are upheld by the belief that their policies are beneficial or necessary to their country's specific situation at the time. No such criteria can be applied to the Russian government from late 1915 onward, since its conduct was not motivated by the need to solve urgent, short-term problems. The tsarina was the most consistent, but her efforts were no more than a ruthless determination that her weakly son should inherit an intact autocracy, coupled with the conviction that this could only be achieved by obeying Rasputin's injunctions and urging her husband's acceptance.

Fate provided her with the opportunity while the tsar was absent with the armies, and since no provision had been made to appoint a council of regency she could fill the vacuum created, taking as her mandate various casual requests from her husband to do this or that on his behalf. In this way, Rasputin the "Holy Man of Tobolsk", became the effective ruler of 170 million Russians, needing no advice since he worked prophetically through oracles!

The "Holy Man" himself — when not at Tsarskoe Selo — moved about the country without trying to conceal his scandalous conduct. There were authenticated stories of his involvement with shady speculators, of drunken orgies, of indecent exposure, seduced women and cuckolded husbands; there were his own lying boasts of intimacies with the empress and her daughters which were nevertheless widely believed. Yet the surest way to immediate royal disfavour was to bring his activities to the attention of the tsarina, who refused to credit that a man who in her presence exuded the very aura of sanctity could behave in a way which others hesitated to describe to her prim ears. The tsar, too, sacrificed even long-standing friends who ventured hints of this nature: men like Dzhunkovsky, the honest deputy Minister of the Interior, or Count Orlov with whom he had served in the army.

The most expendable, then, were those who failed to acquiesce fully in the empress's crypto-policy, who did not "venerate Our Friend" with sufficient enthusiasm, or who actually dared to oppose him. Irrespective of ability, they were eliminated from government. So the voice of honest counsel fell silent, to be replaced by the flatterers, the spineless, the shiftless, amoral or neurotic riffraff who debased themselves in adulation of Rasputin.

Among the first to go were those whose names had appeared on the letter urging the tsar to reconsider his self-appointment as commander of the armies, and to nominate a new chairman for the Council of Ministers. The empress was especially eager to be rid of the Foreign Minister, Sergei Sazonov, who — she told the tsar in early September — was not attending meetings of the Council over which she now presided. He replied the next day: "This man's behaviour is beginning to drive me mad." Only lack of a successor delayed his immediate dismissal.

There was no such reprieve for Prince Shcherbatov, Minister of the Interior, since the tsarina had already met his ideal successor in the person of Alexis Khvostov, nephew of the Minister of Justice. He had a seat in the Duma, but even in this predominantly right-wing body his views were so extreme as to isolate him. An overt careerist, his associates included some extremely shady characters. Nevertheless, when Shcherbatov ensured his own downfall by refusing to muzzle press criticism of Rasputin, this was the man who succeeded him.

The tsar and tsarina were also unhappy with Samarin, Procurator of the Holy Synod, who was bound to come into conflict with Rasputin if he exercised his function with any integrity. The actual breach came about when Varnava, the Bishop of Tobolsk, took it upon himself to canonise a predecessor, whereupon

Samarin and the Synod objected and had Varnava and his supporters sent to monasteries. When Nicholas heard the order, he promptly reversed it, and on 9 October Samarin and Shcherbatov were both dismissed. A month later, the Minister of Agriculture, Krivoshein, who had also been a signatory to the letter, anticipated dismissal by asking to be relieved of his post.

With the question of transport crucial not only to the continuation of the war but also to the maintenance of supplies to the civil population, the next minister to leave was Rukhlov; he was replaced by A. F. Trepov, who soon came in for criticism from the tsarina for not being sufficiently subservient to Rasputin.

Neither the elder Khvostov nor Polivanov, the War Minister, had signed the famous letter; Polivanov because he claimed that service rules precluded active officers from taking part in politics. For the time being the two were retained, as was the President of the Council himself, the doddering Goremykin who, at Rasputin's suggestion, was given the title of "Chancellor of the Empire" as a personal accolade.

It could be concluded from these changes that the tsar and his consort were bent on displaying wanton contempt for national opinion, as voiced through the elective assembly's call for a "Ministry of Confidence", but the real reason for their actions lay in the fact that, for them, the Duma had no significance. When expressing patriotism, loyalty to the tsar or unanimity with government it was scrambling on the bandwagon of patriotic sentiment activated by the "True Russians", whom the tsar, unlike the deputies, had always understood and had relied upon. When criticising or calling for governmental changes it was no more than a nuisance, which because it nourished discontent, ought to be suppressed in wartime. A meeting of moderate socialists secretly held at Kerensky's flat was no more representative of "True Russia", even if the sovereigns had deigned to take note of its occurrence. Four points were agreed: (i) that tsarism was discredited by the public disorders, government inefficiency and military defeats; (ii) that the nation was so sick of the war that reservists were refusing to go to the front; (iii) that despite protestations of solidarity with the other Allies, Russia was likely to be forced to a separate peace; (v) that any peace negotiated by the existing government would be a reactionary one. As a corollary to all this, they resolved to secure a democratic, socialist peace.

Nor would there have been any great royal concern about a conference in Berne attended by Lenin and the dissident Leon Trotsky, where Lenin enunciated his latest thesis: "Civil war — not civil peace, that must be the slogan."

The French and British governments who were aghast at the damage to national stability caused by the latest changes, found some solace in the fact that the Russians were able to report fresh successes early in the year. The grand-duke, now viceroy in the Caucasus, agreed with Yudenich on the necessity to consolidate their victory against the Turks, especially in view of their advantageous position with regard to men and munitions.

Plans were prepared in strict secrecy, and when the attack was launched on 11 January, the Turks were taken completely by surprise. Three columns advanced. One moved up the Araxes Valley, and by 20 January was within twenty miles of Erzerum — the "Turkish Siberia" — the fortress which was the main concentration point for their armies. A second force wheeled northward to capture several mountain positions splitting the Turkish Tenth Corps in half and also cutting it off from the fortress.

The third Russian force, commanded by Yudenich himself, approached from the south where — because this region was believed to be impregnable — the only defenders were Kurdish irregulars. The Russians pushed right through this line and the assault upon Erzerum began; it fell on 16 February after five days of fierce and bloody fighting.

For the Russians this was a heartening victory, and according to their communiqués some 100,000 Turks fell into their hands, though the Turks put this at a mere 600 and described the loss of the fortress as a voluntary evacuation. Whatever the true details, the Turks had been routed and, despite the weather, were closely pursued by the Russians until they were able to re-form and make a temporary stand at Baiburt.

Taking the military situation as a whole, the Russians could boast that even when bled white they were unbeatable. For the Germans, even the previous years' victories had not permitted any significant withdrawal of the troops sent to stiffen the Austrians. The Bukovinan crisis of late December and early January had demonstrated that their eastern enemy would not remain on the defensive for ever, and was likely to recover more quickly than anticipated.

In December 1915, General Alexeiev had left Stavka to attend a meeting of the Allied Chiefs-of-Staff at Joffre's headquarters at Chantilly. Here it was agreed that future offensive action should be co-ordinated by the Allies, so as to nullify as far as possible the Germans' advantage of internal rail lines for moving their troops rapidly from front to front. The following summer was proposed for a combined onslaught on the enemy. The British commanders, whose forces had not yet been involved in a major battle in France apart from the Loos offensive, did not anticipate being ready to move before July 1916, when the Kitchener armies would be coming into line, and Joffre expected to be ready about the same time.

Only Russia, whose armies had fought continuously and at enormous cost that summer, was able to undertake readiness to give battle a month earlier. That this promise could be given was largely due to the achievements of Polivanov as War Minister: he was not just rebuilding the shattered armies, but was equipping, organising and training them on an unprecedented scale.

With only one factory to every 150 in Britain, he had nevertheless so increased home production that rifle ammunition had risen to 100–120 million rounds a year; the output of machine-guns — almost nil in 1914 — was now 500–800 a month. On a sheer percentage basis this was the greatest increase in output attained by any of the belligerents.

A good deal had been accomplished through the bodies set up for the purpose: the Special Council and the War Industries Committee. However, the Council was overloaded with members and hampered by constant internal disputes, while lack of liaison often put the Committee in competition with the War Ministry and other government agencies when buying in the home market, helping to force up prices. Three attempts to "militarise" the munitions factories were rejected by the Council of Ministers who were afraid of the workers' reaction. Credit for what had been achieved was therefore mainly due to the force and will-power of the War Minister himself and a few like-minded associates.

At the onset of winter there were only 650,000 rifles in the whole army, but some 1,139,000 had now been imported, though this was a mixed assortment including American, French, Italian, Japanese and British weapons. The number of guns along the line had risen from 1,920 at the end of 1915 to 3,943 by the end of January 1916, and more shell was available. There was also hope of an improvement in the number of heavy guns, as Lloyd-George had promised 100 4.5-inch howitzers a month.[1] In only a few weeks' time, Knox would write that all units had their full complement of rifles; machine-guns averaged 10–12 per four-battalion regiment; infantry divisions had thirty-six field guns, and most corps a division of 4.8-inch howitzers; many trench mortars and hand-grenades had been provided, and there was a reserve of 8 million rounds of 3-inch shell.

The cost, however, was prodigious. Piotr Bark, the Finance Minister, had visited the western Allies the previous September to obtain additional and extended credits, but his only collateral was the threat of withdrawal from the conflict. The borrowing, which had started in the second week of the war using the excuse that Russia needed to "prove her credit sound", had reached £50 or £60 million by early 1916, with a further £100 million promised. Poincaré did not approve of these transactions: "I could remind Monsieur Bark", he wrote, "that neither the text nor the spirit of our alliance led us to foresee that Russia would ask us at some time to lend our credit." However, he was compelled to give in by the thought of the millions of men, German and perhaps Austrian, who would flood westwards after a Russian capitulation.

Russian purchasing missions went all over the world, even to ex-enemy Japan. Their inspectors were installed in the factories, but being chosen on a nepotic basis and without technical training, they lacked both flexibility and the discretion to allow the slightest deviation from specifications or their own terms of reference. In consequence, American and Japanese contractors were driven to despair by their hidebound methods, and Britain was called upon to mediate.

Transporting the vast quantities of goods which began to arrive from the ports to the battlefields naturally presented fresh problems, but action was now being taken in this direction. November 1915 saw the completion of a railway from the ice-free port of Murmansk, built by abundant prisoner-of-war labour. The

British had simultaneously given financial backing to the plan of a Finn named Bostrom, for a sledge route from the port of Skibbotten to Karungi, near the gulf of Bothnia, which was the terminus for the Finnish railway system.[2]

Fresh drafts now coming from the depots had been trained for a minimum of three months, although the call-up of the 1916 class was delayed for lack of rifles. While the other belligerent nations bemoaned the quality of the troops they were forced to draw upon, those taking their place in the Russian line seemed better than ever, calling forth delighted approval from Pares, the tsar, Rodzianko and Knox. They showed such keenness that, immediately they arrived in the line, they begged to participate in the most dangerous assignments, often without officers.

There was still a shortage of officers, however, the traditional officer corps having been decimated, and those replacing them were sober young men who had worked their way up from the ranks, NCOs who were given their commissions or, in many cases, village schoolmasters — no less courageous than their predecessors, but substituting for wild dash a more serious approach to their duties.

On the training grounds, French and British instructors were inculcating the techniques and methods of modern war as learned from experience, but coming up against an insensate national pride which — here as in every sphere — regarded such help as humiliating.

From the strategic point of view, the abandonment of the Polish salient had shortened the line to something under half its former length, making it easier to defend in depth. Even so, at the beginning of the year it was terrifyingly thin. However, only time was now required for this dearth to be made up, and this the Russians seemed likely to be granted.

Over Christmas 1915, Falkenhayn had submitted a memorandum on the state of the war and prospects for the coming year to the scrutiny of his All-Highest War-Lord. He was opposed to further offensive action on the blank plains of Russia, pointing out in justification that: "Even if we cannot expect a revolution in the grand style, we are entitled to believe Russia's internal troubles will compel her to give in within a relatively short period." Predictably, his complacency in this respect was not shared by Oberost. "We found", writes Hindenburg, "an opinion prevalent that the Russian losses . . . had already been so enormous that we should be safe on our eastern front for a long time to come. After our previous experience we received this opinion with caution."

During recent months, however, the German commander-in-chief had done much to secure his own position vis-à-vis his critics – and potential supplanters – in the east, and he could point to the real achievements of the Russian summer campaign as backing his divisions. He could, therefore, confidently tell Hindenburg and Ludendorff that there would be no major initiatives on their front, and deny them all reinforcements despite their pleas that the extended line was inadequately held. Indeed, he withdrew all German troops from Galicia, leaving its defence entirely to the Austrians although they were themselves fully occupied with defeating Serbia and planning an offensive against Italy.

That the efficient Polivanov had a breathing-space in which to accomplish Russia's military resurgence was not entirely due to the grace of the enemy, or his own prudence in refraining from signing the letter to the tsar. Nor did his first impressive achievements so inspire confidence that he was allowed time to complete his task. From the first he was the particular butt of the tsarina's written attacks: "I don't like your choice of Minister of War . . . He is Our Friend's enemy, and that brings bad luck. . ." On 22 January: "Get rid of Polivanov." And again: "I implore you quickly get rid of Polivanov." However, the temporary brake on the Rasputin-backed campaign to force the entire government to conform with his divinations – and which granted Polivanov a longer lease of office – was the fear that one of the staretz's riots (on this occasion on a river-steamer) seemed likely to end in the public courts. After this had been hushed up, other events supervened.

Goremykin, who regarded the Duma as an open affront to the tsar, had twice lost his nerve and cancelled appointments to attend its meetings, but when courage again failed him in January 1916, all he could do to avoid public wrath was ask to be allowed to resign. Permission was the more readily granted as he had "lost the confidence" of Rasputin. The Duma, while never suggesting that ministers should be made accountable to it, had urged that those appointed should be people they could support. They therefore interpreted Goremykin's dismissal, for which they had long been pressing, as the tsar's acceptance of their arguments, and waited hopefully for someone with at least a modicum of respect for the elected parliament of Russia to be appointed in his place. To their horror, the man chosen was Boris Stürmer, Court Master of Ceremonies and at one time Governor of Jaraslov in Poland, where his financial peculations were well known. He had also served under the reactionary and detested Interior Minister Plehve, ultimately assassinated but not before his brutal high-handedness had helped to plant the seeds of the 1905 revolution. In 1913, Nicholas had even considered foisting him on Moscow as mayor, displacing the man properly elected, until an outcry from the second capital forced him to change his mind. Stürmer was in many respects a worthy successor to Sukhomlinov in the royal affections. According to Sazonov, he was "a man who left a bad memory wherever he had occupied an administrative post"; for Paléologue his face bore the "very expression of hypocrisy"; and Buchanan described him as "a man on whose word no reliance can be placed". However, all this was outweighed by his being a faithful Rasputinite.

The Duma, due to meet in late February, was in an uproar which transcended all party lines. Stürmer's very name denoted this German lineage, and he had no sooner taken office than he sought the tsar's permission to change it to the Russian form — "Panin"; this was withheld because it required the consent of all the other markedly unenthusiastic Panins in the country.

It was widely believed that Stürmer strongly favoured peace at any price, and the Allies noted a considerable increase in pro-German sentiment in the government after his accession to power. Goremykin was reputed to have declared: "They curse me up hill and down dale, but I am guided by the highest motives; when I go peace will be concluded." It now looked as if there were some savage truth in this.

The reaction of the British and French governments was one of the utmost alarm, yet those who precipitated these upheavals during a war in which Russia had known only defeat and slaughter, appeared totally unaware of the effects of their actions. Such confidence was reposed in the tremendous manpower of the armies, their readiness for perpetual sacrifice and the measureless size of the country, that notwithstanding scares like those of the previous August when Petrograd was about to be vacated by the government, they never doubted ultimate victory. As Rodzianko pointed out in 1917 to a foreign diplomat, Russia was a big country and "quite capable of running a revolution and a war at the same time". Such complacency in all quarters allowed the deterioration of government to proceed unchecked.

The Duma's anger boded ill for the new prime minister, who had to fulfil Goremykin's cancelled rendezvous. Rasputin suggested — through his usual mouthpiece, the tsarina — that the accepted practice whereby the deputies present themselves at the Winter Palace for the royal benison prior to a new session should be reversed, and the tsar should present himself at the Tauride Palace instead. This was arranged, and according to Paléologue, the tsar was in an agony of nervousness. He "stopped or stumbled over every word of his speech", and his hands trembled. It was "quite painful to watch". Rodzianko more charitably says the speech was delivered "in a firm, clear voice". In any event, the visit was an enormous success, speaking highly of the House's loyalty to his person. He addressed the assembled deputies for the first time as "representatives of the people", and there was the usual climax of a Te Deum. Rodzianko had been presented with the Order of St Anne some time previously, but it was typical of the ambivalent attitude to the Duma that when this was handed over it was explicitly indicated that the award was for his work in education — not, by implication, in his role as president.

Stürmer was at his master's side, but the deputies could not bring themselves to tarnish the occasion by attacking him. Later, when he tried to pass himself off as a convinced liberal and to extract a promise of silence from them on the subject of Rasputin, they were less co-operative.

Chapter 17

Distant Echoes From Verdun

It was an external event rather than the agitation against him originating at Tsarskoe Selo which first hindered Polivanov's efforts and, indeed, damaged the whole Allied offensive schedule.

In his Christmas report to the Kaiser, the German commander-in-chief rejected all the options available to him and ended by tendering his positive conclusion that the theatre most likely to yield results was France, upon whom "the strain had almost reached breaking point". He proceeded to set out a scheme which, in its originality and understanding of other than purely military factors, must lay claim to being considered the master plan of the war.

The Schlieffen plan was the product of years of thought in the serenity of peace and it was, in the event, modified and mis-applied. Despite the brilliant results of Gorlice, which seemed to bode well for future applications of the plan (under whatever conditions and circumstances), it represented the application of massed technological resources against those who lacked the means to counter them. What now followed was something entirely different; a concept developed by Falkenhayn in a matter of months under the exigencies of war. If it ultimately failed, this was partially through misapplication at field level, but mainly because of the unbreakable courage of the defenders.

Hindenburg had declared that soldiering and politics did not mix, but Falkenhayn saw things differently. In total war, where whole populations and public opinion were mobilised behind armies drawn from those populations and where entire national economies were committed, politics – and the national psycho-logy they reflected – had to be taken into account. The idea of an offensive based on these premises was so novel it failed to permeate the minds of commanders – including Falkenhayn – and they could never quite shake off the habit of thinking in terms of advance as being a tangible gain.

"Within our reach, behind the French sector of the Western Front," he told the Kaiser, "there are objectives for the retention of which the French General Staff would be compelled to throw in every man they have. If they do so, the forces of France will bleed to death . . . whether we reach our goal or not. If they do not do so . . . the moral effect on France will be enormous."

Verdun was one of the two places which satisfied these conditions — the other was Belfort. At Verdun the French trench-line was backed by a system of forts cut in the chalk and reinforced with concrete. They were actually considered of such little strategic value by the French commander that they were partly evacuated in August 1915, and the removal of their guns continued up to January 1916. It was argued that experience of the Belgian, Austrian and Russian fortresses had proved their worthlessness in modern war, though ironically the Verdun forts were to prove stronger than any. They also possessed a high political value. When it was decided that they had become untenable, no effort was made to explain this or even to announce what was being done; they remained, therefore, as the symbols of the unconquerable military heart of France, and as such had to be defended entirely against army opinion.

Falkenhayn's offensive commenced at four o'clock on the morning of 21 February with the explosion of a 14-inch howitzer shell in the Archbishop's Palace in the town. This heralded a tremendous bombardment which was so similar to that inflicted on Radko-Dmitriev's Third Army the previous May as to betray the same hand behind it. It lasted two days and reduced the countryside, in the words of one observer, to "an appearance like the surface of the moon". Such bombardments, not yet experienced on the Western Front, were soon to become commonplace.

Falkenhayn considered he had learnt of the effects of such barrages from experience in Galicia, and while selected shock troops were again used for the first assault, it was not thought necessary to push them right up to the enemy lines beforehand, or to dig special jumping-off trenches. On the basis of Russian experience, the damage done to the defences was expected to be sufficient to clear the way for them, though there was a mile of no-man's-land to traverse. It was here that the strength of the fortresses first proved its value to the French, for the bombardment inflicted much less damage than anticipated and the exposed attackers suffered heavily. But for the fact that the first assaults at the Grand Quartier were taken for a feint (the real ones being expected in Champagne) and Verdun was sent neither reinforcements nor supplies, they would have proved of even greater value. As it was, the German's sheer numerical strength was overwhelming and, by 24 February, the first of the forts – Douaumont – fell. On the 25th, Joffre and his colleagues awoke to the fact that this was indeed the major offensive. Their immediate proposal to evacuate the area was greeted with horror by the French government, which decided to place Pétain in command of its defence.

Now that the scale of the German offensive was revealed, the French were terrified that their own armies were about to re-enact the Russian's experience, and the cry "au secours" was immediately raised among the Allies. Britain could do nothing for she was awaiting the arrival of her new armies. Russia was in the process of re-forming her armies with the summer offensive as a deadline, but every effort was made to persuade her to launch attacks immediately. At Stavka, the French liaison officers pleaded with the tsar and Alexeiev, and when the tsar returned to Tsarskoe Selo, Paléologue presented a cinematograph show to give him and the tsarina some idea of the battle, evoking appropriate comments from Nicholas: "What wonderful dash your soldiers have! How could anyone face such a bombardment? What a mass of obstacles in the German trenches."

Such efforts had not been made since August 1914 and, in fact, popular feeling was successfully aroused in France's support. It is no denigration of her soldiers' bravery to say that she managed to present, throughout the world, the picture of civilisation itself struggling for existence. Immediate judgments are made as much on emotional as on rational grounds, and on this basis it was easy to overlook the negligible strategic value of what was being so resolutely held, in admiration of the manner of its retention. Paléologue records that the tsar and Russian generals frequently expressed this feeling, and it was undoubtedly more than mere formal courtesy.

Conversely, when the world anxiously waited to see the French relieved, it was hard for anyone in whom a romantic and self-sacrificial chivalry was as instinctive as it was in Nicholas to stand objectively by and pursue a coldly logical course. Nevertheless, this was what his Stavka advisers counselled. There must be no surrender to French importunities. The armies were unprepared for the attempt, and to venture now might ruin everything. Furthermore, the thaws could set in at any time, swamping the trenches and making the roads impassable.

This argument was easier stated than obeyed. Unlike those about him, de Laguiche and Paléologue could not simply be dismissed when they offered unwelcome advice. He was most susceptible to their kind of blandishments. He therefore overruled his generals and ordered an offensive. Writing to the tsarina, he said that they wished to attack before the thaws set in or the Germans themselves attacked. "For this reason, therefore," he said, "it has been decided to take the initiative into our own hands, taking advantage of the onslaught at Verdun." Paléologue was relieved and delighted at the news.

It was true that for some time past the Russians had considered an attack by the North Front against Hindenburg's forces in the Dvinsk-Vilna region as the necessary preliminary to any larger offensive in the area. At points between Postavy and Smorgon the Russian line reached within 40-60 miles of Vilna, whose capture, with its rail connections, represented a considerable loss to the Russians. Its recapture – a tempting prize to them – would certainly deeply embarrass the Germans, and the Russians wanted to anticipate a possible blow from this direction.

The Russian staff were also concerned about certain features of their own northern line, in particular the existence of a salient called "Ferdinand's Nose", which lay between the lakes Narocz and Vishniev.

The offensive might have begun under more fortunate portents if the Front commander had been a Brusilov or a Plehve, but Brusilov was at the opposite end of the line and, moreover, there had recently been a reorganisation of command. When he departed for Stavka, Alexeiev's old North West Front had been broken into two separate sections. The West was put under Evert, and as an immediate temporary measure Ruszki was placed in command of the newly created North Front. When Ruszki had to go on sick leave, he was relieved by Plehve, whose body finally broke under the strain. He also left, ostensibly on sick leave, but when brother-officers spoke of his return he told them vehemently: "No, gentlemen, this is the end." A few weeks later he was dead.

Plehve was replaced by Kuropatkin, commander-in-chief in the Russo-Japanese War, who was widely associated with that disaster both by the public and the army and was furthermore generally regarded as out-of-date in his ideas and lacking initiative. The tsar himself was doubtful about his appointment, and wrote to his wife shortly afterwards: "I hope with God's help Kuropatkin will prove a good commander-in-Chief. He will be directly under Stavka and will not have the same responsibility he had in Manchuria." Nonetheless, he was now responsible for a great part of this major effort. It was to be shared with General Evert, a man of Swedish stock, another commander from Manchuria and also extremely cautious.

Along the two battle lines the winter passed with only minor activity. The Russian army, now beginning to learn the art of entrenching, was dug in and living in something like comfort. "Some", wrote Brusilov, "were genuinely cosy." The walls were planked, floors were of wood or stamped earth, stoves used for heating, and ceilings supported by wooden beams believed, quite erroneously, to be proof against all but the heaviest shells. There had even been opportunities for relaxation, and Brusilov describes a day when the troops went en fête for the benefit of their officers.

On the German side, now that they had reverted to the defensive, there had been considerable activity to strengthen their positions, and Hindenburg commented that building trench-lines and roads, erecting hutments, plus the need to supply the troops with war material, food, timber, etc., "made the word 'rest' practically a mockery to both officers and men". The ultimate result was that wherever the Germans were able to impose their own precepts and practices, both German and Austrian trenches could have served as models of their kind. Strongly built in concrete, equipped with light railways and often their own generating plants, they included bomb-proof shelters. Recreation areas had been established not far behind the lines.

Taken as a whole, this sector of the line was adequately though not over-garrisoned, for such was the German confidence in their defensive skill and in the terrain – a zone of lakes, swamps and forest – as well as in the depleted state of the Russian forces, that much of the line was held by Ersatz and Landwehr units.

The attacks planned by the Russians were to be launched in two places: on either side of the Sventsiany-Postavy rail line, and between Lakes Vishniev and Narocz. A third attack was to be launched simultaneously from the Jakobstadt bridgehead further north. It was hoped that the convergence of these armies would envelop the German Twenty-first corps, under Hutier, and by breaching the line bring Vilna, as well as Kovno (fifty miles east) within striking distance. The objective was to break up the northern wing of the German line and throw it toward the Baltic coast, north of the River Niemen.

Even Ludendorff conceded the choice of venues to be a good one, as the Russians were striking where the German line was thinnest on the ground. Both the North and West Front were to be involved; West Front had been augmented by two Guard Corps and the Twenty-fourth Corps sent from the South West to reinforce the Tenth Army, while three divisions came from West Front to reinforce North Front. The Second Army (West Front) was to attack on either side of Lake Narocz; the Fifth Army (North Front) would attack the Jakobstadt bridgehead along an area stretching from Postavy to Lake Drisviaty, while the Twelfth Army (reinforced with the Fifth and First from West Front) were positioned on the lower Dvina to initiate attacks along a line from Jakobstadt to Smorgon. The purpose of this was to detain German reserves and divert attention.

Through late February and early March, Russian concentrations continued. In the Second Army's zone no fewer than 10 infantry and 1 cavalry corps were assembled, but this army had to cover a front of 60 miles of which 16 was frozen lake.

For purposes of attack the Second Army was divided into three of which the two outer groups were bearing the main weight, seeking to curve round the sides of the defence. The commanders of these two groups were both soldiers of high standing, and their forces included a strong backbone of Siberians, classed among the best troops.

When the build-up of forces had been completed, it was estimated that the Russians had a numerical superiority over the Germans of five-to-one. At the same time, the Russians assembled weapons on a scale hitherto unknown. The artillery backing for the three main attacking groups included 271 guns, ranging from 4.2-inch quick firing guns to 6-inch howitzers. Quantities of shell equivalent to an average daily expenditure of 100 per gun were also amassed. In Knox's view, the two sides were for the first time evenly matched in "matériel".

By mid-March, with the French still begging for relief, all was ready. The forces and the necessary munitions had been concentrated as secretly as possible (since the middle of 1915 the Russians had learnt to be more discreet in their use of radio) but it had all taken longer than anticipated. Some delays were due to problems inherent in large-scale operations, others arose out of sheer incompetence, as when parts of the Twelfth Army had to be withdrawn from the line because they were found to be unfamiliar with the Japanese rifles issued to them.

During the winter of 1915/16, Alexeiev — with his mind still on 1812 — had ordered the formation of guerrilla bands under Cossack aegis. Supplied and paid by the nearest army headquarters, they were particularly intended to harry enemy lines of communication. This was another instance of failure to understand the essential differences in the two wars. In the Napoleonic campaign, with the invading armies advancing in columns like snakes, it had been possible to nip through their supply lines; now, with the enemy occupying a broad belt of the country, it was physically impossible to do this on an effective scale. These bands degenerated into mere groups of uncontrolled marauders, terrorising villages, ravishing their women and committing armed robberies; later that year they were disbanded. Nevertheless, on the night of 27 February, one such band of thirty-two men, led by Cossack officers, crossed the frozen Lake Narocz, penetrated enemy lines and reached Vilna disguised as Lithuanian peasants. Armed with explosive, their object was to destroy communications to the front about to be assailed, but having passed safely through several German checkpoints they were spotted by a sentry and caught. The Germans naturally concluded that the Russians were planning to attack in this region. This was confirmed by concentrations which were observed early in March, and the whole line was reinforced.

By mid March both sides were in an equal state of preparedness, and along the battle line Russian troops could do nothing but await the final orders which would begin the offensive or cancel it. Many of the Russian commanders believed it would be called off, for while the area still lay under deep snow with rivers and lakes frozen, the thaw might set in at any moment and the whole region would lapse into its annual "roadless period", when all but the very few metalled roads would disappear under water for weeks at a time, and communication and movement would cease.

The waiting, and the conviction that the attacks were in any case doomed to failure, proved too much for the commander of the Second Army, Smirnov, who was taken ill. His place was taken at the last moment by General Ragosa, a fiery and resourceful officer seconded from command of the Fourth Army.

Mid-March passed and the thaw held off. Then on the 17th it began. This meant that the ice over the lakes across which Pleshkov's groups were to have advanced to the flanks of the German trenches in the isthmus was unsafe and could not be used, and the swamps forming much of the intended battleground, though frozen at night, were under a foot of water by day. The trenches would now have to be forced by frontal attack.

However, the heaviest pre-attack artillery barrage of the war so far had already started. According to Hoffmann there was "such an expenditure of ammunition as we had not yet seen in the east". During the eight-hour bombardment the Russians fired 30,000 rounds of 3-inch and 9,000 rounds of heavier calibre shell, the weight falling on the eight-mile stretch of isthmus between the two lakes. As Knox points out, this was an extravagance in view of the comparatively limited resources; it left the batteries short thereafter and, as there was little opportunity for accurate observation, much of it was wasted.

Furthermore, as was to be the experience on the Western Front, this kind of bombardment did little more than destroy the more advanced trenches when falling on deep defensive positions. When at 10.20 a.m. on 18 March Baluiev's Fifth Corps began storming the isthmus, followed an hour later by Pleshkov's Thirty-fourth Division, the Russians were repulsed by accurate German artillery and machine-gun fire. At noon, Baluiev switched his attack to the right of the German line, but was still held, while the minor attack made on other sectors of the front was recognised by the Germans as diversionary and failed to affect their defensive dispositions.

Next day the Russians resumed attack, Ragosa's forces concentrating on the left wing of the German defence at Postavy. Heavy pressure was also applied at Vidzy and at Jakobstadt in the north, but the Germans held their lines though at times, as Hoffmann says, the situation became critical.

Pressure continued on 20 March, with persistent attacks at Postavy and fresh assaults of great bravery by Baluiev's forces on the isthmus. Still there was no gain and once more the diversionary attacks failed in their purpose.

That night the thaw came to an abrupt, though temporary, end. The temperature fell to 13°F and snow began to fall. At midnight Baluiev ordered a fresh artillery bombardment accompanied, according to German reports, by the release of gas. At 1.30 a.m., four Russian corps poured across the isthmus and at five in the morning penetrated the German trenches near Postavy, taking approximately one third of a mile of the front line, while a German reserve division, defending the south of Lake Narocz was forced from its first two lines by the Fifth Siberian Corps.

The price for this small gain had been exorbitant: the barbed wire in front of the German trenches was hung with the corpses of Russian attackers as far as the eye could see. The break in the thaw had frozen a swamp through which the Russians were advancing, and early on 21 March 300 men had to be hacked alive from the ice which gripped them.

The greatest advance was on the isthmus, where there had been a penetration 2,000 yards deep on a front 4,000 yards wide. Yet, as the Russians were quick to point out, this would have been hailed as a great victory on the Western Front. "I could never understand", wrote General Gourko, "how it was that our allies ... had one law for their advances and another law for our advances." Ludendorff now regarded the position of the Tenth Army as critical, and ordered immediate reinforcements to retake the lost ground, but by the end of 21 March this had not been done. Throughout the next day further Russian attacks were repulsed, but in the early evening they succeeded in taking a position at Postavy which threatened disaster for the Germans.

The thaw had now resumed and the temperature was rising. In this exceptionally hard winter, the snow which had begun falling in November reached a depth of 18 inches only a few weeks before. This now turned to mud and slush, making the conduct of the battle even more difficult. It soaked the Russians' greatcoats and came over the tops of their high boots; shell craters were filled with water; roads ceased to exist and even the trenches were filling. These conditions afflicted both defence and attack, and the German Tenth Army reserves took hours wading through swamps to reach the front from the Vilna-Dvinsk area. As the temperature rose, thick fogs caused units to lose contact, and all reconnaissance aircraft were grounded.

Nonetheless, more Russian attacks reached the first line of German trenches south of the Postavy railway line, but by dawn a heavy and accurate German bombardment accompanied by heavy machine-gun fire had forced them to withdraw from all their gains, including those of the previous day.

The Russians had characteristically attacked at the junction between two command zones, where enemy co-ordination was predictably poorest and where it would be easiest to create confusion. The Germans had now corrected this situation by reshuffling their commands. As the attacks continued, the only weak spot from the German viewpoint was in the Riga area where their troops were reinforced by men brought up from the Austro-Hungarian front who were positioned south of Mitau.

By 24 March, the Russian offensive was a week old and the Germans felt they had the situation under control. The only enemy gains had been the two lines of trenches between Lake Narocz and Lake Vishniev; repeated attempts to take a hill overlooking these positions failed with heavy losses.

The thaw had now slowed all movement, and the twenty-mile journey from the nearest station to Baluiev's headquarters took seven hours. In the trenches the water was more than three feet deep. In the centre of Baluiev's front the marshes were impassable, but on the 26th a further assault was attempted with the Russians – in Ludendorff's words – "wading through swamp and blood" and suffering enormous losses. Finally, with his front reduced to a lake, Pleshkov was forced to abandon all further operations.

German intelligence believed the Russians were withdrawing troops from the front, and this was confirmed by air reconnaissance. On 3 April, monitored radio messages, when decoded, confirmed that the offensive had petered out, but corps commanders were warned that this might only be a temporary lull until the roads had cleared.

Baluiev's Fifth Corps made several unsuccessful attempts to dislodge the defences in the "Ferdinand's Nose" salient, on 25 and 27 March and finally on 7 April, though by this time his heavy guns and aircraft had been recalled by Stavka.

On 28 April the Germans began their own efforts to retake the captured trenches, commencing with an artillery bombardment. The shelling was carried out under the orders of a certain Lieutenant-Colonel Bruchmüller of the Landwehr, whom Hoffmann dubbed "Durchbruchmüller" (roughly Breakthrough-Miller). He was regarded as an artillery genius, able to instinctively judge the weight of shell needed to render a target harmless, and he more than lived up to his reputation. After his bombardment gas was released, but the Russian troops were still unprotected although stocks of Allied respirators were available and the tsar had seen them demonstrated the previous month. In the infantry attacks which followed, the Germans easily regained all their lost ground. Thus, in one day, the Russians' entire campaign achievements were wiped out.

The offensive was a total failure. Russian losses amounted to something between 110,000 and 120,000; the Germans lost about 20,000. Furthermore, not one German soldier had been transferred from the Western to the Eastern Front. An offer of troops made by Falkenhayn at one stage was declined as unnecessary by Oberost.

There was widespread fury at the fiasco throughout the army and the nation, particularly as — in view of the time of year — the rawest recruit could have predicted the outcome. In line with Russian opinion, Falkenhayn wrote: ". . . these attacks by the Russians were simply carried out under pressure from the Western Allies. . . No responsible leader, unless under constraint from outside, would have let such inferior troops attack well-built positions like those held by the Germans. Even if the enemy had met with initial successes, they would not have been turned to good account, owing to the state of the roads."

Junior officers told Knox: "We Russians are . . . noble we are always ready to sacrifice ourself for the sake of our allies; no one does the same thing for us, though." Similar sentiments were expressed throughout the army. Golovin commented that the Allies did not respond to Russian sacrifices "in coin of equal value", and Paléologue was told: "France is letting Russia carry the whole burden of the war."

In June, Grand-Duke Boris Vladimirovich predicted in the presence of British officers that the next war would be between Britain and Russia, because Britain was so greedy. "England doesn't care a straw about this war," he declared, "she is letting her allies be killed." Although the tsar was deeply concerned and successfully demanded that the grand-duke apologise, this could not remove the underlying national indignation.

The Russian and Allied press and public were told that "small-scale" attacks had succeeded in improving the Russian defensive position. Such misrepresentations could not, in the long term, alter the effects of this battle, for it was the first time since early 1915 that the Russians had taken the initiative against the Germans only to meet with disaster as before. Baluiev, a big man given to emphasising points by smashing his fist on his desk, declared he had been forced to counter technical superiority with nothing but the lives of his men, and stressed that only one of his few aircraft had radio. This habitual excuse made by Russian commanders was not as valid in 1916 as it had been in 1915, the truth being that despite overwhelming superiority of manpower and (on this occasion) no shortage of artillery, they had been outwitted and out-manoeuvred.

The inferiority complex this engendered had more far-reaching results than the loss of a single battle. The Russian army and, worse, its commanders like Kuropatkin and Evert, had ceased to believe they could defeat or match their opponents Hindenburg and Ludendorff.

Had the Russians been allowed to remain on the defensive, offering no more than sufficient force to stop the Germans robbing their own lines; had they attacked against Austria, where it had been proved they were the masters, infinitely more might have been achieved and a crisis created for the Germans, of which the echoes would have resounded at Verdun. As it was, all they had been asked to do was to throw their lives uselessly away.

As the battle was running out, yet another blow came to shake the Russian people and its allies.

The tsarina did not let up in her campaign against Polivanov, and on 17 March she told her husband, "Remember about Polivanov", on the 19th, "Get rid of Polivanov." At last the tsar wrote: "I have found a successor to Polivanov", and she replied: "After Polivanov's removal I shall sleep in peace."

Matters were brought to a head when the infuriated Polivanov discovered that, over his head, Stürmer had supplied Rasputin with four of the fastest War Ministry cars so that he could shake off the police when they followed him. On 2 April, Polivanov, the man who had saved and rebuilt the Russian army, was dismissed without even an Imperial Rescript, a particular mark of disfavour. He was told in a letter from the tsar: "The work of the war industry committees does not inspire me with confidence, and your supervision of them I find insufficiently authoritative."

One of the principal reasons for the tsar's lack of confidence may have arisen from the dislike and suspicion felt by many right-wingers toward working people on the war industry committees. These men, solid trade unionists but unswerving patriots, had done much to assist the war effort, arguing against those like the Bolsheviks who asserted that the only way to bring about changes was to ensure the country's defeat.

Polivanov's place at the War Ministry was taken by General Shuvaiev. "A nice old man", Knox called him, using almost the same language Poincaré had earlier employed to describe Goremykin, "quite straight and honest. He had no knowledge of his work, but his devotion to the Emperor was such that if . . . His Majesty were to . . . ask him to throw himself out of the window he would do so at once."

Chapter 18

The Glorious Fourth Of June

On account of their losses at Verdun, the French were compelled to tell their British allies that their own contribution to the midsummer offensive – a joint effort on either side of the River Somme – would have to be rigidly pruned. Of the forty divisions they were originally to have provided, a mere sixteen would now be available, so that the British would be making the major effort in putting twenty-five divisions into the field. The Russians, who had exceeded their brief by launching an unscheduled and extremely costly relief offensive at Narocz, gave no indication that they would be unable to meet the bargain struck at Chantilly, and were proceeding with their arrangements for an attack in the north, notwithstanding the fact that the Germans might be expected to have increased their defensive strength in the area. On this occasion the main thrust was to come from Evert's West Front advancing from Molodechno toward Smorgon and Vilna, while Kuropatkin's North Front wheeled inward to protect it. Meanwhile, the rest of the front was to remain purely passive, including the South West, where Brusilov had recently succeeded Ivanov as commander-in-chief, and which was considered unsuitable for offensive action.[1]

On 14 April, a council of war was summoned at the governor's house at Mogilev, where Stavka was based; the tsar presided, and all front commanders were present. Its purpose was to finalise details of the coming attacks. Brusilov suggested that one reason for previous failures had been that – unlike the enemy – they had not adopted the policy of "pinning down" to prevent one part of the menaced front being reinforced from the more passive sectors. Furthermore, it seemed to him that the apparent unsuitability of the terrain was a good reason for activity there, since the Austrians would no doubt have drawn similar conclusions and felt secure in weakening their defences.

Following his invariable rule of attacking vigorously at every opportunity, he proposed, therefore, advancing in concert with Evert and Kuropatkin to give these attacks a better chance. The meeting somewhat grudgingly assented, emphasising that Brusilov could use only those resources he currently possessed, could expect no reinforcements and must limit his action to exerting sufficient pressure on the enemy to prevent his moving troops. The two other front commanders, who had shown extreme pessimism about the outcome of their own offensives, might have been expected to be grateful for this unsolicited assistance, but instead privately expressed considerable surprise that he was willing to hazard his military reputation when not called upon to do so, and took a discouraging view of his proposed operations.

The South West Front ran from the Pripet Marshes to Czernowitz and comprised four armies: the Eighth, formerly commanded by Brusilov and now under Kaledin; the Eleventh under Sakharov; the Seventh under Shcherbachev; and the Ninth under Lechitski. At his own headquarters in Berdichev, Brusilov called these commanders together to convey the meetings' decision and explain how he proposed to act upon it. The central problem of the war, afflicting both the Western and Eastern Front, was that of keeping offensive preparations secret and so preserving the element of surprise. When trying to breach tenaciously-held trenchlines by frontal attack, the necessary colossal concentrations of troops, guns and supplies could rarely be hidden from the enemy for long, consequently he could bring up reinforcements in advance ready to meet the assault. On the Eastern Front the enemy had the advantage in this, since he commanded the best developed part of the Russian railway system, backed up by his own railways.

Brusilov's answer was to order all four commanders to begin simultaneous preparations, preventing the enemy from anticipating the direction of the main attack. Furthermore, with simultaneous attacks delivered over such a wide front, it would be impossible for the enemy to move his troops from one point to another. Moreover, Brusilov particularly hoped and expected that one or more of these attacks would uncover weak points along the defence line where a breakthrough could be made. Kaledin was to make the main attack, but Brusilov's whole plan hinged on the ability of his forces and their commanders to exploit such openings as presented themselves. He was accordingly, as Hindenburg has agreed, in the position "of a man who taps on a wall to find which part of it is solid stone and which lath and plaster". His colleagues, though surprised by his "unorthodox methods", readily fell in with them and each was left to make his own plans for attack in his sector.

Brusilov's preoccupation with surprise led to the adoption of highly complex and ingenious devices to ensure secrecy. Extra trenches were dug, others were left half-dug, and in some places representations of trenches (to deceive air reconnaissance) were painted on the ground, all calculated to confuse.

Under the triple incitements of a high casualty rate leading men to take a pessimistic view of the odds on survival; of concern for their families struggling to exist at home; and of defeatist propaganda, heavily subsidised by the Germans and disseminated by groups like the Bolsheviks, desertion was now assuming dangerous proportions. Brusilov was no less troubled by desertion than the other fronts, particularly now there were rumours of an offensive. Trains bringing reinforcements could lose as many as half their passengers before reaching their destination, and by mid-summer nearly 70,000 men were absent from the four armies of South West Front, significant numbers having deserted before the attacks began. Special preventive measures had to be taken in the rear, including the application of the death penalty for desertion.

There was also a rising tide of discontent, and letters home from the South West Front were highly critical of the government, the Duma's impotence, war profiteers and the rear in general, all indicative of the sense of injustice felt by men called upon to suffer and die at the front.

Brusilov felt all the more reason for secrecy because of an incident along his front at Easter, which fortunately occurred before the War Council meeting on 14 April. The Austrians, following the precedent of previous Easters, had called an informal truce, and Russian troops and officers crossed over to the opposing trenches and fraternised freely. It appeared, however, that this was something more than a spontaneous outburst of goodwill on the occasion of a religious festival, for two Russian officers had been detained, presumably for intelligence questioning. Brusilov rebuked all concerned and forbade all commerce with the enemy save "by gun and bayonet". Penalties were severe.

This was not the only quarter where he had to be vigilant, for there was considerable anxiety at headquarters about the tsarina's habit of reporting everything she heard to Rasputin. On 22 April, when Brusilov was summoned by the tsar and asked when his preparations for attack would be complete, he was told 25 May. At the same time, Nicholas said the empress was anxious to see him; Brusilov could not understand this invitation, but it emerged during the subsequent interview that the tsarina's sole purpose was to try to discover when his action would commence. By various subterfuges he was able to keep this from her, and at their parting she gave him as a memento a small tin medallion of St Nicholas, her husband's patron saint. Within days the paint had worn away leaving the bare metal – a symbol perhaps of her enmity.

Back at Berdichev, planning was continuing under Brusilov's supervision when an ally called yet again for Russian help. In early May, Italy found herself within "days or even hours" of capitulation to Austria as a result of Conrad's offensive in the Trentino. On the 24th, the King of Italy appealed to the tsar, asking the Russians to help by attacking the Austrians. Before making any commitment, Alexeiev telephoned Brusilov to enquire the earliest date by which they could move. To his surprise the South West Front commander answered that his men were ready, his plans laid, his preparations were so complete that he might as well start now as wait until 1 July, the scheduled starting date for both the Eastern and Western Front offensives.

It was finally agreed that he would start on 1 June, though Brusilov stipulated that Evert must also ensure that no reinforcements would have to be drawn from his part of the front. Unlike Brusilov, Evert was far from ready, and it was ultimately decided that the South West Front would strike on 4 June and Evert on the 13th.

Only now did Stavka come to know Brusilov's precise plans, in which it had not previously been interested. Being an unbending military conservative who was horrified by anything unusual, Alexeiev urged a traditional attack concentrating on one point, but finally gave way to Brusilov's inflexibility. On the night of 3 June, twenty-four hours before the offensive was due to begin, he telephoned the South West Front Headquarters to order changes not only in his own name but in that of the "commander-in-chief", the tsar, offering extra time for them to be made. Brusilov protested that it was too late, and asked that this fact be conveyed to "the commander-in-chief"; this was impossible, Alexeiev told him, as the tsar was in bed. However, when Brusilov angrily refused to change his plans, Alexeiev again relented and told him: "Well, God be with you. Have it your own way. I will report our conversation to the emperor."

As it happened, 4 June was the birthday of Archduke Frederick, the Austrian commander-in-chief, and many of the officers from the Galician front had gone to his headquarters at Teschen for celebrations. There was a mood of high confidence. Italy was about to collapse, and there was so little apprehension about the Russians that Conrad had had no hesitation in thinning his lines to give added weight to the Trentino attack. This left the defences against the South West Front manned chiefly by Slav troops, though the German South Army was also present as part of a group including the Fourth and, subsequently, the First Armies.

In the early hours of this day of Austrian celebration, Brusilov's artillery opened up along the whole of his front. He had carefully husbanded a fortnight's supply of ammunition, which was now expended in one hurricane bombardment. For the first time, the Russians used aircraft equipped with radio to direct the gunfire accurately. The barrage continued throughout the day and well into the night to prevent the enemy from repairing his barbed wire under cover of darkness, but was temporarily halted between midnight and 2.30 a.m. so that scouts could inspect the damage. This "exceeded all expectation"; with the exception of some deep shelters, the Austrians' first, second and third lines were all destroyed.

The first assaults were to be made by Kaledin's Eighth Army, the right of whose line adjoined the West Front; this move being intended to ease the way when Evert began the main attack on the 13th. The Eighth Army, advancing toward Lutsk from trenches dug as far forward as possible, took Archduke Josef Ferdinand's Fourth Army by surprise, causing his entire front to collapse. Meeting only minimal resistance, the Russians were able to push a wedge between this and Böhm-Ermoli's Army group consisting of the First and Second Armies. By the following day 40,000 prisoners had been taken and the number swelled rapidly as the offensive spread along the line.

The Austrians were anxious to retain Lutsk for more than tactical reasons, for it was the headquarters town for the Fourth Army. Its fate, however, was contingent upon that of nearby Krupy, held by the Hungarians. By next day, the 7th, the Russians had already caught up with the forces fleeing across the River Styr from their first assaults; the Russians stationed their guns on the heights round Krupy and fired into Lutsk, which fell to the Russian cavalry following this bombardment. In the panic, fleeing troops were caught on the barbed wire of their own second line defences and many were crushed and torn against it before they could get through. Frightened Austrian engineers blew up the Styr bridges prematurely, leaving thousands of men and enormous supply stocks of every kind stranded on its banks.

The Russian bag of prisoners rose to 60,000, many from Slav units which had seen little reason to be fighting Russians anyway. Some, such as the Fortieth Regiment, consisting mainly of Ukrainians, surrendered without firing a shot and with hardly a casualty.

The Austrians did not attempt to hold the Styr, and pulled back thirty miles beyond it. The Russians could have pushed on to Lemberg, but Kaledin could scarcely believe in the magnitude of his own victory and suspected a trick. He was also concerned for his northern-most flank — exposed until Evert advanced and vulnerable to further exposure by a deeper penetration.

There were similar successes in the far south where Shcherbachev's Seventh Army, after being initially held up, drove the Austrians back across the Strypa. Lechitski's Ninth Army, at the extreme left, first of all moved southward to reach round the flank of the Austrian right wing, then wheeled north toward Shcherbachev. The commander of the Austrian Seventh, defending this sector, was von Pflanzer-Baltin, one of their best generals who, although in hospital when the Russians struck, insisted on directing the battle from a telephone by his bedside. In an effort to stem Russian onslaughts, he refused to allow his field commanders to retire, but to little avail. By 9 June, Lechitski's army had penetrated to a depth of twenty miles, nearly matching the Eighth's advance of twenty-five. There were now huge gaps in the Austrian defence, and about 125,000 prisoners had been taken.

Only in the centre was there little progress. Here Sakharov's

Eleventh had met Bothmer's German-Austrian South Army which repulsed all assaults upon it, though its right flank advanced slightly toward Brody, north of Tarnopol. Here the Austrian Second Army, shaken by the failure of the Fourth and First on its left, was forced to give ground to maintain conformity of line. The steadfastness of his centre was small consolation for Conrad, who had been taken so completely by surprise by the Russian assault that at first he refused to believe in it. Even if Bothmer held, the advance of the two forces on his flanks would threaten him with envelopment.

The invasion was obviously more than Conrad's own forces could withstand, and again he had no option but to beg Falkenhayn for more troops. These were made available on condition that the offensive against Italy be abandoned. Thus Brusilov and the Russian army had succeeded in their task and had rescued their ally. This was only the beginning of the aid they were to give.

With his own forces still advancing, Brusilov waited for his fellow front commanders to deliver the main blow. Kaledin's advance on Lutsk had created a salient, along the north side of which the Austrians had formed a defence line and were resisting all attacks. There could be no further advance nor any measure of security for the Eighth Army until the salient had been flattened. Several ineffective attempts in this direction had been made with attacks on the towns of Kolki and Czartorysk, but the position could be drastically changed if Lesh's Third Army (forming the left wing of Evert's West Front) attacked from the north so that the defenders were threatened with envelopment.

Brusilov telegraphed the Third Army command with a request to this effect, which was refused by Evert who would not move until mid-June. Then Alexeiev told Brusilov that his attack would have to be delayed until the 18th because of the weather; in any case the West Front commander expected little to come of it. Under pressure from an angry Brusilov, Alexeiev ordered Evert to keep to the original date, but allowed him to alter the venue from Vilna to Baranovichi further south, an extraordinary decision involving a reconcentration of forces.

Despite all this Lesh, anxious to help a companion-in-arms, attacked as soon as he was permitted, but by this time the

Austrians in front of Kaledin had reinforced and, apart from 8,000 casualties sustained by the Guard Corps, nothing was achieved.

A day or two later Ragosa, commander of the Second Army, telephoned Brusilov. As a favourable opportunity had presented itself along his front at Molodechno (where the original attack was to have been launched), he had asked Evert's permission to attack immediately. This too had been refused. It was becoming increasingly obvious to Brusilov that he would be left on his own, and in fact the Germans were already reorganising their lines so as to send troops south.

From Kuropatkin at North Front, there was no sign of movement. The truth was that both the other front generals quailed at the thought of meeting the Germans: the memory of the horrors of Lake Narocz were too recent. To add to the problem, Alexeiev had been subordinate to Kuropatkin and Evert in Manchuria and now lacked the will to overrule them.

The attacks launched at Baranovichi and Lake Narocz on 13 June were easily pushed aside by Woyrsch's detachment and nothing was achieved. Ragosa later complained that aircraft used for artillery-spotting were too slow compared with the German planes, which in any case were present in overwhelming numbers. The ground troops were insufficiently supplied with machine-guns and were wiped out by the Germans.

Offensive preparations were in fact proceeding along Kuropatkin's front, but at a dilatory pace; not only did he lack confidence in their execution, but at Stavka there was little confidence in his own ability. His intentions had already reached the ears of Hindenburg and Ludendorff. Oberost had now moved to Kovno, where Hindenburg spent all his free time hunting in the neighbouring forests.

In late May they were visited here by their All Highest War Lord and petitioned him for six extra divisions to stem the coming onslaught. These were refused on the grounds that they were needed at Verdun which was, they were told, "a great success". Though they do not record actually mentioning it to the Kaiser, Ludendorff and Hoffmann did not share this opinion.

Neither the conduct of Kuropatkin and Evert, nor the pinning down of Kaledin's advance at the northern end of the South West

Front had affected the pace of advance elsewhere, and there was scarcely a point along the line at which the defenders had not been forced to give ground. The position was worst in the south where Pflanzer-Baltin was till trying to halt Lechitski. His worn-out Seventh Army, which had no reserves, had been deprived of many of its heavy guns for Conrad's Trentino offensive, while the remainder were running out of ammunition. Retirement ultimately became so confused that Baltin lost control, and only one-third of an army originally 90,000 strong reached the line of the River Czeremosz by mid-June.

This last remnant might also have been destroyed, but Lechitski himself was short of reserves and — now the hoarded stocks were used — suffering from the old shortage of shell. His position was additionally complicated by the expectation that Rumania would shortly enter the war on the Entente side, making it essential to keep their right clear. In view of all this, Lechitski decided to turn south once more; by 17 June Czernowitz was taken and, on the 21st, the entire province of Bukovina. By the 23rd, the Russians were in Kimpolung and once more threatened the Carpathian foothills. On 30 June, Lechitski took Tlumacz, and had reached a point well to the west of the right wing of Bothmer's South German Army. Bothmer, still menaced by Sakharov, counterattacked and recaptured the town, but Delatyn was swallowed up on 8 July and the threat to his right increased.

Falkenhayn had been most urgently concerned for the Lutsk salient, and in the absence of effective Russian opposition was able to build up an army of eight mixed Austrian and German divisions along the Stokhod, under a German general, von der Marwitz. On German insistence, the Archduke Joszef had been removed from command of the Austrian Fourth Army and replaced by the Hungarian Tersztyanski in whom, after his failures in the Carpathians in early 1915, the Germans had only slightly more confidence. On 16 June all these forces struck in the Kovel area, and in four days' fierce fighting recovered only a few miles of ground. The action reaffirmed a lesson learnt at Verdun and on later battlefields, that counter-attacks achieve very little against an enemy engaged in an all-out offensive.

Brusilov's offensive was far from halted. His gains so far included about 350,000 Austrian prisoners, 400 guns and 1,300 machine-guns, besides which the enemy had suffered heavy casualties. A 200-mile long front had been penetrated, in some places to a depth of forty miles. "Never", as Liddell-Hart puts it, "has a mere demonstration had a more amazing success . . ."

However, the cost was high, particularly once artillery became short. Brusilov, while understanding he could expect no reinforcements, at least anticipated being adequately munitioned, and this shortage was yet another blow he had to sustain from his countrymen. At a meeting of the Special Council in Petrograd, it was alleged that a number of supply trains had been held up at the express orders of Stürmer because − it was suggested − a Russian victory would jeopardise the case he was urging in the tsar and tsarina for peace with Germany. Whatever the cause, as a result of the shortage the South West Front casualties had totalled 300,000 since 4 June. Moreover, if Brusilov's methods of attack prevented the enemy from calling upon his reserves, they equally meant that he had no margin with which to exploit success.

The fact was that the unexpected and spectacular events in the south had faced Stavka with a fresh dilemma. Should it press forward with the proposed July offensive or make the most of Brusilov's gains? Brusilov was prepared to continue provided he was given more support than hitherto, but some still argued − with French agreement − that only by defeating the Germans could the war be concluded.

At this point, however, another factor began to affect the Russian Army's decisions. The prophetic voice of Rasputin which had already influenced affairs in the realms of government and administration, now extended to that of military strategy. Thus the tsarina wrote on 17 June: "Our Friend sends his blessing to the whole Orthodox army. He begs we should not yet strongly advance in the north, because he says if our successes continue being good in the south they will themselves retreat in the north or advance and then their losses will be very great." The tsar replied in due course: "Some days ago Alexeiev and I decided not to attack in the north, but to concentrate all our efforts a little more to the south." He entreated: "But I beg you not to tell anyone about it, not even Our Friend" − which injunction the tsarina ignored.

Rasputin's involvement in military affairs (which the tsar's caveat implied) was to be proved in 1917, when the tsarina was found to possess a map detailing army dispositions along the entire front. "Only two copies were prepared . . ." says Alexeiev, "one for the emperor and one for myself." It was currently believed in Petrograd that the staretz was in German pay, and Admiral Grigorovich, the Navy Minister, claimed to have proved it by feeding Rasputin false information on which the Germans were later observed to have acted. As Pares points out, the prudent Rasputin was unlikely to have risked his influential position by accepting German bribes; it seems more likely that any information reaching German ears did so because their energetic agents kept close to him. His indiscretions were notorious, especially in his cups, and his shady entourage of largely German-Baltic origin was one to which they could inconspicuously attach themselves.

Despite the tsar's assertion, Stavka was still undecided, and did not convey orders to the relevant commanders for nearly a fortnight. Yet the fact remained that a strategic decision had been taken which coincided with Rasputin's desires, hence it is impossible to ignore his influence here.

As a military decision it represented a disastrous wasting of opportunities. Brusilov's offensive had only been mounted to pin down the enemy and had been denied resources because they were needed for the principal attack. Now these would have to be moved from one extremity of the line to the other and, since the enemy would be reinforcing too, they would have to be thrown into the current battle piecemeal, as they arrived. Of the outstanding armies, one was able to move its reserves quickly along good railway lines, the other only with agonising slowness. The Fifth Siberian Corps, which had fought so ferociously at Lake Narocz, took over a fortnight to reach the South West Front when sent there by Alexeiev in early June. The Twenty-third and First Divisions, as well as the First Turkestan Corps were equally late in arriving when moved from Evert's and Kuropatkin's fronts.

At the same time, Brusilov's offensive had achieved the anticipated diversion. It led to a panic robbing of the enemy line to meet it, especially in the north, thus leaving opportunities to be exploited. Says Hoffman: "If the Russians had now attacked the German line regardless of the losses they might incur, they would have prevented the Commander-in-Chief East from sending forces for the support of our allies and without this help the crisis would probably have developed into the complete defeat of the Austro-Hungarian Army."

As it was, Falkenhayn made full use of his superior communications. Austrian troops were beginning to arrive from the Italian front and German troops were scraped together from every possible place, including the Balkans, while more than eighteen divisions were moved from the France-Flanders Front. In this way the Brusilov offensive had achieved what Narocz failed to do, and brought about the final winding up of the Verdun attacks.[2] Even the Turks were called upon to require the help they had received by sending troops to Galicia. For the Austrians, the price they had to pay was the sacrifice of most of their remaining independence. Pflanzer-Baltin, whose sector was well south of Lemberg, on the right of the South Army and who had hitherto escaped German supervision, now had Seeckt (mastermind of the Ninth Army's Gorlice drive) foisted on him as chief-of-staff.

The Galician victories might have been expected to provide a tonic for the war-weary Russian people, especially as they followed close on fresh successes against the Turks by Yudenich. On 15 April, Trabzon (Trebizond) on the Turkish coast fell to a combined sea and land attack, but only an unrepresentative minority still believed that Russia had anything to gain from victories in Turkey now that the Dardanelles attacks had failed. "The failure of the Gallipoli expedition", wrote Sazonov, "was a great misfortune for Russia." The descent on the Bosphorus and the taking of Constantinople were both dead letters.

Galicia aroused some manifestations of the old patriotic fervour, and Brusilov received thousands of congratulatory telegrams including one from the former commander-in-chief, the ever-magnanimous Grand-Duke Nicholas. Both Joffre and Haig were represented in this complementary flood, but there was the usual failure in the west to understand the effect of his achievements upon enemy planning; the soldiers undervalued them for fear that they would lead to a diversion of effort from their own projects. Haig appears to have sincerely believed that Brusilov's success would be likely to enhance the chances for his Somme offensive, and it certainly had its interactive effect. Falkenhayn had intended to disrupt British preparations, but was compelled to abandon plans of this sort when it became essential to use every available man to halt the Russian advance.

Nevertheless, Brusilov, who felt foresaken by his compatriots, could not complain that the western Allies failed to keep to their schedules. On 1 July, as promised, after the heaviest and most sustained artillery barrage of the war, the British attacks began. They succeeded only in taking a narrow sliver of ground at the cost of the wholesale destruction of the new citizen army. Falkenhayn, momentarily discomfited, quickly recovered his equanimity when he saw there was no real threat to his defences. He redirected his attention to the eastern problem, knowing that the British could achieve little through "the tactics of attrition" to which they were reduced. He was sufficiently confident to withdraw troops from the Western Front at the height of the battle.

It never seemed to occur to Haig that neither planning nor tactics differentiated his attacks from those earlier attempts which proved repeatedly that a determined defence — even with slender resources — can repel and inflict heavy toll on an attack. Least of all would he have considered that his resources could have been better used elsewhere: "One third of the Somme guns and ammunition," says Lloyd George, "transferred in time to the banks of . . . the Dniepr, would have won a great Russian victory." The British and French generals had been alike determined that no such transfer should be allowed to imperil their own opportunities for glory.

A patriotic few apart — the Russian peoples' main reaction to events in the war on both foreign and home fronts was apathy. Lost or gained, the names of the Galician towns had recurred with tedious frequency in communiqués since 1914, and if taken now they would doubtless be abandoned again later. There was much more concern at the Russian lives thrown away time after time to retake the same territory, coupled with an angry contempt for those commanders too pusillanimous to risk battle. Generally, however, especially in the towns where life had reverted to a primitive struggle for survival, there was only the belief that the country was finished. By June the price of bread was up 47 per cent in Moscow and 80 per cent in Odessa. Firewood had

Food — Supplies

increased by 100–150 per cent and sugar, when obtainable, 65–70 per cent. Wood and eggs were both four times the 1914 price; butter and soap five times. Meat was unobtainable in the towns, but Petrograd workers saw cartloads of carcases being delivered to the soap factories. Contractors asked to be allowed to build new refrigerators; because of inter-departmental squabbles, they were given neither permission nor funds.

Government printing presses continued to roll off paper roubles, but the public showed distrust of this scrip by contributing virtually nothing to the 1916 War Loan. In an effort to institute a measure of order, some rationing had now been introduced, together with control of wholesale and retail prices, but as these were below true market values, goods were hidden and sold illicitly.

The transport situation had deteriorated from the disorganised to the anarchic. Meat stocks sent to Siberia for preservation through the winter for lack of cold storage could not be brought to the towns, and with summer began to rot.

Although the railways were supposed to be almost entirely devoted to the war effort, Paléologue learnt that 1½ million rounds of ammunition, 6 million grenades, 50,000 rifles and 70 heavy guns from France were still on the quay. Shipments from the US were arriving at Vladivostok, but the Transsiberian Railway was no more able to cope than the others, and within a few months the Pacific port was in the same condition as Archangel — its wharves and piers piled high with undelivered freight left in the open. The limited number of Russian locomotives were now wearing out, while the shortage of rolling stock was further aggravated when the army requisitioned a large number of carriages for use as billets. At one stage all passenger traffic between Moscow and Petrograd had to be stopped for six days so that food and other essential goods could be rushed to the capital.

Because so many of its supplies failed to arrive, the army had been forced to set up special factories in the rear to try to meet its needs in other ways. By the summer of that year, Shcherbachev's Seventh had a tannery, two soaps works, three tarring plants, four sawmills, a foundry, rifle and machine-gun repair shops and two workshops for making carts; a kerosene refinery had been added by the autumn. Soldiers and prisoners of war were used as labour, but no attempt was made to organise this latter resource though there were now nearly 2 million prisoners in Russian hands. Germany, on the other hand, was known to be keeping her industries running on prisoner of war labour, the greater part of which was Russian.

For the war-profiteers who so antagonised the fighting soldiers, these times of shortage were no more than an opportunity for gain, and they had no scruples about using subterfuge to acquire it. When the government turned down Putilov's request for a subsidy of 36 million roubles for his factory engaged on essential war contracts, he simply arranged for the Russo-Asiatic Bank (of which he was manager) to end government credit, and blackmailed the Finance Ministry by threatening to close if the subsidy was withheld. Rodzianko proposed to the Special Council that Putilov should be nationalised, but through the offices of Rasputin he was able to circumvent this move. To the government, nationalisation smacked of socialism. Similarly a plan by Minister of Agriculture Naumov to organise food supply in collaboration with the "zemstvos", who had the advantages of being close to the producers, was rejected by the Cabinet though accepted by the Duma allegedly on direct orders of Stürmer. His government continued to preside paralytically over the growing chaos. In this situation industrial unrest began to grow, and pamphlets appeared in factories and works urging strikes for peace.

In mid-June, Alexeiev proposed to the tsar that a military dictatorship was the only way to bring order to the country, and Grand-Duke Serge Mikhailovich was considered for the post. On another occasion it was discovered from a secret ukase that Stürmer had actually been appointed, but neither appointment was ratified and ultimately the tsar went no further than an appeal to the Council of Ministers, begging them "to serve unitedly in the national cause, equally dear to all."

Calls for a "Ministry of Confidence" were still being made, and continued to the end of the year when a secret motion by Zemgor, passed at a prohibited meeting, demanded the creation of "a government worthy of a great people at one of the gravest moments of its history." Like every cry which preceded it, this fell on deaf ears.

The Council of Ministers was now as little representative of the government as was the Duma. Authority had passed to Rasputin and the imperial puppet of his bidding, Empress Alexandra

Feodorovna; they continued to pursue their course of suspicion, resentment and mystical revelation. At one point (having seen reports from the secret police) she told the tsar that Guchkov and Alexeiev were writing to each other. At another, the elder Khvostov, Minister of Justice, came in for her indignation. Early in 1916, following the Duma decision, he had set up a commission to investigate the affairs of Sukhomlinov, the discredited War Minister. Once his association with the traitorous Miassoiedev was officially established, Sukhomlinov's detention was ordered pending further inquiry, but this treatment of an old favourite inspired the empress to shrill fury. The Justice Minister, who had already offended by refusing to receive Rasputin, was summoned and she spent two hours urging him to release the ex-War Minister. When he repeatedly refused she shrieked: "Why not, if I order you to do it?" "My conscience, ma'am," he answered stoutly, "forbids my obeying you and freeing a traitor . . ." It was known thereafter that his days were numbered. They were even more anxious to be rid of Foreign Minister Sazonov, the last remaining member of the group which had signed the letter against Goremykin.

Recent events had again raised the question of Poland's future and, despite right-wing opposition, it was decided that the grand-duke's pledge of autonomy must be honoured. A twelve-man commission under the chairmanship of Sazonov was detailed to draw up a programme which was in due course submitted to the tsar. Under it the Government of Poland was to be vested in the emperor, whose delegate would be a viceroy, together with a Council of Ministers and a bicameral parliament. Upon this three-tier government would rest the entire administration of the Polish Kingdom, except defence, foreign affairs, customs, finance of common interest and strategic railways, which would remain in the province of the Petrograd government. Administrative disputes between kingdom and empire would be laid before the Senate of Petrograd, of which a special section would be created with equal Russian and Polish participation. The absorption of Austrian and German Poland into the autonomous kingdom was provided for, but was of course dependent on the success of Russian arms.

The scheme was fair to both sides, and was communicated in secret to Paléologue and Buchanan. Sazonov then went to Stavka, where the tsar gave it his wholehearted approval. "Gentle and good-natured, he was pleased to meet any desires which seemed to him just", Sazonov records. On 13 July, he burst in upon Buchanan and Paléologue and told them: "I have won all along the line." At the tsar's suggestion, he then went to Finland for a short holiday.

As far back as March, the tsarina had written to her husband: "Wish you could think of a good successor to Sazonov – need not be a diplomat." Now she took up the cudgels again. The right-wing newspapers had attacked the Polish plan and she wrote gleefully to Mogilev: "How the papers are down on Sazonov, it must be very unpleasant for him, imagining he was worth so much . . ." Shortly after she was at Mogilev herself, taking the children and Virubova with her to plead the cause of "Babys" [the tsarevich's] future rights.

Sazonov was still in Finland when told of his dismissal. The British and French ambassadors, with whom he had worked closely and harmoniously for years, were so shocked that they asked Allied liaison officers to make representations on their behalf to the emperor at Stavka, but were told through Count Frederickz, the Court Chamberlain, that their petition was hopeless. The displaced Foreign Minister was allowed to accept the Order of the Bath, conferred on him by George V, but although the tsar showed every sign of pleasure at this honour, mention of it was censored from the Press, causing Sir George Buchanan to pay a furious visit to Stürmer, whose hand he saw behind it.

The Allies were even more alarmed when it was announced that this very man – already suspected of pro-German sympathies – was to take over Sazonov's portfolio in addition to his functions as chairman of the Council of Ministers.

This was only another stage in the plans of the Rasputin-tsarina-Stürmer coalition. Khvostov now received the punishment merited by his refusal to release Sukhomlinov. Aged and in poor health, this honourable man was not dismissed but shuffled from the Ministry of Justice to the far more onerous one of the Interior.

Amid these upheavals, Petrograd was visited at that time by Réné Viviani, French Foreign Minister, and Albert Thomas, French Minister of Munitions. The Russians appeared greatly impressed by the decisiveness these representatives of democracy showed, enabling them to answer Russian requests by issuing immediate instructions; the minions of Russian government, carrying the weight of autocracy behind them, seemed totally unable either to give a straight order or ensure its execution. When Rodzianko asked them what they considered Russia most needed at that moment, the candid Albert Thomas answered: "Authoritative government."

The French ministers promised the Russians more guns; but demanded in exchange renewed attacks along the whole front, and revived the request for 400,000 Russian troops for the French front. There was never any lack of suggestions for fresh places in which the Russian soldier could die.

Chapter 19

The Offensive Halted

The fact that Brusilov had been set to run a race in which the advantage lay with the other contestants did not deter him from trying to win.

In the centre of his line, Shcherbachev's Seventh and Sakharev's Eleventh had made comparatively little progress against Bothmer's South German Army. Heavy rains in early July brought fresh delays, allowing the enemy to collect his forces, and with these accretions plans were laid for a counter-offensive against Sakharov to begin on 18 July. However the weather cleared, the floods subsided, and Sakharov — warned by his intelligence — anticipated Bothmer with an attack of his own on the 15th. This not only took 13,000 prisoners, but captured much of the ammunition stockpiled for the German action. Advancing from Demidovka, he crossed the Styr and swung south on Brody, after which concerted efforts by himself and Shcherbachev carried them both toward Lemberg and the Dniestr, taking further hordes of prisoners. At the same time, Lechitski was advancing in the south having recaptured Tlumaczh and re-entered Stanislau.

At the northern end of the line, Kaledin's right wing had made some progress against the Austrian Fourth Army round Lutsk, and he was now trying to reach the railhead of Vladimir—Volynskiy; however, his forces were divided as another area also claimed his attention. Lesh's Third Army on Evert's left had been placed at Brusilov's disposal, and on 4/5 July it advanced with elements of Kaledin's forces across the Styr on Czartorysk, driving the Austrians back on the Stokhod. Here Lesh was able to gain a number of bridgeheads over the river, menacing the key town of Kovel and taking some 12,000 prisoners. Not surprisingly, this area with its vital communications centre had been one of the first to be reinforced by the Germans as fresh troops arrived, and Linsingen's forces had been regrouped into a so-called Army of Manoeuvre, including among its mixed Austrian and German divisions, four German divisions from the Western Front. They formed a line on the Stokhod and, well-equipped with artillery, held the combined forces of Lesh and Kaledin.

The Kovel area still remained the principal barrier to Russian advance at the pivotal point between Brusilov's and Evert's fronts. What was more, with the constant transfer of troops from elsewhere, the going was becoming increasingly difficult and the offensive was losing its impetus. The capture of Kovel now became a major preoccupation. Particularly since his succession as commander-in-chief, Nicholas had wanted to group all the Guards Corps together as "a personal reserve". In the previous October this wish had been fulfilled when an army was formed under Bezobrazov, with Count Ignatiev as chief-of-staff, comprising some 134,000 men of the First and Second Guard Corps, First and Thirtieth Infantry and the Guard Cavalry. Through autumn and winter it had been undergoing intensive training for Evert's Molodechno offensive, but when this was abandoned it was decided that the capture of Kovel was precisely the sort of action for such an élite unit. It was therefore moved down to a section of the front between Lesh's Third Army on Evert's left and Kaledin. The plan, which Pavel Rodzianko considered "ridiculous", was for the infantry to break through and then for the cavalry to attack, routing the Germans' defence.

Like Rodzianko, Brusilov was not only unimpressed by the plan but also by the generals who were to execute it. Since these were the personal nominees of the tsar and subject only to his supervision, no changes could be made. The place chosen required that the troops deploy over marshy ground where the three causeways along which they must pass would expose them to fire from enemy artillery and machine-guns positioned on higher ground.

On 27 July, the tsar reported to his wife that the guards were moving forward for the attack. During the next two days he claimed they had advanced considerably "thanks be to God", were attacking and "performing miracles".

To close observers matters appeared differently. The attack of 27 July had been launched without artillery support, and with such insufficient preparation that the troops had to cut their way through barbed wire before they could move. Nevertheless, the Thirtieth Corps gained some ground on the left bank of the

Stokhod and took 11,000 prisoners, forty-six guns and sixty-five machine-guns. Knox, who was with the Guard Army, described the German prisoners as "a sorry a looking lot as one could wish to see." Losses in both the Thirtieth Corps and the accompanying First Corps were so heavy that by 2 August the units were down to one-third of their strength, a loss of 30,000 men in under a week.

The Grand-Duke Paul, commander of the First Corps and uncle of the tsar, had been told to make a flank movement. He considered this beneath the dignity of his troops and chose to attack frontally, using two of the finest regiments: the Preobrazhensky Guards and the Imperial Rifle Regiment. Casualties were so heavy on the causeways that many preferred to wade waist-deep through the bog, their slow progress leaving them prey to the machine-gunners and the German planes which circled and bombed them. Since they had not been expected in this particular place – the grand-duke having told no one of his altered plans – they were additionally subjected to shelling from their own guns.

All along the line men sank in bubbling mud, only the injured struggling a little before they disappeared. Even for the wounded who were rescued and sent to the nearest military hospital at Rozhitsch, there was little relief. Drugs were short and further casualties occurred when a dump of fuses – stored with incredible carelessness near the hospital – exploded.

Even so, they continued advancing up the hill from which the Germans were maintaining their fire, the second-wave troops climbing over their comrades' bodies. They finally succeeded in capturing the rising ground at a cost of 70 per cent of their number, but the cavalry, instead of coming round the rear, withdrew and they were forced to abandon their gains.

It now seemed that Kovel would not be taken, and every pause in the assault gave the Germans time to regroup and bring up more forces. Nevertheless, on 8 August another attempt was made as part of a re-opened offensive right along the South West Front line. At first it appeared to be succeeding, especially when a crowd of about a hundred prisoners began to reach the rear. Then came news that the support units on the flanks had failed and were retiring, followed by an almost unbelievable report that the Guards themselves were withdrawing. By the following day it transpired that the Guard Army, "physically the finest human animals in Europe" had lost 55,000 men.

Throughout the army and the country there was an almost speechless fury at the whole catastrophic and futile episode. Mikhail Rodzianko, visiting the Guard Army, found it seething with anger and dissatisfaction. A letter to Brusilov on the subject ultimately found its way to Stavka, and called down on the Duma President's head a rebuke from the tsar (through Alexeiev) demanding he refrain "from direct interference in war matters which did not concern either the President of the Duma nor a member of the Special Council" — though the tsar later withdrew this.

It appeared that on the first day of the attack, Kaledin had protested to the arrogant Bezobrazov at his failure to co-ordinate activities with his colleagues. What particularly incensed the Eighth Army commander was that if the Guards had been at his disposal, his knowledge of the area and the state of the defences could have enabled him to capture Kovel.

In response to the general outcry, Bezobrazov, the Grand-Duke Paul and Count Ignatiev were all dismissed, the highly competent General Vasili Gourko being given command. The army, renamed "The Special Army" was moved back to the West Front with the rest of Lesh's Third Army, and Brusilov's command reverted to its normal four armies.

Elsewhere along the battlefront waves of grey infantry were surging forward on the tide of the new offensive. On 28 July, Brody fell to Lechitski after bitter fighting; he was then joined by Shcherbachev in an advance along the Korobtsa toward Monstriyiska, which was occupied by the Seventh Army on 7 August; on the 12th, the Ninth took Nadworna. By this time, Russian armies were across Bothmer's communication line and the German South Army had no option but to evacuate its entire line, pull back from the Strypa to the Zlota Lipa in order to defend Lemberg which was threatened by this latest move.

From 4 June to mid-August, Brusilov's troops had taken 15,000 square miles of territory, an area slightly less than that of Belgium. They had captured 400,000 prisoners, and the probable losses of the Central Powers were around ¾ million. It was by far the greatest military feat of the Entente armies in two years of fighting.

Taking account of the disadvantages under which it began, and that it was fought by an army decisively beaten a year earlier, everywhere outnumbered by its opponents, it is arguably the greatest achievement of the entire war.

The struggle was by no means over, since the Russians were once more ascending the Carpathians and Brusilov and Stavka could contemplate the possibility of realising their twice-thwarted ambition: the assault upon the Danubian Plain. They now faced an Austro—Hungarian enemy infinitely weaker and more demoralised than fifteen months previously, but the South West Front had been considerably lengthened by its own advances, with a consequent thinning out of manpower.

On the enemy side command had been reshuffled to increase efficiency, and Oberost was made responsible for the entire eastern front. The new arrangement was to have commenced on 2 August, but at the last moment the Austrians jibbed at this sacrifice of their independence and insisted on retaining control of their forces south of Lemberg — the South German Army and the Austrian Seventh. With this reorganisation, the Russians were meeting increasingly tough resistance, while their enemy still had the advantage of his railways.

Moreover, the Russians were deficient in resources, and these factors combined to produce the standard feature of their campaigns — casualties immediately became enormous, and these could not be afforded with attenuated lines. Brusilov's losses were 450,000 and his reserves reduced from 400,000 to 100,000. Total Russian war losses were now 5½ million. The army which was 4,800,000 strong at the end of the Austro—German summer campaign of 1915 had been increased as a result of Polivanov's measures to 6 million by May 1916, and this was to rise by another 100,000 by the end of the year. Nevertheless, high losses were becoming less tolerable because, although the depots were still full, the country was coming to the end of its manpower resources which were being used more quickly than they could be replaced. Shuvaiev, Polivanov's successor, wrote to Stavka urging the economical use of reinforcements and that, wherever possible these should be found by reducing the number of non-combatants (of which it was reckoned there were two to every fighting man) When the contents of this letter became known to them, i produced scornful replies from South West and North Front pointing out that there were bound to be losses in war.[1]

External forces arising in two widely separated quarters were also conspiring to defeat Brusilov. One of these was in the form of a campaign by the tsarina and Rasputin, to persuade the tsar to terminate the offensive.

In essence their argument was simple, humane and of undoubted sincerity; like many Russians, they were horrified at the scale of the casualties and considered no price too high if it ended such carnage. The empress, working as a nurse, saw something of the cost; Rasputin had a certain rapport with peasant opinion, for he both came from and moved among the "mouzhiks" and was still revered by millions not only as a holy man but as their spokesman with the Little White Father. All the same, there is no indication that he or the tsarina realised the cost of ending the campaign.

The other external force was the indirect result of Allied foreign policy. Rumania had first been considered a useful ally with the inception of the Salonica Expedition early in 1915. Later, when Bulgaria came into the war, it was suggested that the Rumanians attack here in a southerly direction, aiming to meet the Allied forces assembling in Salonica. This would have countered the increased strength Austria and Germany gained from Bulgaria's belligerency and, had she acted promptly, she might have saved Serbia from defeat. The Rumanians, however, had no interest in acquiring Bulgarian territory, having obtained all they wanted by the peace of Bucharest in 1913. They were more concerned to recover those parts of their own land they regarded as having been unlawfully wrested from them: Transylvania and Bessarabia. Unfortunately these provinces were shared between the two belligerents, for Austria had seized Transylvania in 1868 and Russia had taken Bessarabia a decade later. The Rumanians were thus torn between joining the Entente to recover one, or remaining in the Triple Alliance (to which they actually joined by a secret protocol signed by the king in 1883) to recover the others. King Carol, who was connected with the House of Hohenzollern, favoured the latter and the Liberal prime minister, Ionel Bratianu, the former alternative. In the event, the protracted haggling outlasted Serbia's powers of resistance, but the Entente continued to regard Rumania as a force worth acquiring, largely because they accepted at face value the purely notional size and efficiency of her army, and on 17 August their efforts were rewarded by her signing a treaty of alliance. She hesitated to declare war, however, and would obviously continue to do so until the Entente produced a sufficiently convincing victory to persuade her that her best interests lay in this quarter.

Such a victory had now been achieved by Brusilov, with the additional merit of apparently clearing the enemy wolf from her back door. Neither Brusilov nor Alexeiev was enthusiastic about the new ally, and Alexeiev totally opposed her entry but said, "I have been forced to agree to it by pressure from France and England." The Russians knew her real strength. Her army, ½ million strong and largely made up of reservists, was weak in artillery and ill-provided with ammunition, particularly since an explosion at one of the main arsenals in Bucharest had destroyed 9 million rounds. It was anticipated that if she went to war the Russian army would speedily be called upon to mount another rescue operation.

On the western side the only person to share these misgivings was Lloyd-George, who in a memorandum to the Chief of the Imperial General Staff mentioned en passant: "I can hardly think that the equipment of the Rumanian Army would enable it long to resist an attack from an Austro-Germanic-Bulgarian force."

Although continually exhorted to enter the fight, she was finally forced to action by the Russians themselves despite perfectly just protests that she was not yet ready. Stürmer, whose secretive methods in dealing with the Rumanians and their claims exasperated Poincaré, once more donned his foreign minister's cap and — without telling France his intention — warned the Rumanian government that they risked losing all that had been promised if they did not enter the war forthwith. Compelled by this ultimatum, she entered the fray without a formal declaration of war on 27 August.

To encourage their new allies Brusilov, who had already cleared the enemy from her right flank, was asked to make a fresh effort. The chosen target was Bothmer's Southern Army, which on 29 August was attacked by Shcherbachev at Brzezany. After repeated efforts, the town of Potutory was taken. The real purpose of the attacks was to flatten out the dangerous salient created in the

RUMANIA

Russian lines by Bothmer's stubborn defence, but this failed completely and Bothmer held his ground, though Niziov (on the Dniestr) fell and the Austrians were forced back upon Halicz.

Fighting continued at this point until the end of September, the Russians scoring some local successes at great cost. The heavy reinforcement of Bothmer, standing between the Russians and Lemberg, continuously diminished opportunities for the attackers.

The first cry for help came from Rumania sooner than even the Russians expected. She had enemies on three sides and, having decided to employ almost all her modest active forces in a northward attack on Transylvania, she was threatened by her southern enemy, Bulgaria. Without hesitation she asked for Allied aid, which she may well have expected to come from the Anglo-French Salonica army, but they had failed to equip themselves with transport suitable for the mountainous terrain and were immobile.

Only Russia remained and she was asked to lengthen her already over extended line to Dobruja. To take Transylvania would not directly benefit them or the Alliance, but they had no alternative but to comply. Brusilov categorically refused to extend his own command, and Alexeiev appointed Zayonchkovski as commander of a special Dobruja Detachment. Since the Rumanian Army was under the nominal command of King Carol himself, Zayonchkovski was required to be something of a courtier and diplomat as well as a soldier. Regrettably, in this atmosphere of intricate politics and interracial passions, no thought was given to the constitution of the forces assigned to the new detachment. The Bulgarians would hardly have evinced any enthusiasm at fighting the Russians, whom they regarded as their liberators from the Turks in 1877, but Stavka — anxious to pull together some sort of force without delay — was imprudent enough to include large numbers of volunteers from Serbia, a traditional enemy.

However, the first actions in Transylvania resulted in several Rumanian successes, largely because the only defence the Austrians could muster was five tired divisions; this situation could not be expected to continue. For one thing, the final admission of failure at Verdun had proved too much for Falkenhayn's reputation as commander-in-chief. Hindenburg and Ludendorff were moved to GHQ to take his place, while General Field Marshal Prince Leopold of Bavaria succeeded at Oberost with Hoffmann as chief-of-staff and hence virtual commander.[2] More important, the new high command, unwilling to let the Rumanian situation drift and needing a job for their predecessor, sent Falkenhayn south to take control of the Rumanian front on 6 September. At the same time three Bulgarian divisions, a division of cavalry and part of a German division were moved from the quiescent Salonica front under the command of August von Mackensen. They burst upon the Rumanians and Russians in Dobruja, steadily pushing them back throughout September, while Falkenhayn began probing attacks from the north.

Within a short time the Rumanians had used all their ammunition. Since they were in an enclave where the only way to supply them was via Russia, Allied goods for Rumania had to be sent by way of Russian ports already choked with cargo, and then consigned to the over-taxed railways. Brusilov's offensive was thus being further jeopardised for the sake of a feeble ally, but he was nevertheless striving to carry out the mutually contradictory tasks of helping that ally while trying to pursue his own plans. A reorganisation of the front transferred the burden of attacking Bothmer from Lechitski to the Seventh Army, and a corresponding shift leftward was made all along the line. The Ninth Army was now free to attack southward from Delatyn to Kimpolung with the ultimate objective of recrossing the Carpathians. Once again the plains-dwelling Russian soldiers were challenged with unfamiliar country and this time faced Mackensen's howitzers supported by German mountain troops instead of the exhausted Austrians of 1915. Against this they could make little progress, though they did take the Jablonitsa Pass at the end of September.

In Dobruja things were meantime going from bad to worse. The Rumanians were easily swept aside, though Zayonchkovski's detachment resisted stubbornly. In an effort to save the situation, he was relieved; a new Army of the Danube was formed under Sakharov, the Eleventh Army commander, which was made the keystone of a new "Rumanian Front" with the king as commander-in-chief, Klembovski taking over command of Eleventh Army. But on 19 September, Falkenhayn undertook a new drive, and after defeating them at Kronstadt forced the Rumanians into general retreat. To save them, the Russians threw in twenty infantry and seven cavalry divisions — of which the Danube Army alone had ten — but when the Rumanians on Lechitski's left in the Carpathians were thrown back in disorder, Brusilov's front had to be extended 400 kilometres into formerly neutral territory to cover them while Lechitski had to abandon Jablonitsa. This new responsibility had to be paid for and the price exacted was that of Brusilov's own offensive.

Parts of Kaledin's Eighth Army were moved south to the right of Lechitski, who sidestepped leftward to fill the gap caused by the Rumanian failure. The Special Army (the former Guard Army) under Gourko took their place on the right of South West Front beside the remainder of the Eighth.

Russian officers, bitterly aggrieved at the unexpected failure, were perhaps unduly sharp in blaming an ally. Lemberg, they insisted, would have been Russian but for Rumania's untimely intervention. This ignored such realities as the abandonment of other offensive plans to concentrate on one intensive effort; the failure of other generals to support this by their own determined initiatives; the persisting Russian deficiency in arms; and overall, the growing shortage of men. Against these handicaps, the Russian offensive effort had already been slackening before Rumania entered the war, mainly because of the enemy's ability to reinforce. Thus the balance of strength had shifted. At the beginning of the battle 39 Russian infantry divisions opposed 37 Austrian and one German division. By 12 August, reinforcements from other fronts had increased South West Front to 61, but they were opposed by 72 enemy divisions of which 24 were German — 18 having been sent from the west.

Another factor not taken into account was the increasing clamour from the tsarina and Rasputin. The tsarina wrote on 24 August: "Our Friend hopes we won't climb over the Carpathians", and in October: "Oh, give your order again to Brusilov to stop this useless slaughter." Such an order had gone out on 4 October, but at Brusilov's insistence the attacks continued for a few days longer.

On 16–17 October, Gourko threw fifteen divisions into the attack toward Vladimir-Volhynskyi and its railway lines. Lack of spotter aircraft prevented Russian batteries from locating the Germans, while they — under no such disadvantage — punished the Russian infantry severely. Considering that casualties since June exceeded the million mark, the abandonment of the battle after two days is hardly surprising. However, it marked the end of yet another campaign mounted by Russia on behalf of one ally (Italy) which the Russians considered had been destroyed by another (Rumania).

That the last campaign of the Russian Imperial Army should end in this way was considered by many Russians to be symbolically appropriate: it was the essence of the nation's whole war effort.

Chapter 20

Coming Of the Storm

Winter comes sooner in the northern latitudes, following hard on the harvest, so that the battle which began in the ripening corn ended in mud and stubble under lowering skies. Along the city streets the passers-by were already wearing thick clothes and the evening mists were permeated with the smell of wood smoke from household fires.

It was only October, but food and fuel were already short and prices rising. The old problem of transport was partly responsible. Before the War northern Russia's main source of coal had been Cardiff, but now — with all shipping needed for war supplies — it was entirely dependent on coal from the Donetz basin, about a thousand miles away, and only about half the wagons needed for transportation were available. There were other reasons, too. Although there was still no basic food shortage over the country as a whole, under the price-fixing regulations the peasants felt they were not only receiving insufficient reward for their labours, but insufficient to keep them through the winter under inflation; they were therefore hoarding their produce. Consequently, a number of mills in Petrograd and elsewhere had stopped grinding, and when bakers received their flour allocations the price they could ask for their bread was often so low that they preferred to sell the rye to stables for feeding horses.

The position in the Russian capital was summed up in a police report for October: wages had increased 100 per cent on pre-war levels, but prices by 300 per cent. There was growing distress at the impossibility of obtaining necessities even for cash, and the time spent in queuing. Cold and damp, combined with an inadequate diet, was making people (particularly children) prone to illness. The prohibition of all, even the most innocuous, public gatherings and the closing of the trade unions forced the working masses toward extremism. The report expressed the view that the capital was on the verge of despair and that "the smallest

223

outbreak, due to any pretext, will lead to uncontrollable riots with thousands and tens of thousands of victims."

Strikes were now rising toward 1914 figures, but even more ominous were the signs that dissatisfaction was spreading to the armed forces. In August, outbreaks among troops travelling by a circuitous route to the Salonica front resulted in an officer being beaten to death at Marseilles, and the French garrison had to be called in to quell the disturbance. On 21 August, twenty-six of the rioters were tried, eight were sentenced to death and executed. Zhilinski, chief of the Russian military mission (and architect of the East Prussian disaster of 1914), who conducted an inquiry, attempted to place the blame on the working-class French families with whom the troops had been billeted, but since the disorders had started while they were still at sea, they obviously had an earlier origin. In fact, discontent in the Russian navy and merchant marine was already apparent, and in 1915 there were mutinies in the Baltic Fleet aboard the "Gangut" and "Imperator Pavel". The Black Sea Fleet had been less troubled, but no explanation had been found for an explosion aboard the "Imperatriza Maria", one of the finest ships of the navy, which sank while at her moorings in Sebastopol harbour.

In late October there was a no less ominous incident in Petrograd when, during the autumn wave of strikes, the French Renault factory (still operating) was invaded by strikers demanding that the men show their solidarity by also coming out. When the intruders ignored the management's orders to leave, police were called, but they asked for troops. Men of the Petrograd garrison arrived, and fired not on the agitators, but on the police. Ultimately, four Cossack regiments had to be sent for and they drove the troops back to their barracks where they were confined and tried. On 8 November 150 of them were shot, and as soon as the news became public there was a fresh wave of strikes.

Amidst these manifestations of unrest, the government remained paralysed by internal upheaval. The task of providing a bodyguard for Rasputin had been entrusted to a certain Manasevich-Manuilov, whose ready wit, sparse scruples and superficial charm, had enabled him to insinuate himself into the bizarre court government of Tsar Nicholas. Manuilov had been a hack-journalist, secret police spy and blackmailer, and once his past became known even Stürmer had no option but to dismiss him. He thereupon returned to blackmail, for which he had acquired a wealth of raw material through his contacts with Rasputin. Khvostov, as Interior Minister, was determined to have done with him and his investigators gathered enough evidence to have him arrested.

It is difficult to reconcile the tsarina's actual behaviour with the assertions of those who knew her closely that she regarded stories about Rasputin's conduct as pure slander. If she was convinced of their insubstantiality, why was she alarmed at the thought of what might emerge if Manuilov was tried in a public court? He had plenty of opportunity to know a great deal about the staretz and – using his blackmailer's skill to the last – announced his intention of revealing this at the trial. The only answer is that the empress subconsciously recognised what her conscious, puritanical mind rejected. In any case, Rasputin had made himself psychologically as well as materially indispensable, so in order to save him the incorruptible Khvostov must go. The dismissal was conveyed by the slimy Stürmer, who told him: "You brought me the unpleasant news of Manasevich-Manuilov's arrest. Now I have news for you: you are no longer Minister of the Interior." The spirited old man is said to have answered: "It is the first time I leave you with a feeling of sincere pleasure."

The empress had a successor waiting in the wings. In the spring, a delegation from the Duma had visited Britain.[1] Its spokesman was liberal deputy A. D. Protopopov who comported himself with "tact and dignity" according to Rodzianko and Kerenski. They returned by way of Stockholm, where it became known that he had been in contact with the German minister in the city; confronted, he swore that his sole purpose had been to emphasise Russia's firmness in the war and to convince the German government there was no hope of a separate peace. None of his Duma colleagues knew that Protopopov was a Rasputinite of some years' standing (having first visited him for a cure) and that the Royal Friend was awaiting an opportunity to introduce him into the government. This opportunity now arising, the tsarina immediately embarked on a campaign to persuade the tsar to install him in Khvostov's office. Mentioning his membership of the Duma, she said: "It will have a great effect among them and shut their mouths" – an idea no doubt originating with Rasputin. The tsar had once met Protopopov when Rodzianko was considering him for Minister of Commerce, and although at the time he made a favourable impression, a feeling of doubt appears to have been left in the tsar's mind. Protopopov was not completely unprepossessing; though rather short, he had a well-structured, aristocratic face and neat moustache. He apparently succeeded in dismissing any lingering doubts from the tsar's mind, for on 25 September he answered his wife's request that Protopopov be appointed Interior Minister by writing "It shall be done."

If the tsarina hoped that his appointment would silence the Duma, she was badly deceived. A storm of anger broke about his head, and he was reviled for joining a government presided over by Stürmer; still at that time believed to be the true power. Protopopov was impervious, however, and it was obvious that he had been nursing delusions of a providential mission for some time. "I feel I shall save Russia", he told Rodzianko. Kerenski, who visited him in his office, found him wearing – quite improperly – the uniform of a general of the gendarmes and sitting under a large ikon to which, he claimed, he submitted all his actions and decisions. It was obvious to his former colleagues that they had missed a fundamental aspect of his personality: he was mad. Later, a doctor diagnosed "creeping paralysis", a disease affecting the cerebral regions. The admixture of religiosity they found so alarming was just the characteristic to commend him to the empress, a devout believer in divine missions of her own.

The public thought differently. They had long since concluded that the tsarina was in league with the enemy, and even believed an absurd story that a radio on the roof of Tsarskoe Selo enabled her to communicate directly with the German Kaiser. The appointment of Stürmer, suspected of similar pro-enemy sentiments, had supported this view which was further confirmed by the advent of Protopopov. The conviction that the government was about to make peace began to spread, and it was even suggested that the Ministry of the Interior was responsible for fostering agitation in the factories and elsewhere as part of a campaign to win the tsar over to the cause of peace.

Until Protopopov's appointment, Rasputin's various nominees had kept their association secret and, in some cases, had even professed to be planning his downfall. Since the new Minister of the Interior made no such pretence, the full extent of Rasputin's influence was now realised, and with it the imperative need to remove him. All over Petrograd, groups drawn from every class discussed ways of doing so, ranging from assassination to keeping him permanently drunk.

Conservatives like Rodzianko persevered in their efforts to make the tsar see the need for better government which would relieve the (often unnecessary) hardships now inflicted on the Russian people. Both Buchanan and Paléologue added their own warnings at separate audiences. A third group, realising the long-awaited revolution was moving closer, began looking ahead to what would follow, and all over the city various political groups met secretly to consider their programmes, hoping to be prepared when the storm broke.

The ordinary people grumbled and queued, stamping their feet to keep them warm, murmured at passing gendarmes or shouted at the rich as they drove by. Almost invariably, supplies ran out before everyone had been served and they were turned angrily or desperately away.

On 14 November a new session of the Duma opened. Urgent matters for discussion such as food, fuel and transport were now in the hands of the tsarina herself, who neither understood them nor had any head for figures. Rasputin suggested they should be handed over to the Minister of the Interior, who at least had the police to back up his measures, but Protopopov had no more understanding of the complexities of the job than his sovereign. His solution for Russia's salvation was so far limited to a nebulous plan to revive the "Black Hundreds," an extreme right-wing organisation which pursued a campaign of terror, pogrom and the assassination of "liberals" after the 1905 revolution.

Moreover, the tsar was already losing faith in the new minister, whose entire administration was once more under public scrutiny and attack. In parliament, Pavel Miliukov, a leading Cadet deputy and member of the so-called "Progressive Bloc", itemised the failures of the government, asking rhetorically after each count: "Is this folly or is it treason?", and named the empress and Stürmer as among the forces of national sabotage. The House's support was almost unanimous, which was all the more amazing since some right-wing members of the Duma were actually in receipt of secret police subsidies. Censored from the press,

Miliukov's speech was distributed secretly and became common knowledge.

About this time, Stürmer himself had been shouted down when appearing before the House. Such behaviour normally produced a counter-reaction in the tsar, but this time it coincided either with a period of doubt or perhaps the revival of a mood in which he sought to identify himself with his people. Even the tsarina was now having doubts about Stürmer, and on 20 November she wrote: "Stürmer ought to say he is ill and go for a rest for three weeks . . . it's better he should disappear a bit, then in December when they have cleared out return again." The following day Nicholas replied in similar vein. The tsarina was therefore perfectly prepared for his departure and accepted with reasonable equanimity his succession by A. F. Trepov, a colourless bureaucrat of the extreme right, who nevertheless possessed the inestimable virtue of being no friend of Rasputin. However, she was not prepared for the simultaneous dismissal on 23 November of her latest favourite Protopopov, and sent letters begging the tsar to reconsider, as on 24 November: "I entreat you don't go and change Protopopov now, . . . give him a chance to get the food supply matter into his hands and I assure you all will go." In the same letter: "Protopopov is honestly for us." Correctly divining the hand of the hated Duma in this decision, she wrote on 25 November: "The tsar rules the Duma"; and later: "Have the Duma cleverly shut." When letters seemed ineffective she made the twenty-four hour journey to Mogilev, and succeeded in having Protopopov reinstated. He was immediately put in charge of food supplies.

The less favoured Stürmer had now relinquished his posts as chairman of the Council of Ministers and as Foreign Minister, leaving that office without even the customary farewells to ambassadors. There was now no Foreign Minister, but it was realised this gap would have to be filled quickly, if only because the Polish question was once more in focus. As one of his last acts, the Austro-Hungarian Emperor Franz-Joszef had signed a decree granting independence to Galicia. The fury of the Russian imperialist dinosaurs was immediately directed toward the British and the French for their meddlesome insistence that Russia honour the grand-duke's pledges which, they said, had kept the whole question in the open.

By this time, Russia was quite convinced that her allies were bent on the total dismemberment of her empire, and Buchanan was said to be actively intriguing with the revolution, even attending meetings of revolutionary groups in disguise. Buchanan was so completely the model of old-school British diplomacy, both in aristocratic appearance and immaculate dress, that it is fascinating to imagine him in worker's cloth cap and false beard among the revolutionaries, whom he loathed as whole-heartedly as did the most right-wing Russian. However, Paléologue (who regarded him as the soul of honour) points out a kind of precedent for this strange delusion, in that after the assassination of Paul I in 1801 it was alleged that the British had planned the crime. In fact the then British ambassador, Lord Whitworth, had left Russia in April of the previous year.

In early December, Trepov appeared before the Duma. Feeling that he must produce some evidence of the government's determination to compensate for the possible loss of Poland to the empire, he chose without prior consultation to give the House the full text of the inter-Allied agreement on Constantinople and the Straits. The news that this opened to the nation "the glowing future, decreed by history" was greeted apathetically by both Duma and public.

On 27 December Miliukov again took the rostrum to press his attack on the government, warning of the "coming storm." On the 28th, an illegal meeting of Zemgor carried by acclamation a motion condemning the government's fatal incompetence and the "dark forces behind the throne," a chilling phrase echoing one used at a meeting of the highly conservative Assembly of Nobles on 20 December.

The thought of this "coming storm" struck terror in many breasts, particularly those who realised they were likely to be victims of the mob if rioting started. From all quarters there were frenzied demands for a fundamental change of government. Plots and conspiracies spread like a plague, and normally harmless people planned the murder of the tsar, tsarina, Protopopov and Rasputin. The loyal Alexeiev was made party to one plot whereby he was to arrest the tsarina when she was visiting Stavka and insist to the tsar that she be confined at Livadia, their summer home.

Her own formula for the current troubles was to combine pious observance with exhortations to her husband to be "more autocratic." In November, the grand-duke was due to visit Stavka. She was in a dither: "I shall be anxious while Nicholasha is at Headquarters, hope all will go well and you will show you are master." In fact the meeting was, as always, extremely cordial. On 17 December she predicted: "Now comes your reign of will and power," and on the 26th: "Draw the reins in tightly which you let loose . . . Russia loves to feel the whip . . . ." On the 27th: "Be Peter the Great, Ivan the Terrible, Emperor Paul — crush them all under you — now don't laugh, naughty one." And the tsar signed his reply: "Your poor, weak willed little hubby."

Only one of these conspiracies came to fruition. On 29 December a trio including Prince Felix Yussopov (married to a niece of the tsar) killed Rasputin. He was invited to the Yussopov palace and given a massive dose of cyanide in cakes and wine — enough, it was said afterward, to have killed thirty men. When he survived this, a revolver was emptied into his body, after which he was seen to open one eye and Yussopov set upon him, battering his head with a lump of steel. He was then thrown into the Neva, weighted and with hands tied. When his body was later recovered, water found in the lungs indicated he had still been alive when thrown into the river; one of his hands, freed of the ropes, was raised as though about to make the sign of the cross over a supplicant.

As news of his death leaked out there was widespread jubilation in many quarters, but only anger among the "mouzhiks" who regarded the staretz as one of themselves. To them he was a martyr, killed by "Pridvorny" — the court folk.

At Tsarkoe Selo, added to grief was the recollection Rasputin had once predicted that if he died at the hands of any member of the royal family the dynasty would fall within a year, and that its principal members would suffer violent deaths. It was also recalled that he had behaved and spoken in recent days as if he knew death was near.

The body was buried amid deep mourning in which the tsar participated. But they buried more than the dead Holy Man of Tobolsk that day.

Warnings continued to come from all sides. Sometimes Nicholas listened courteously and attentively, sometimes he was cold and disinterested. Rodzianko was cut short in the middle of a report: "Couldn't you get through this a bit quicker? The Grand-Duke Mikhail Alexandrovich is expecting me for tea."

Sturmer's successor at the Foreign Office was sixty-year-old N. N. Pokrovski, who took up his appointment on 14 December. According to Paléologue, he had no knowledge of foreign problems or of diplomacy, but was liked and trusted. Although he too urged the tsar at least to get rid of Protopopov, for the present the latter remained safe in his seat. Shuvaiev was relieved as Minister of War, and General Belaiev — a "typical military bureaucrat" — appointed in his stead. Bobrinski, who had succeeded Naumov as Minister of Agriculture, was himself replaced by Rittich, the fourth holder of the office since autumn 1915. On 9 January, Trepov was allowed to resign and his place was taken by the aged Prince N. N. Galitsyn, totally unknown outside the court, who vainly begged to be excused.[2]

In January, the railway situation reached crisis proportions. Coal stocks were exhausted and 1200 overworked locomotives broke down, boilers frequently exploding in the intense cold. Protopopov, however, had virtually abandoned his task of endeavouring to supply the populace in order to attend spiritualistic séances with the tsarina at which attempts were made to contact the dead staretz. By way of preparation for the coming storm, his achievements were limited to diverting machine-guns sent from Britain (for the army) to the gendarmerie, who were instructed in their use. At the same time, the Petrograd garrison was detached from the North Front for use in the city, although officers of the Guard Depot Cavalry Regiment petitioned against such employment and begged to stay at the front.

The crisis of discontent always begins in the rear, as General Serrigny pointed out, and along the front itself the troops were still outwardly untouched, particularly in the south. Indeed, campaign prospects looked better than ever before. Through the autumn and winter of 1916/17 there was the usual recouping of strength, and the troops' morale was so good that when on 29 January Paléologue told General Castelnau — visiting Russia and just come from the front — that revolution was near, he regarded it as a gross exaggeration. Supplies of every kind were reaching the armies, putting them on a parity with the enemy even in aircraft. After discussions with the other Allies, it had been recommended that Russia should receive four batteries of 6-inch, two batteries of 8-inch and one battery of 9.2-inch howitzers per month. By January of that year they had received from Britain: Sixteen 60-pounders with wagons; one 9.2-inch with caterpillar tractor; thirty-two 6-inch howitzers and 400 4.2-inch howitzers. The spirits of the troops were further raised by the manifest depression of the enemy, which Pares commented upon.

Generals like Brusilov might have put an official stop on the easy-going fraternisation across the trenches, but this did not prevent the two sides from exchanging messages by means of banners raised above the parapets, which often indicated both the Austro-German war-weariness and the effects of blockade. Indeed, at times they crossed the lines to beg the Russians for food.

The Germans were aware of the Russians' growing strength; Hoffmann at Oberost and Ludendorff and Hindenburg at General Headquarters were all anxious. "No intelligence came through to us," wrote the latter, "which revealed any particularly striking indications of disintegration of the Russian army . . . . We had . . . to anticipate that attacks by the Russians might once again mean the collapse of the Austrian lines. It was in any case impossible to withdraw direct German support from the Austrian front."

Although the Foreign Ministry reported that all attempts to persuade the tsar to a separate peace had met blank refusal, German spirits were dampened by signs of a fundamental readiness for peace among their Allies.

Throughout his lifetime, Franz-Joszef's reluctance to make the slightest concessions provided a stumbling block to any realistic approach, while in his last weeks of life the dire seriousness of Austria's situation had to be kept from him. The Archduke Karl, who assumed the imperial diadem on 21 November 1916, had quickly shown himself more flexible, and among his first public utterances was the promise to restore peace "as soon as the honour of my Arms, the vital interests of my States and its faithful Allies and the malignity of my Enemies will allow." Although the Germans were not aware of it, approaches had been made in December through the emperor's brother-in-law, Prince

Sixte of Bourbon who — by the chances of royal relation-
ships — was an artillery officer in the Belgian army.[3]

At the beginning of 1917, Russia could have been said to be
reaching a point where the reward for long and bloody struggles
were coming within her grasp. Churchill has summed it up: "No
difficult action was now required; to remain in presence; to lean
with heavy weight upon the far-stretched Teutonic line; to hold
without exceptional activity the weakened hostile forces on her
front; in a word to endure — that was all that stood between
Russia and the fruit of general victory." Besides, fresh resources of
strength were soon to reach the Entente.

In February 1916, Woodrow Wilson the American president,
sent out Colonel Edward House as a special peace envoy to sound
Germany, France and Britain about their attitudes to a peace
conference under Wilson's chairmanship. The German emperor
dismissed House in a single sentence of medieval arrogance: "I and
my cousins George [V of Britain] and Nicholas [the tsar] will
make peace when the time comes" — as if, House comments, "war
was a royal sport". After this high-handed rebuff, he concluded
that the only way to persuade Germany to submit to mediation
was to threaten American intervention on the Entente side.
House's visits to Britain and France were conditioned by his Berlin
experience, and he urged the Allies' acceptance of any presidential
invitation to a conference, so that Germany's refusal might be
regarded as due cause for American intervention to bring the war
to a speedy close and ensure a durable peace. The British Cabinet
felt they needed to be told exactly what terms were acceptable to
the president so that when matters reached the negotiating table,
they would know where to expect his support; with this object in
view they put forward their own conditions which were, broadly:
the restoration of Belgian and Serbian independence; the return of
Alsace-Lorraine to France, with Germany compensated for the
losses incurred by territorial concessions outside Europe; and the
adjustment of the Italian and Austrian frontiers to free the Italian
communities now under Austrian dominance. Russia was to be
given her outlet on the Mediterranean — though nothing was said
about the annexation of Constantinople or other Russian aims.

This represented a purely British résumé, though they insisted
that the other Allies must be consulted before final decisions
about participation in a conference were taken. All the same,

House considered the terms reasonable enough to submit to Washington for study, and Wilson's reply was forwarded in due course. At this juncture, the whole enterprise collapsed, for the pacific president, suddenly timorous at the thought of being committed to war if Germany refused his overtures, interpolated the word "probably" before his threat of intervention. To the British, this so weakened it as to nullify it — in which circumstances they were disinclined to press upon the French and the Russian terms implying the abandonment of some of their most cherished war-ambitions.

However, hope for peace was not entirely dead, and on 18 December the American government communicated to the Allied governments the text of a note from Germany offering peace negotiations. This was rejected on the strange grounds that its emphasis on German victories so far (plainly no more than a bargaining base) was in Lloyd-George's words, "the language of a conqueror," not that "of an enemy suing for peace."

Ten days later, nonetheless, President Wilson asked the tsar to divulge his pre-conditions for a cessation of hostilities. Nicholas hardly had time to answer before the die was cast in favour of American intervention — by a German throw. On 31 January, they informed Washington of their intention to wage unrestricted submarine warfare, and on 28 February the first American ship was sunk with some loss of life; on 1 April, the second. Five days later the United States of America entered the alliance against Germany and Austro-Hungary.

In November, the Allied military staffs had assembled at Chantilly for the customary annual meeting. It had been hoped that this would be preceded by a conference of political leaders, but those of Russia felt they could not leave the country at the moment, while Joffre refused to postpone. Plans for the third year of the war were thus made without the politicians having any opportunity to scrutinise them (as was doubtless the generals' intention). At a preliminary conference of statesmen held in the absence of both the Russians and Italians, it was decided to hold a fully representative meeting in Russia as soon as feasible. This was tentatively fixed for early in the new year, but postponed after Rasputin's death until the third week of January.

Protopopov was horrified that the storm might break while the Allied delegates were actually in the capital, or that their presence might spark off some demonstration; on 13 February, in the middle of the conference, he lost his head completely and ordered the arrest of eleven of the worker-representatives on the Central War Industries Committee, to whose presence he had always taken exception "for plotting a revolutionary movement." This group, regarded by the Bolsheviks as class-traitors, had supported the continuation of the war against Germany and consistently exerted a moderating influence on their fellows. The workers of the capital responded to this action with fresh strikes and demonstrations, and the Allied visitors had to be hurried past barricades in the process of erection. Even now, Protopopov forbade the publication of an appeal from other "defencist-worker" groups for the strikers to resume work for the sake of the war effort. In its schizophrenia, the régime was turning on its friends, while enemies continued to thrive undisturbed.

Perhaps the implications behind this made Gaston Doumergue, French plenipotentiary and a future president, decide to lose no more time in gaining Russia's formal approval to France's war aims. The precise details were approved in discussion with Pokrovski, the Foreign Minister. In exchange for the acceptance of French demands for Alsace-Lorraine, the Saar and an independent protectorate along the banks of the Rhine, Russia was to swallow up the whole of Poland (Austrian, German and Russian) into a single autonomous province within the empire, and to have a free hand in demarcating her own western frontiers.[4]

The conference meanwhile endorsed the minutes of the Chantilly meeting. Undeterred by past events, it was again declared that 1917 would be the year of victory over the Central Powers, toward which an offensive must be launched by all the Allies in May. Russia would attack along her entire front with some 70 divisions; and vigorous attacks would be launched on Bulgaria by the French, British and Russian forces in Salonika on the one side, and by the Russians and Rumanians on the other, so as to compel her withdrawal from the war.

In mid-February, after the conference delegates dispersed, the Duma once more assembled. Before the meeting, the chairman Rodzianko had another audience with the tsar, and once more warned him of the menaces surrounding the nation. Again he was ignored. Four days later, Alexander Kerenski was loudly applauded in the predominantly conservative House when he openly demanded the removal of the tsar "by terrorist means if there are no others."

The tsar was to have addressed them in response to yet another appeal for a ministry in which the country could have confidence, this time originating from Prince Galitsyn. He intended to tell them that he accepted their demands, so that this second royal visit to parliament would – in its way – be as important as the occasion in 1906 when he agreed to the granting of a constitution and the very birth of the House. At the same time, he felt he was needed at Stavka, and his brother Grand-Duke Mikhail Alexandrovich, unaware of his plans, urged he delay his return no longer.

That evening, Galitsyn was summoned to the palace and told by Nicholas that he was leaving for headquarters. Galitsyn was amazed. "What about a responsible ministry?" he asked. "You intended to go to the Duma tomorrow." The reply came: "I have changed my mind . . . I am leaving for headquarters tonight." Before leaving he gave the President of the Council a sheaf of undated forms, bearing his signature, for the prorogation of the Duma – "to be used if need arose."

It was 7 March. The country had from two to – at most – five days' supply of coal; half the blast furnaces of the Donetz had stopped work; metal output had fallen from 260,000 tons to 100,000. At the huge Putilov works, the Tula works and the Tambor and Baranovski powder factories, all production was at a standstill because the labour-forces reckoned they were getting insufficient food to enable them to work.

On 8 March, the Duma itself criticised the government's inability to feed the people – and it was that day that the people began to take matters into their own hands.

A squadron of Cossacks sent to drive off women looting food stores, instead fraternised with them. This was not the first dereliction of duty by Russian soldiers but it was to have the most far-reaching effects, like a flash of lightning through the lowering clouds.

As the thunder crashed in reaction and the streaming rain fell, the planners of both the revolution and its aftermath were caught unawares as they ran hither and thither in a vain attempt to escape.

Chapter 21

The Rising Of the Sun Of Freedom

In March 1917, a soldier returning from leave was asked by an officer if anything had happened in his village while he was there. "No, nothing happened," he answered, "except some agitators came from another village and said the tsar had been turned out and suchlike nonsense. But we caught them and beat them." The remark was a fair assessment of the Russian Revolution of March 1917 which, like the French one 130 years earlier, was a metropolitan phenomenon. Its preparation and execution were carried out without reference to either the countryside or the armies at the front, on both of whom it left little immediate mark.

The soldiers' reaction to the change of government and the fall of the monarchy varied. Some of the older men wept openly when told of the abdication; others demanded the imperial monogram be removed from the regimental colours before they would take the oath of allegiance to the Provisional Government. All, however, expected that the war would continue and they would have to go on fighting; indeed troops of the Caucasian Front were actually engaging the Turks at that moment.

The finer political points were simply incomprehensible to illiterate peasants bred in the political atmosphere of autocracy. When the soviet passed a motion demanding immediate peace negotiations on the basis of "no annexations and no indemnities," the terms were so unfamiliar that, according to Knox, many soldiers believed "Aneksiia" and "Contributsii" to be two Russian towns and, since they had never heard of them, they hardly mourned their loss! The revolutionary soldiers of the Petrograd garrison were wholeheartedly condemned as "cowardly rubbish" and agitators sent to soldiers' meetings were booed and given a scant hearing.

In the early days of upheaval the Soviet of Workers' Deputies, born in the 1905 revolution and forcibly dissolved a year later, had sprung back into existence. Now renamed the

238

Soviet of Soldiers' and Workers' Deputies, it consisted of representatives elected in the capital on the basis of one per company of the Petrograd garrison, and one per hundred employees in the factories. It had taken over part of the Tauride Palace, so that there were effectively two governments under one roof, and as the Provisional Government did not feel strong enough to rid itself of this rival, it was allowed to coexist. The Labour Deputy Alexander Kerenski had been made Minister of Justice in the new administration because he was a lawyer. He now persuaded himself that he was the only person trusted by the working people and acted as an informal and self-appointed liaison officer with the Soviet, persuading it to accept this or that government proposal, and warning the government what the Soviet would or would not tolerate. Through the Soviet, the troops of the Petrograd garrison obtained an undertaking that as architects and sole guardians of the revolution, they would not be sent to the front; this news formed the basis of the contempt and dislike with which they were regarded by the front line soldiers.

Whatever the Soviet's intentions, it was actually hastening the army's disintegration. A baseless rumour that a group of officers were planning a counter-revolutionary coup led to the Soviet drawing up the now famous Order No 1 on 14 March, directing that soldiers' committees be established in all units stationed in Petrograd, which would take charge of all arms. The order also introduced a number of other reforms: the saluting of officers when off-duty was abolished, as was the use of courtesy titles such as "Your Excellency" and "Your Nobility" which were replaced by simple titles somewhat in the French style of "Monsieur le Géneral," "Monsieur le Colonel." It further forbade "rudeness" by officers in talking to soldiers, and specifically the use of the familiar second person singular.

They showed this document to Colonel Engelhardt, chairman of the Duma's Armed Forces Commission who, in a stormy interview, questioned the existence of any officers' plot and did not intend to be railroaded into accepting proposals beyond the needs of the situation. When he refused to promulgate the order, the Soviet deputation did so themselves, but according to Kerenski it was sent by mistake to the whole army, instead of only the Petrograd garrison, and its ambiguous terminology implied that it had universal application. Thus, the system of double authority already existing in civil government was extended to the army, and officers found themselves having to consult the soldiers' soviets before giving orders — an immediate cause of friction.

The order was particularly significant in that it provided the first example of the troops directing the actual running of the army. Having had their first taste of power, the men soon became addicted. This situation might have been avoided had Engelhardt been less uncompromising, for a government order ameliorating some of the injustices under which the Russian troops laboured would have won support for its authority while avoiding the dangerous impression of impotence. As it was, Order No 1 spread further and cut deeper than its authors ever intended.

At the same time both the Duma and the Soviet were sending "commissars" to the front, ostensibly to explain the governments' intentions and to calm down the troops. The Soviets' delegates were often Bolsheviks who used their office to further undermine military authority and attack the Provisional Government, while to increase confusion a commission appointed to revise military law, headed by former War Minister Polivanov, abolished the death penalty and other drastic punishments, at the very time when officers felt that such correctives as were available should be retained. Witnessing the disintegration of their armies assisted by government action, officers like Brusilov and Gourko asked to be freed of their commands, though their requests were refused.

High Command was also assisting the process of osmosis by which the philosophy of the revolution was permeating the army. In November 1916, Alexeiev had been taken ill (hence the plan for him to "arrest" the tsarina was stillborn), and his place was taken temporarily by the commander of the Special Army, General Vassili Gourko, under whom a plan for reorganisation was put in hand in January 1917.

Divisions in the Russian army were larger than in most others and were therefore particularly unwieldy. The 1916–17 drafts would add 132 battalions to army strength, and by pruning divisions from sixteen to twelve battalions a more uniform distribution of fresh equipment would be made possible. A corps, previously two divisions, was now to be three divisions strong, into each of which 8 gun machine-gun sections could be incorporated. Asked to relinquish a third of their men, the divisional commanders naturally chose the most troublesome units, and the so-called "Third Divisions" were centres of disaffection. Men felt they had been torn from their comrades and that this was simply an application of the principle of "divide and rule" by those of whom they were already suspicious. Furthermore, the reorganisation was bound to call for more officers than were available. It was then decided to disband the "Third Divisions" as plainly unfit for combat, but the soldiers interpreted this as an attempt to silence them, and threatened mutiny. Disorders broke out among the regiments of the 163rd Division of the Sixth Army, who only laid down their arms under threat of infantry fire and artillery bombardment.

Similar convulsions had shaken the navy, especially the Baltic Fleet where fresh mutinies had broken out in March and in which some officers were killed.

In an effort to impart a revolutionary character to the entire fleet, many vessels were renamed by the Navy Ministry of the Provisional Government. Thus the "Imperator Pavel", scene of an earlier mutiny, became the "Republic"; the "Tsarevich", the "Citizen"; and so on. This made no difference. As in the army, soviets were formed on a basis of one per ship. The Black Sea Fleet was less rebellious but its commodore, Kolchak, felt his authority sufficiently undermined to insist on resigning his command. He later became one of the focal points of resistance to the Bolsheviks.

Astonishingly enough, in the armed services these changes were taking place as if the war had been dismissed as easily as the tsar. Not a shot was fired along the battlefront by either side, although now there was the best ever chance for Germany and Austria to end Russian resistance before the Americans, about to declare war, began arriving from the west.

Petrograd was reputedly crawling with German spies, and Ludendorff was supposedly better informed than the Provisional Government as to what was happening there, but the truth was completely opposite. The Germans were so ill-informed that their early propaganda accused the British of causing the revolution, believing it was unpopular with the troops. The idea so far survived that Hoffmann, in a book published in 1925, accused Buchanan of joining Kerenski and Guchkov "in deposing the tsar."

As realisation dawned, however, the Germans saw that they might be able to gain a cheaper victory from the revolution than from assaults which would force the Russian troops to defend themselves. They therefore decided to play upon the continuing dissatisfaction, on the Provisional Government's difficulties in enforcing its authority, and in particular on the hostility shown to officers. A propaganda rather than a military campaign was launched. German Socialists, normally detested particularly by the army, were enlisted and, according to Sazonov, some RM70,000,000 budgeted for their use. There was one short break in the informal truce when the Germans mounted an attack in the River Stokhod region on 21 March, wiping out one corps, but Hindenburg quickly apologised for the action as "an accidental misunderstanding," which would not be repeated. Neither German nor Russian troops had any wish to see this pleasant interlude in a bloody war ended, and to avoid any danger of this happening from their own side the infantry cut the telegraphs to the artillery and promised to bayonet any artilleryman who opened fire.

The Germans' campaign of words was materially assisted by the Soviet, fast becoming the only authority to which the troops would listen. The Soviet was convinced that the German and Austro-Hungarian armies were as ripe for revolution as they had themselves been, and it passed a motion in this vein on 24 March urging that negotiations with the working men of the enemy be opened at once; that systematic fraternisation be organised at the front and that all schemes of conquest be abandoned. This was followed by an appeal to the German proletariat to "follow our example and shake off the yoke of a semi-autocratic power by refusing any longer to be the instrument of conquest," and then on 22 April by a demand for peace with "no annexations and no indemnities," quickly taken up by the Bolshevik press of Petrograd.

In putting forward these lofty peace proposals, the Soviet had one eye on America whose president, in a note to the Russian government in May 1916, had advanced the premise that no people was to be "forced under a sovereignty under which it did not wish to live"; no territory must change hands except to give its inhabitants a "fair chance of life and liberty"; no indemnities were to be insisted on except those that "constitute payment for manifest wrongs done." America was regarded not only as the citadel of anti-imperialism, but also as a provider of assistance in building the new society, and even the Bolsheviks did not at first abandon this courting of American opinion.

The policy of fraternisation by which the Russians hoped to advance their case proved to be one-sided. Usually German officers successfully prevented the Russian missionaries of "proletarian peace" from reaching the men, and were also able to pass them their own propaganda sheets, "Tovarich" (Comrade) and "Ruskii Vestnik" (Russian Messenger). There thus evolved the bizarre situation in which the Russian troops read articles under the name of Crown Prince Leopold of Bavaria, the German commander, which not only demanded publication of the secret treaties between Russia, Britain and France and the sloughing off of their subjection to the "warmongering imperialists," but also urged them to distrust their officers and the "hirelings of Franco-British finance," the Provisional Government.

Throughout the country there was a feeling of a new era dawning which spread through every sector of society; almost every day there were processions of support for the revolution through the streets of Petrograd and Moscow. Paléologue witnessed demonstrations by Jews, Mohammedans, Buddhists, orphans, deaf-mutes, midwives and even prostitutes; Knox saw children parading under the banner "Down with the Parental Yoke"; prisoners of war struck for better pay and conditions and Moscow thieves passed a resolution undertaking to refrain from stealing for two days! The "Sun of Freedom" cast its rays even upon hospital patients who, in asserting their sovereign rights, refused to accept doctors' orders to take unpalatable medicines, and a number of hospitals were consequently closed. In industry and commerce, celebration of the new dawn took the form of a refusal to return to the tedium of day-to-day work.

Gratified by these manifestations of popularity for the revolution, its makers — men like Rodzianko, Guchkov, Muliukov and Prince Lvov, the new prime minister — were yet alarmed by all the symptoms of anarchy. They had been expecting a more "gentlemanly" revolution, a simple transfer of power, and were particularly depressed by the growing arrogance of the Soviet whose wishes had to be taken into account in every decision made. Even when the tsar and his family were offered asylum in Britain, acceptance had to be postponed because the Soviet disapproved. A small consolation was that Lenin, allowed to return to Russia by the Germans, had been booed on his first appearance before it on 17 April.

In the Allied countries, where there was little knowledge of the true state of affairs, the public's great enthusiasm for the revolution was shared by politicians of the left and centre. Shortly after its occurrence, socialists in the French governments despatched a congratulatory telegram to their Russian counterparts, hailing the achievement of a free government and urging them to "fight on". Another was sent on behalf of the British Labour Party by Arthur Henderson, its representative on the War Cabinet. Despite the fulsome felicitations, the appeals to continue the war embodied in both messages represented the first breath of disillusionment, the first fear that the revolution might, after all, bode ill for the war-making Alliance. Henderson's appeal had been suggested by Sir George Buchanan as early as 15 March, two days after the tsar's abdication.

The Soviet's ceaseless calls for peace turned this fear into real alarm, especially when Kerenski proposed to the Allied ambassadors that their countries should modify their peace aims to conform with Russia's. On 22 April a combined deputation from the French Socialist and British Labour Parties, led by Albert Thomas, arrived in Petrograd "to preach wisdom and patriotism to the Soviet." Since the pacifist British Independent Labour Party declared in a message to the Soviet that the visitors were the paid emissaries of their government and did not represent British labour, they were given a cool reception which neither an official denial nor their appearance in pro-revolutionary demonstrations in Petrograd entirely thawed.

The Provisional Government was clearly failing to restore order, and by April there was every sign of a total breakdown. In Petrograd, the metal industry's output was down 20–40 per cent; in Moscow, 30 per cent. Nearly 130 factories were closed in the capital and over 9,000 workers were idle. Extreme tension between employers and employees expressed itself in physical assaults, even in those factories still working. Factory committees often threatened the complete takeover the business, despite attempts made to curb their power and appeals for a return to work.

These measures had little success, and the committees were becoming deeply infiltrated by Bolsheviks who saw them as "the organs of insurrection." All this was aggravated by a worsening food and supplies situation, since the locomotives of the overworked railway system could not be repaired because the works were closed for lack of labour. In this situation of uncertainty, Britain stopped the supply of war materials until authoritative government had been established, while France confined herself to protesting that failure to prosecute the war was a "betrayal" of her "vital interests." The Provisional Government was furious at what it considered coercion.

In May, Miliukov resigned as Foreign Minister and Guchkov as War Minister; the latter was replaced by Kerenski, former Minister of Justice. Though the rest of the government survived, its tenure was increasingly insecure. Albert Thomas remained in Petrograd after the Franco-British delegation left, as a kind of Allied plenipoteniary and like Buchanan, he saw Kerenski as the country's future leader. In his partiality, Thomas suggested at the British embassy that Britain should abandon her programme of post-war annexations, and even that the restitution of Alsace-Lorraine to France should be made contingent upon a plebiscite.

Chapter 22

The Last March

Notwithstanding the turmoil, the government — including the socialists — never wavered from their determination to continue the war. Public support was such that not even the Bolsheviks, who were wooing the Soviet, dared at that moment to intimate that they would consider a separate peace. An article under the name of Josef Stalin in "Pravda" on 15 March declared: "The war will go on, because the German troops have not followed the example of the Russian army and are still obeying their emperor, who avidly seeks his prey on the battlefield of death . . . . The revolutionary soldiers and officers who have overthrown the yoke of tsarism will not leave their trenches to make room for the German or Austrian soldiers and officers."

Kerenski, for his part, declared that the continuation of the war "was dictated by Russia's interests and followed from the very logic of the revolution." The revolution, he wrote, had been partly a protest against the movement for a separate peace, and it could only consolidate the freedoms won if Russia defeated her enemies.

Words were not action, and the western Allies demanded more than mere declarations of principle. Desertions from the Russian forces were increasing, the position of officers was becoming impossible, and the troops spent more time at political meetings than in soldiering. However, France, Britain and America specifically wanted Russia to mount its May offensive for which preparations had been in train before the tsar's abdication. In fact, the French Grand Quartier and the British HQ had set the date for their own campaigns forward almost a month. On 12 December, General Nivelle became commander-in-chief in place of Joffre, "kicked upstairs" as military adviser to the government. The new commander-in-chief immediately produced a plan which he convinced everyone would bring about the long-promised breakthrough, and on 21 March in a telegram to Alexeiev, now Russian commander-in-chief, he instructed rather than requested him to advance the date of the Russian offensive.

"I would . . . ask you to launch the Russian offensive around the beginning or middle of April", the astonished Alexeiev read. "It is essential that our joint operation be begun simultaneously . . . otherwise, the enemy will be free to utilise his reserves, which are large enough to enable them to halt the offensive at the very outset." The message closed sardonically: "I should add that the situation has never been as favourable as now . . . nearly all available German forces are fighting on our front, and the number is increasing from day to day!" — a statement of whose untruth Nivelle must have been fully aware.

Alexeiev's reply of the following day, pointing out the impossibility of acceding to this request, drew from Nivelle on the 24th the information that the British had already begun offensive operations in the Arras-Soissons area, and the "insistence" that the Russians launch an immediate offensive; since Alexeiev had emphasised the demoralised state of his troops, Nivelle added that "the best solution to the problem would be to resume offensive operations." An enraged Alexeiev answered that because of the political situation and the unsettled state of the troops it would not be possible to launch even sporadic attacks before the early part of May.

When the Anglo-French attacks encountered fierce German opposition, the notes (passed on to Alexeiev by General Janin, who had succeeded the Marquis de Laguiche as head of the French mission) became increasingly harsher in tone, and ultimately resorted to reminding Russia of her enormous debts and the continuing sums she was receiving, and threatening sanctions against her. This threat presented the Provisional Government with a new dilemma, for sanctions would have the effect of isolating a country whose new rulers had been at great plains to drag her into the comity of western nations. It was plain that the action demanded by the Allies could not be postponed much longer, and fresh efforts had to be made to restore the army.

Shortly after his appointment as War Minister, Kerenski made a speech-making tour of the front which earned him the title of "persuader-in-chief". His hypnotic demagoguery varied in its effect on the troops, though they usually clapped and cheered his exhortations to scale new heights of revolutionary heroism and sacrifice.

The tour brought him into close contact with Brusilov, who had his own ideas for restoring the army by building up "shock units" to be used both to impose order and to lead the way in attack. Alexeiev opposed the proposal on the grounds that it meant drawing from the main body of the army precisely those elements on which any attempt at rebuilding must be founded, but Kerenski was so completely persuaded that Brusilov was the man Russia needed, that he not only backed the "shock units" plan but appointed him as commander-in-chief in Alexeiev's stead. The new generalissimo immediately embarked on a patriotism-rousing campaign of his own, boasting of his victories and his "good luck" in an effort to instil confidence. At the same time, the disciplinary units were actually recruited and used to crush some of the more extreme exhibitions of revolutionary zeal.

As a result of these measures, Kerenski deceived himself that by mid-June a new warrior-like spirit was abroad. Never needing more than the slightest evidence to confirm his own opinions, he found this in the Soviet, which passed a resolution "demanding a revolutionary offensive." There was no doubt that the army was tiring of inactivity and now realised, as Stalin's article indicated, that the Germans were not to be recruited to world revolution; many Russian commanders felt that only action could provide the antitoxin to disintegration and indiscipline.

On the other hand, there were equally strong reasons for supposing that the army was far from being in a sacrificial mood. For all the rousing appeals, the troops had a natural antipathy toward dying in battle before the "Sun of Freedom" had reached its zenith, hence thousands decided to absent themselves from the scene of hostilities altogether. Desertions, which from the beginning of the war to the revolution, totalled 195,130 or 6,846 per month, reached 85,921 or 34,270 per month between March and May and this figure was rising.

Of all the motives conspiring to drive men from the battlefield, the strongest was undoubtedly the hope of benefiting from a revolutionary redistribution of the land. On 2 June the Central Land Committee, set up by the Provisional Government, declared that its guiding principle was the "transfer of all land to the working agricultural population." This might seem an imprudent moment to choose for the deliverance of such an unsettling pronouncement, but the government's hand was forced into making de jure what already existed de facto: the peasants in a number of areas, including Kursk, Tula, Tambov, Kazan, Voronezh, the Ukraine and Bielorussia, were in the process of seizing land owned by the big estates, which they traditionally regarded as having been taken from them in the first place. This was being divided up among them under the administration of cantonal committees, and no-one who sprang from the land — as did most of the troops — would want to miss this long-awaited reform.

Nevertheless, preparations for the offensive began in late June. The first scheme involved nothing less than the complete execution of the plans agreed at Chantilly in November 1916 and ratified at Petrograd in January, whereby some 70 Russian divisions would be launched against the length of the enemy line. There were plainly not enough men, and those available were insufficiently reliable for conceptions of such bravura. Finally, it was decided to attack in Galicia for several reasons. The troops most affected by the revolution were those of the North Front, who were not only within easiest access of Petrograd and its hosts of agitators, but had suffered appallingly in the various abortive and ill-conceived offensives against the Germans, such as Narocz. Moreover, they were commanded by men whom they no longer trusted.

South West Front, conversely, was furthest away, had enjoyed a run of victories and still retained relatively good relations with its officers. Also, the Austrians were less formidable opponents, but a startling victory such as the recapture of Lemberg would restore army morale. Kerenski, having in mind the French revolutionary army of 1789, began to talk of another Valmy.

The plan evolved was one whereby the Seventh Army, now under Belkovich, was to strike the main blow along a forty-mile front against Bothmer's Southern Army at Brzezany on 1 July. They would cross the Zlota Lipa and aim to take Lemberg from the south, while the Eleventh Army would simultaneously try to take it from the north.

Among the number of feints and subsidiary attacks, the principal one would be by the Special Army toward the communications centre of Kovel; another would be started in Rumania on 6 July by the Eighth Army now commanded by Kornilov.

Planning was haphazard, and officers felt themselves betrayed. Men who had won the 1916 victories, drawn from classes temperamentally well-disposed to the revolution, found it now disdained them as allies while displaying what they considered a craven readiness to make every concession to the men. For their part, the troops had lost interest in anything but politics, and disliked obeying men they regarded as no better than themselves.

Nevertheless, an enormous weight of material was concentrated along the front, including 800 light, 158 medium and 370 heavy guns with vast reserves of shell. In addition, there were 120 spotter aircraft, many being flown by British and French pilots, challenging German air supremacy for the first time; there was also a British armoured car division.

The one problem was insufficient men, but some 200,000 were ultimately mustered, specially picked from those units least infected with the revolution. There was a strong stiffening of Siberians, and even instructors were sent to the front. Believing that, for the first time, they could exact revenge in kind for 1915, the Russian commanders placed total reliance on supremacy in material; they made no effort to hide their preparations or, as Brusilov had done, to confuse the enemy about their intentions. While the enemy watched, bridges were thrown over rivers, railway lines laid, even ammunition dumps were left uncamouflaged.

Since the liberal-minded Provisional Government objected to censorship on principle, its problems were now increased by having to combat an intensive Bolshevik propaganda campaign in the press and in the Soviet against the offensive. At the front desertions increased and no one could be bothered with such tedious labours as entrenching – in battle, one officer had to take his troops up to the line by advancing on all fours along a shallow ditch under heavy German shell-fire.

Fully aware what was happening in the opposing trenches, Ludendorff telephoned Hoffman a few days before the offensive. Could it be nullified by a counter-action, he asked? Yes, but this would need extra troops. How many? Say four divisions. Ludendorff told him they would be coming – the last troops to move from west to east.

On 30 June, with the observation posts crammed with pressmen, political commissars, "soldiers' delegates," etc., the Russian bombardment began along a thirty-mile front. The enemy consisted of three nations: Germany represented by four divisions; Austria, three divisions; and Turkey, one. The bombardment was clearly destroying the front line, but it was still uncertain how the troops would behave. When the order to advance was given on 1 July, the men of the Seventh Army climbed over their trench parapets and advanced in the old waves, just as before the revolution. They penetrated some miles into the lines, taking prisoners and guns, but then began to find sheer weight of metal was not enough.

As the British had found at Loos, and the French in Champagne, the Germans had developed a new defensive strategy in depth since Gorlice. Bothmer therefore pulled behind new lines. Although these had not been "softened up" by bombardment, the Russians adopted their time-honoured system of hurling men against them; hence the third line was reached, but at the usual appalling cost. This was too much for the troops, who had been promised that this time the guns would do the work for them. When the Germans counter-attacked, whole units retired; officers were killed trying to set an example and the men so far lost the will to fight that they refused to dig in and demanded immediate relief. The reserves then refused to move up, and some detachments at the spearhead of the advance turned round and walked back to their lines. Every effort was made to shame them into going forward, and physical struggles broke out between men, officers and NCOs.

Kerenski, elated by the early successes, behaved as if it had been a magnificent victory. He telegraphed Lvov, the prime minister, asking him to sanction "in the name of the free people, my presentation of red revolutionary standards to the regiments which took part in the Battle of 1 July." In consenting, Lvov wrote: "1 July has shown to the whole world the might of a revolutionary army based on democratic lines and inspired by a fervent belief in the ideals of the revolution." The ex-tsar, who also only knew of the early successes, ordered a special service of thanksgiving at Tsarskoe Selo, where he was now a prisoner.

Amid all this unfounded satisfaction, events in Petrograd were taking a sharp turn against the Provisional Government. For some days there had been casual talk of a Bolshevik coup, but Kerenski, who had returned to the capital after the offensive began on 1 July, left for the front on the 16th for the next phase of the attacks. That morning lorries travelled the barracks calling on the soldiers to join an uprising. Thousands turned out carrying banners and placards with the now familiar slogan: "Bread and Peace"; or calling for "All Power to the Soviets," and "Down with the Offensive".

By the 17th the uprising of the "July Days" was spreading. During the next few days several members of the Provisional Government had to go into hiding, and in the end only the loyalty of the Cossacks and the Preobrazhenski Guards prevented the capital falling to the Bolsheviks.

This was an appalling humiliation for the government, which tried to redress matters by a counter-demonstration organised by the Cadets. As a result of the revolt, arrest-warrants were issued against a number of leading Bolsheviks including Lenin and Trotsky, but Kerenski cancelled these two as their membership of the Soviet supposedly entitled them to the same immunity from arrest as members of the Duma. Both Bolshevik leaders went into hiding.

On 18 July Brusilov had been superseded as commander-in-chief by Kornilov, and despite events in Petrograd, part of the offensive went forward as planned on the day of his appointment, striking in the direction of Halicz and Dolina. The Third Austrian Army, under the Hungarian Tersztyanski, was surprised and overwhelmed. There were advances of up to twenty miles in the centre of a sixty mile front. Large numbers of prisoners were taken, mostly from the disaffected and weary Slav units, including the entire Eighty-first Czech Regiment which surrendered to the Eleventh Army's Sixth Corps and the following day marched through Tarnopol into captivity with flags flying, bands playing and a Cossack escort. It later became part of the Czech Legion fighting on the Russian side.[1]

The Russian advances now threatened the oil wells at Drohobiez, and reserves had to be hurried in against this hardening resistance; the advance faltered, then stopped.

Among the devices employed to buttress military morale had been the formation of a Women's Battalion. The idea came from a peasant girl, Batchkerova, one of those female prodigies history occasionally throws up — the woman who passes herself off as a man successfully enough to penetrate the masculine enclave of the army. She had served through most of the war, and on the thesis that "when the men saw wives and daughters fighting they would be ashamed and would follow," she formed the battalion with War Ministry backing. After a solemn dedication at Kazan Cathedral in Petrograd, their First Detachment went to Kornilov's front and took its place near Tarnopol. In the battle they took 200 prisoners despite heavy casualties, but far from inspiring the nobler instincts of the male units on either side of them, both of these deserted and left them to hold out alone.[2]

It was the same all along the front; faced with strong enemy resistance the men had no stomach for the fight. Even the so-called "Iron Division" refused to dig in, and though Kornilov tried to restore discipline by terrorism and hangings, nothing would move the broken-backed Eighth Army — they simply fled before the assault. Tarnopol fell on 24 July, and the Kaiser and Mackensen entered in triumph. Next day Stanislau was re-entered; on 3 August Czernowitz, which during the struggle had changed hands fifteen times, was finally back in Austrian hands. Everything gained in the Kerenski offensive had been lost and within a fortnight the enemy held all Galicia except a strip near Brody, and all the Bukovina provinces. They took 30,000 prisoners and 200 guns, as well as large quantities of other war material. Further advance was only prevented by a shortage of troops and fierce attacks on the Sereth by a reorganised Rumanian army under French staff.

Once the Russian advance had been halted, the Germans began to concentrate for the counter-offensive. Hoffman summoned Bruchmüller south to organise the artillery bombardment. On 19 July, in pouring rain which turned the Galician clay into slimy mud impeding movement, the infantry began to move forward. Bruchmüller's artillery had already done its work and the attack penetrated ten miles in one day. Then they wheeled southwards, and one after another the Austrian armies joined in rolling back the Russian front.

The Russian imperial army, broken and remade again and again, had broken for the last time. Yet this was not quite the end, even though the greatest optimists in Petrograd were now convinced it was too demoralised ever to fight again. For two years the Germans had been concerned about the bridgehead which the Russians managed to maintain along the lower Dvina, covering Riga. Ludendorff — unlikely to relinquish his cherished plan for a march on Petrograd — now saw a chance to implement it, partly because although Petrograd was well over 300 miles away, such a threat might panic the rattled Russian Provincial Government into suing for peace. He seemed unsure, however, and twice telephoned Hoffmann to ask for the return of the divisions sent from the west. Each time Hoffmann pointed out that without them the offensive would be impossible, and Ludendorff gave in.

The invincible Bruchmüller was moved north once more, and on 1 September opened fire without even registering his guns. After a five-hour bombardment, infantry from Hutier's Eighth Army began to advance across the river on pontoon bridges. Uxküll (several miles downstream from Riga) fell, and a few days later Riga itself. The Russian command, thoroughly confused not only about the action of the enemy but also the behaviour of its own men, could not even try to re-group its forces.

A Siberian brigade broke, and by 21 September Hutier had a seventy-mile gap through which to deploy his armies. The Russians retreated so hastily that only about 9,000 prisoners were taken.

The Provisional Government sought to blame the debâcle on the demoralised state of the Russian army as a result of Bolshevik propaganda. Hence it was forced "to take extraordinary measures for the purpose of restoring order and discipline." These measures included restoration of the death penalty and the establishment of Revolutionary Courts Martial. The accusation that Bolshevik influences had been at work was answered by an enemy declaration that the regiments which fought best were those most affected by Bolshevism.

This was the end. Casualties of the Kerenski offensive totalled 17,339 killed, wounded and missing: not vast by that front's standards but a contribution to the nation's total war losses computed at between 7 and 8 million, i.e. half the total army of 14 million men called up. Desertions, however, increased manifold, and entire units of deserters commandeered trains leaving the front. By November, it was estimated that the army had probably lost 2 million men in this way, amounting, as Golovin points out, to a "spontaneous demobilisation."

Various attempts were made to re-form the army. Knox put forward a six-point plan, including not only the re-introduction of the death penalty, but also the punishment of the July agitators, military censorship of the press, the introduction of a militia in Petrograd, and the disarming of all units refusing to comply with these conditions, which would become labour battalions.

Such theses were largely academic, however. Besides other difficulties, food supplies were no longer reaching the fronts, and many units were reduced to their last week's or even day's supplies of flour, biscuit, fat, meat, fish and canned food. Prokopovich, Minister of Supply, said he could not feed an army of the present size, and in October measures were put in hand for its reduction to 5 million men.

The Russian imperial army, the largest in the world, the great "Russian steamroller", was dying of inanition. Time and again, even in the last battle for which German troops were sent from the Western Front, it had helped its Allies, rarely fighting at a time or place of its own choosing, always — because its resources were believed unfathomable — under pressure to do what others refused.

Yet it had repeatedly come within striking distance of victories which could have changed the whole course of the war. At that time, Austria was desperately seeking peace, notwithstanding its recent Galician victories, a situation for which the Russians (who in prisoners alone had deprived the Austro-Hungarian armies of nearly 2 million men) were largely responsible. The Russian army won a few battles and lost many, but it was never defeated: it was simply broken. Finally, in Lenin's phrase, it voted for peace with its legs. Hardship, enormous casualties, a ruthless and well-equipped enemy, promised victories which always turned into endless retreat, commanders so interested in their own aggrandisement that they became jealous and suspicious of their colleagues — all these things bent it to and fro until it eventually snapped.

It is said that many armies have been goaded into overcoming fear of the enemy by a greater fear of their own officers: what lies ahead becomes less terrible than what awaits them if they fail. The essential flaw in this is that the day may dawn when the enemy actually becomes preferable, and is granted victory without a struggle, which is the position into which the Russian armies were pushed. Enemy occupation, defeat, death itself could hold no greater terrors than those they daily faced.

This factor was ignored not only the tsar, the Russian government and the army commanders, but also by the Allies who continued making demands even when the breaking point was near. Equally, it was forgotten that a man did not turn into a rootless automaton when he became a fighting unit. Prepared to tolerate suffering himself, his pains were infinitely greater when he saw that those he loved at home — whom he was supposed to be defending — were also victims of intolerable hardship.

Broken, and bitter, torn against herself, the only course open to Russia was to seek an independent peace. Paléologue told his government that "in the present phase of the revolution, the Russians cannot make peace or war." Buchanan, in a message jointly composed with Knox, went further: "In my opinion the only safe course left to us is to give Russia back her word and tell her people that . . . we leave it to them to decide whether they will purchase peace on Germany's terms or fight on with the Allies." Lloyd-George supported this view. Not so Italy or France; Clemenceau declaring that if "all the celestial powers asked him to give Russia back her word, he would refuse."

Her Allies, who had asked so much of her, now asked that she pull herself up from the ground and — somehow — fight on.

The final blow came from one who, had fortune decreed otherwise, would have been in an Austrian prisoner of war camp: General Kornilov, whom Kerenski had made commander-in-chief in mid-July.

The new generation of Russian officers, totally disillusioned with the government, felt that to change their own situation the power of the Petrograd garrison and the Soviet would have to be broken. In late August Kornilov found an excuse to do this when there were reports of a new Bolshevik rising, to forestall which he decided to march on Petrograd, take over city and government, and set up a military dictatorship until a Constituent Assembly could be elected. The march began on 22 August. Organisational difficulties were formidable; sympathetic officers were spread out over a number of depots and along the front, hence communication was slow and difficult, and Kerenski heard that something was afoot. He dismissed the commander-in-chief and took over the post himself in addition to his other functions; he was now prime minister and virtual dictator. Furthermore, as they only learned when the march had begun, no Bolshevik coup was planned at that time; therefore the Kornilov group had to find a raison d'être for their action, while the general ignored his dismissal and urged the whole army to rise against the Provisional Government.

Kerenski responded by sending telegrams to all the soldiers' soviets, denouncing Kornilov as a counter-revolutionary rebel. The men telegraphed back begging Kerenski to court-martial him, and all over the country officers were massacred as "Kornilov supporters." Kornilov himself showed every intention of resisting until Alexeiev persuaded him that this would put the whole revolution at risk, whereupon he surrendered to the government in early September.

On 20 October, Count Czernin sent a message to Petrograd that Austria-Hungary was ready to conclude peace. It was decided that representatives from Vienna should attend a Conference on Peace Aims (Kerenski's brain-child) to be held in Paris in early November.

Peace talks with Turkey and Bulgaria were also going on, and it was hoped they would be successfully concluded on 15 November. These were the first hopeful signs from the war which had cost Russia so much, but they came too late for the Provisional Government had been weakened and discredited beyond recovery. On 7 November, Kerenski's Provisional Government was overthrown in a new Bolshevik rising, and he himself only escaped by disguising himself as a sailor.

On 21 November, a radio-message was received by all Russian Army units: "Soldiers, Peace, the great peace, is in your hands, you will not let the counter-revolutionary generals make peace a failure . . . . Let the regiments holding the line immediately select delegates for formal negotiations with the enemy looking to an armistice. The Soviet of People's Commissars authorises you so to do. . . . Soldiers, peace is in your hands."

This was picked up by German radio-monitors at Brest-Litovsk, the Oberost headquarters, and conveyed to Hoffman who was utterly mystified by it and the name of its author, Lev Davidovich Trotsky. When matters became more definite he telephoned Ludendorff: the new Russian government wanted to negotiate peace.

"Is it possible to negotiate with these people?" he was asked. "Yes," he answered, "it is possible. Your Excellency needs troops and this is the easiest way to get them . . ."

Chapter 23

The Last Word

The revolution, now complete, began sweeping away the last traces of the ancien régime, those who had stood out against it as much as those who supported it. In the great purges and accompanying upheavals, many of the principal actors have been lost to history.

Some left the country and survived, such as the Grand-Duke Nicholas Nicholaievich who reached France and died in Antibes in January 1929, when the French nation displayed its "undying gratitude" by according him a funeral with full military honours. Gourko, too, reached the west; Miliukov, Guchkov and Kerenski were reunited in Paris. Mikhail Rodizianko died in poverty in Yugoslavia; his son came to Britain, and made a career as a cavalryman. Sukhomlinov was set free and went to Switzerland where, in due course, he published his memoirs, dedicated to the deposed German Kaiser with whom he always thought (perhaps rightly) Russia should have been in alliance.

Some died. Kornilov and Alexeiev continued to resist the Bolsheviks, and were killed fighting. Ruszki, Radko-Dmitriev and Prince Galitsyn were shot as hostages. Kaledin killed himself when the Cossacks, of whom he was leader, deserted him and went over to the new government. Goremykin was strangled by an angry mob; Nicholas Maklakov, Shcheglovitov, Manuilov, the younger Khvostov and the half-crazy Protopopov were all executed.

Some, like Brusilov and Polivanov, simply went over to the winning side and served Trotski more happily than they have ever been able to serve the tsar. Others, like Kuropatkin, who eked out the remaining days of his life as clerk in his native village, just survived.

In the meantime, after lengthy haggling the Bolsheviks armistice became the Peace of Brest-Litovsk, one of the most punitive ever inflicted upon a fallen nation. Thus Russia was out of the war; the Bolsheviks had brought peace, but most of the bread went to the Germans and Austrians.

The ironies were not over, however. The Germans had permitted Lenin's return because they believed that by destroying the Provisional Government and its loyalty to the Alliance, he would make peace in the east possible and so release their own divisions for the west. So harsh were the terms they exacted, and so distrustful were they of the Russian government in consequence, that they dared not risk any weakening of the front thereafter. In peace, as in war, the Russians had made their contribution.

Nor was this quite all. Under the terms of the peace, prisoners of war from both sides were repatriated   but many of those who returned to Germany were found to be so imbued with the ideology of revolution that they had to be separated from their comrades. This "quarantine" was insufficient to prevent their ideas infecting the navy at Kiel, whose mutiny was the first signal of disintegration in the German forces. In the end it was fear that what had happened in Russia might be repeated in Germany. This, as much as the Allies' mixed successes on the war front, persuaded Ludendorff that the time had come to ask for peace. That, too, was the Bolshevik contribution to the "imperialists'" war.

The enormous territorial concessions which Lenin had been forced to make left him with an Achilles heel exposed, hence he was as susceptible to attacks from his enemies within the party as from those outside it. In November 1918 his security was restored. Under the terms of the armistice with Germany, Russia's annexed provinces were returned, and the capitalist nations – France, Britain, the United States – had made their contribution to the future of Bolshevism.

Ward Rutherford
Brighton, 1975

Notes

CHAPTER 1

1   Since the sale of vodka was a government monopoly, this ban deprived
     Russia of one of their principal sources of revenue. The annual loss to the
     exchequer was estimated at £68 million.

CHAPTER 2

1   The incident was finally closed when Russia agreed to pay compensation
     to the families of those who lost their lives in the action. It was later
     alleged that the incident had been engineered by Germany.

CHAPTER 3

1   This gave a strength of one cavalry division to three of infantry,
     compared with a ratio of one to eight in the German army. Cavalry, it
     was claimed, were particularly suited to the broad Russian plains.
2   There were 360,000 Cossacks, regarded as the cream of the Russian
     army, drawn from the eleven so-called "Cossack regions": Don, Kuban,
     Terek, Astrakhan, Ural, Orenburg, Siberia, Semirechnie, Trans-Baikal,
     Amur and Asuri. They came under special regulations for national service
     and, unlike the rest of the army, were called up at 18.
3   In his efforts to put the Russian army on an equal footing with those of
     other European nations, Miliutin had turned to the fountainhead of all
     military wisdom, Prussia, which had just defeated the French. Large
     numbers of German instructors arrived, but the experiment was short-
     lived because, it was said, of the "incompatibility" of Russian and
     Prussian temperaments. Having taught their pupils to goose-step (a skill
     they retain), they quickly (and to the delight of the Russians) left their
     parade grounds for good.
4   It was claimed in 1914 that 50 per cent of reservists were literate. Knox
     regarded this as a gross exaggeration. Golovine put the figure for literacy
     at about 20 per cent.
5   When a unit broke at the Battle of Krasnik in August 1914, it was driven
     back into the line by Cossacks (often employed as military policemen),
     wielding nagaikas or whips, and Knox witnessed the flogging of a
     shrieking man accused of pillaging.
6   Generals Ivanov (commander of the West Front), Kornilov (commander
     of the Petrograd garrison and, briefly, commander-in-chief) and Alexeiev
     (chief-of-staff to the tsar) had all risen from humble origins, and Kornilov
     was the son of a peasant-farmer.

7   Knox recalls a case of two officers who shared a single camp bed at the front because one of them was too lazy to fetch his own from the station.
8   Lloyd George, vol I, p. 426: "We are . . . justified in demanding candour from Russia. Germany knows all about the Russian forces, their numbers, their dispositions and equipment. All we want is that our great ally should supply us with information which her enemies already possess."
9   This plan was revived and came near to being applied in the last days of July 1914 when the tsar wanted to put pressure on Austria without antagonising Germany.
10   The rouble was worth approximately 11p. or 26.4 cents at that time.
11   In 1904, the War Minister, Kuropatkin, had been appointed commander-in-chief of Russian forces in the Far East in the war against Japan.

CHAPTER 4

1   He told an Austrian officer: "I hate the Slavs. I know it is a sin to do so. We ought not to hate anyone. But I can't help hating them."

CHAPTER 5

1   The tsar had told Nekliudov, Russian ambassador in Bulgaria in 1911: "It is out of the question for us to face a war for five or six years — in fact until 1917 — although if the most vital interests and honour of Russia were at stake we might, if it were necessary, accept a challenge in 1915." All planning and preparation by the Russian War Ministry and General Staff was based on the supposition of no war until 1917.
2   Even the questioning of prisoners was deputed to junior officers untrained in interrogation techniques. Knox was once present when questioning was carried out during a game of bridge, whichever officer was "dummy" slipping out of the room to put a few questions before returning to the game. Officer prisoners were not interrogated, it being maintained that this would have been asking them to impugn their soldierly honour. In contrast, the Germans knew every Russian move, largely through the wide and accurate spy-network built up among the alienated Jewish population of Poland and elsewhere.

CHAPTER 6

1   This habit of sending out secret material uncoded has been much discussed. One explanation is sheer carelessness, but Cyril Falls suggests that higher ranks considered lower ones so stupid as either to be unable to decode messages, or to be so slow that there would be no time to act upon them. Several factors probably contributed: the size of the army, the brevity of training, the difficulties in getting code books printed and distributed. Russia's sole consideration at that time was to get men into the ranks and fighting.

CHAPTER 8

1   No relation to Manfred Freiherr von Richthofen, the German air ace.
2   It was already too late for such hopes. The stipulation of the Franco-Russian Treaty of 1892 that neither side should enter into a separate peace had been endorsed by a similar undertaking in the Pact of London of 4 September 1914, signed by all three Entente partners.
3   The British naval presence amounted to five submarines — though their effect was considerable. The E1 and E9 arrived in October 1914 and the E8, E13 and E19 followed early in 1915.
4   They had, as Hindenburg acknowledges: "More troops came to us from the West, but they were anything but fresh . . . Some of them had come from an equally hard, perhaps harder struggle — the Battle of Ypres — than we had just fought."
5   On the Eighth Army's front where men were fighting in mountain snowdrifts, in places up to their knees, the army commander had to send purchasing commissions into the nearest towns to find warm clothes.
6   The other two were the abolition of the neutral buffer states on Germany's frontiers and the termination of Britain's "intolerable hegemony" in the international scene.

CHAPTER 9

1   The Foreign Office version was that the king had said, "Oh, Constantinople is of course a town which must in the future become Russian"; that this meant at some time in an indeterminate future; and that a lunchtime remark in no way represented a promise which George V, as a constitutional monarch, had no right to give over the heads of his own government.
2   The urge was short-lived; as so often with things Turkish, months later the batteries were still in such a state of disrepair they were unusable.
3   According to Nogales, the Ottoman Army had no part in the massacres; disapproved of them and would have forcibly prevented them had this been possible.

CHAPTER 10

1   By his action, Falkenhayn merely demonstrated his own jealousy, and received a serious rebuff, which led to greater reversals.
2   Gas was first used at Neuve Chapelle in October 1914. This was such a complete fiasco that the defenders never knew of it, and its employment was not revealed until after the war.
3   It was true that in the north they had been forced from an offensive to defensive posture, but this took an active form. On 17 and 20 March, a Russian reserve division, divided into two task-forces, moved on the town of Memel (Klaypeda) on the Baltic coast and Tilsit (Sovetsk) on the Niemen. Memel gave in after a brief struggle, though it was recaptured in a speedy and vigorous counter-attack by the Germans, whose forces included battlecruisers of the Baltic Fleet from Danzig sent to bombard the town. Two days later the situation round Tilsit was also restored, and the Russians were back in their pre-attack positions.

CHAPTER 11

1   Figures issued in April 1915 showed that, in killed and prisoners alone, the Russian armies had then lost 1,900,000 men. Added to this were an estimated 75 per cent of the total wounded who would never return to the fighting line. Because of the poor medical services the Russian recovery rate was lower than that in the British or French armies. This compares with total French and British casualties (including wounded) of 1,491,870 (British 145,870; French (officers excluded) 1,346,000).

2   The correspondent was Pares who was to have visted the line between Gorlice and Tarnow.

CHAPTER 12

1   There were twenty-two infantry divisions in the Austro-German armies assigned to the offensive compared with fourteen Russian. In cavalry divisions, however, the Russians had a 5:1 superiority. Unfortunately, the defensive role of cavalry in the type of warfare now being waged was small, while for the attacker it was a means of pursuing a retreating foe. This is not to say that the Russians, particularly the Cossacks, did not develop highly sophisticated defensive tactics involving the use of cavalry as mounted infantry. The Cossack ponies were, for example, trained to lie down and provide cover for their riders who fired from behind them. Employed in this way they were often able to provide rearguards while the infantry lines were re-formed behind them and the enemy successfully held. They had also evolved a number of combat techniques which speak highly of the rapport between horse and rider. A typical ploy was one in which some of the troopers appeared to be fleeing the field, leaving behind their dead. An over-enthusiastically pursuing enemy would find himself caught up in a melée of sabre-sweeping Cossacks as the "dead" rose up behind them.

2   The forerunner of the "creeping barrage".

CHAPTER 13

1   The Zemstvos founded by Alexander II and their urban equivalents — the Municipal Dumas — were responsible for local government, education, medical services, etc., and had done much extremely valuable work in developing Russia.

2   Pre-war Russia exported 400—600 million puds of cereal of a total annual production of 1,200 million puds. In the last year of the war the government had to purchase 300 million puds for the army alone. By 1916 the army was consuming 1,000 million puds. (NB: Pud = 35 lb)

3   Daughter of the British ambassador, who frequently met the royal couple.

CHAPTER 14

1   Brusilov gives several examples of the offensive puerilities of tsarist

anti-semitism which, for example, prohibited Jews from earning medals for bravery — even where, in one case, a Jew converted to Orthodoxy was concerned.

2 Among works he mentions in his letters to his wife are: William Le Queux, "Room of Secrets"; Marchmont, "Millionaire Girl" Florence Barclay, "The Rosary".

CHAPTER 15

1 This decision was later reversed by the tsar personally, who promised a contingent would be sent by way of Archangel; this promise was kept. (See p. 224 "The Coming of the Storm").

CHAPTER 16

1 When he heard of this, Kitchener — appointed by the grand-duke as his purchasing agent — tried to make the British Minister of Munitions reverse his promise. The Russians, says Knox, regarded Lloyd-George as a better friend than Kitchener in consequence.

2 The plan came to nothing, though Bostrom bought 2,000 horses. When the spring came only a small quantity of supplies had been hauled to the railhead. Since the sledges operated in relays, freight was desposited all along the route where it was prey to saboteurs — believed to be German-backed — who blew up the munitions.

CHAPTER 18

1 Ivanov had been appointed military adviser to the tsar.

2 It is important, however, to note that the troops moved from west to east were actually replaced by new formations raised in the German interior, so that by October 1916, there were actually 11½ more German divisions in France than in January (127½ instead of 115½). But these were untried soldiers as compared with the veterans sent east, indicating that Falkenhayn regarded the crisis here as the more urgent.

CHAPTER 19

1 This could not alter the basic fact of growing antipathy to the war. The government had proposed to call up men over 43, but decided against it for fear of revolt. There was also strong reluctance to go to the front among depot troops, and in the countryside men hid to avoid the draft.

2 On 16 September, a Supreme War Council vested the entire effort in this theatre in the Kaiser, whose power was delegated through Hindenburg.

CHAPTER 20

1 It was characteristic that the Russian ambassador conspicuously ignored

his compatriots' visit, though they were welcomed by influential and well-known people in all walks of English life, and George V put his personal train at their disposal for travelling the country.

2   Before the Provisional Government commission in 1917, Prince Galitsyn was asked how he came to be appointed prime minister? "I have never succeeded in finding the answer to that question," he answered with laudable candour. The commission president went on: "You are a stranger to politics?" "An absolute stranger."

3   Informal negotiations of one sort or another, which recognised Russian interest in Constantinople but conspicuously omitted Italy, where the military situation was more favourable to Austria, continued for months. When Italy's interests were brought into the discussions, France's old suspicion that an ally once satisfied in his war aims would abandon the contest, asserted itself, and in October, having kept the Austrians waiting six months for a reply, France terminated them. Lloyd-George is impelled to comment: "These considerations appear to have outweighed the immense military advantages to be secured by eliminating Austria from the conflict", reiterating in virtually the same words a view expressed by Paléologue about his own government 2½ years earlier.

4   According to Count Czernin, the Austrian Foreign Minister, the Russians had at this time approached his country through a neutral with an offer of peace "on favourable terms." It was assumed that the Dual Monarchy would be allowed to keep Hungary and Bohemia. Although Austria was prepared to consider these representations seriously, they were never developed because of "events in Russia."

CHAPTER 22

1   It was the Czech Legion, seeking to return home after the Bolshevik takeover, which threatened Ekaterinburg where the royal family were held prisoner in July 1918, panicking their Cheka (secret police) guard into murdering them lest they were freed.

2   It is less for this baptism of fire than for the fact that they were guarding the Winter Palace at the time of the Bolshevik takeover in November that history remembers the Women's Battalion.

Sources

Of the large number of books about the First World War, Russia and the personalities involved in the War which came my way during the writing of this work, some inevitably played a more predominant role than others. For convenience these are given in a shortened form in the following pages. Abbreviations and full titles are as follows:

Abbreviation	Full Title
Tsaritsa	Alexandra, Empress of Russia. "Letters of the Tsaritsa to the Tsar." Duckworth, London, 1925.
Brusilov	Brusilov, General A. A. "A Soldier's Notebook." Tr., London, Macmillan 1930.
Buchanan	Buchanan, Sir George. "My Mission to Russia." Cassell, London, 1923.
Dissolution	Buchanan, Meriel. "The Dissolution of an Empire." Murray, London 1932.
Churchill	Churchill, W. S. "The World Crisis." Mentor Books, London, 1968.
Interrogatoires	"Chute du Régime Tsariste, La, Interrogatoires des Ministres, Conseillers, Generaux, Hauts Fonctionnaires de la Cour Imperiale Russe par la Commission Extraordinaire du Gouvernment Provisoire de 1917." Payot, Paris, 1927.
Danilov	Danilov, General Yuri. "La Russie dans la Guerre Mondiale." Payot, Paris, 1917.
Falkenhayn	Falkenhayn, Erich von. "General Headquarters 1914–16 and its Critical Decisions." Hutchinson, London, 1919.
Golovin	Golovin Lt.-General N. N. "The Russian Army in the World War." University of Yale Press, New Haven, 1931.
Gourko	Gourko, General Vassili. "Memories and Impressions of War and Revolution in Russia." Hutchinson, London, 1921.
Hindenburg	Hindenburg, Marshal Paul von. "Out of My Life." Cassell, London, 1920.
Opportunities	Hoffman, General Max. "The War of Lost Opportunities." Tr., International, New York, 1925.
Hoffman	Hoffman, General Max. "War Diaries." Tr., Secker, London, 1929.
Memoirs	Kerenski, A. F. "The Kerenski Memoirs." Cassell, London, 1966.
Catastrophe	Kerenski, A. F. "The Catastrophe." D. Appleton, New York, 1927.
Knox	Knox, Maj.-General Sir Alfred. "With the Russian Army 1914–17." Hutchinson, London, 1921.
Liddell-Hart	Liddell-Hart, Sir Basil. "History of the First World War." Cassell, London, 1934, with revisions.
Lloyd-George	Lloyd-George, David. "War Memoirs." Ivor Nicholson and Watson, London, 1933.
Ludendorf	Ludendorf, Erich. "My War Memoirs." Tr., Harper, New York, 1919.
Tsar	Nicholas II, Emperor of Russia. "Letters of the Tsar to the Tsaritsa, 1914–17." John Lane, London; Dodd, Mead, New York, 1929.
Letzter Krieg	"Osterreich-Ungarns Letzter Krieg, 1914–18." Verlag Militärwissenschaftlichen, Mitteilungen, Vienna, 1931.
Paléologue	Paléologue, Maurice. "An Ambassador's Memoirs." Hutchinson,

London, 1933.

Pares   Pares, Professor Sir Bernard. "The Fall of the Russian Monarchy." Jonathan Cape, London, 1939.

Poincaré   Poincaré, Raymond. "Memoirs." Heinemann, London, 1928.

Rodzianko   Rodzianko, Mikhail V. "The Reign of Rasputin." A. M. Philpot, London, 1927.

Tăslăuanu   Tăslăuanu, Octavian C. "With the Austrian Army in Galicia." Streffington, London, 1919.

Woodward   Woodward, David. "The Russians at Sea." William Kimber, London, 1965.

It is perhaps proper to comment on the accounts of battles and campaigns. The actions were fluid and extremely complex, covering huge land areas and encompassing vast armies. Each one would make a book and some have. It seemed preferable therefore to give balanced summaries, notwithstanding the inherent risks in this kind of précis rather than to try for a "blow by blow" description or the inclusion of a great deal of anecdotal material, fascinating and seductive as this often was. This has meant telescoping information derived from a large number of sources, and for this reason I finally had to abandon (though reluctantly) any attempt to provide detailed source references. The accounts represent the synthesis of the available and mutually corroborative material and sources are given in regard to battles only where they represent the sole statement of a single person or where some personal statement throws a light on the situation as whole.

CHAPTER 1: WAR FEVER IN ST PETERSBURG

Page

1   Poincaré's arrival in St Petersburg: "Memoirs", 120.

1   The smell of burning pinewood from forest fires: "Dissolution", 77.

1–4   Poincare's visit to St Petersburg: Paléologue & Poincaré.

3   French ships at the opening of the Kiel Canal: Poincaré, 1914, 139.

3   The president's private talks with the tsar and the subjects discussed: Poincaré, 1914, 168, and Paléologue, I, 15–16.

4   The Lena goldfields inquiry: "Memoirs", 80–83.

4–5   Count Pourtalés tears, described by Sazonov, Sergei, "Fateful Years," Jonathan Cape, London, 1928, 213, also at secondhand and with some embellishments by Paléologue.

5   The crowds kneeling before the Winter Palace: Buchanan, I, 212–213; Paléologue, I, 56; "The Times History of the Great War", 1915, 222.

5   Pourtalés art collection: Buchanan, I, 214. Grand-Duke Nicholas told Knox that Gräfin Pourtalés had warned a Russian friend that the Hermitage and Winter Palace were to be blown up by revolutionaries if Russia declared war. The grand-duke told this story as an example of German credulity: Knox, I, 44.

5   "Now all Russia is involved": Rodzianko, 109.

5   The Duma submitted to "incompetent and criminal tsarist government": "Catastrophe," 89.

6   The tsar's oath: Buchanan, I, 211.

6   The destruction of the German embassy: Paléologue, I, 58.

6   German court titles russified: ibid, III, 122.

6   "The bad days of 1905 seemed to have gone from the memory of all": ibid, I, 75.

6   Ikon-carrying procession: ibid, 57.

6   Poincaré's comment on the renaming of St Petersburg: Poincaré, 1914, 134.

6   German subjects in Russia: Paléologue, I, 75.

Page

7   The police believed Germans supplied funds distributed to Russian agitators: Paléologue, I, 77. The probable truth is that these funds did originate in Germany, but from Russian exiles living there, not from official sources.

7   The tsar's hesitation about mobilisation: "Just think of the responsibility you are asking me to assume! Remember it's a question of sending thousands and thousands of men to their deaths". His face was said to have been "deathly pale": Paléologue I, 45. The tsar accepted the French and German thesis that "mobilisation means war".

7   The army — "unending lines of khaki men": "Dissolution", 96.

8   Girls flocked to work in the hospitals: ibid.

8   "As if we were going to the Crusades": Rodzianko, Col. Pavel, "Tattered Banners", Seeley Service London, 147.

8   Appointment of the grand-duke, text of ukase: "The Times Documentary History of the War", V, Military, Part 1, London (1918), 270.

8   The tsar at the Kremlin and Buchanan's doubts: Buchanan, I, 215.

8   "Every war has brought the Russian people a deep domestic crisis": Paléologue, I, 77.

8   The visit to the Kremlin is reported, at secondhand, by Poincaré, 1914, 20.

8   The eager young officers who thought fighting Austrians inferior to fighting Germans: quoted, inter alia, by Knox.

8   Loss of revenue to the Russian exchequer by prohibition on vodka: "The Times History of the Great War", 1915, 222.

8   Wives accompanying the reservists: "Dissolution", 96.

8–9   "Wives and mothers with children accompanied the reservists from point to point, deferring the hour of parting, and one saw cruel scenes": Knox, I, 39.

8–9   The young mother with her baby running beside her husband: Paléologue, I, 64.

9   Witte's visit to Paléologue: Paléologue, I, 122.

9   Witte interviewed by "Novoie Vremlya": Buchanan, I, 236.

CHAPTER 2: THE VEIL OF SUSPICION

11   "The Russian alliance": Poincaré, 1912, 146.

12   Russia's "system of interdependent tiers": Hargave, Sidney, "First Blood", Bodley Head, London, 1964, 17 et seq.

12   Russia had undergone "no revolution, political, religious or industrial": Paléologue, I, 156. Russia was, he goes on, "exactly where Europe would have been if we had had no Renaissance, no Reformation, and no French Revolution" — he overlooked the industrial revolution, to modern minds the most important of all.

12   Kerenski, among others, was forcibly struck by the tsar's distaste for power to which he refers several times in his "Memoirs".

13   Tolstoy's attack on the Franco-Russian Treaty: "Memoirs", 14.

13   Nicholas I on "constitutional monarchy": Paléologue, II, 265.

14   Witte persuaded the tsar of the impossibility of implementing the Björkö Fiord Treaty with Germany: Paléologue, I, 122.

14   Arguments for Russo-German cooperation: Golder, F. A., "Documents on Russian History, 1914–17", New York, 3–24.

14   Two centuries of relations with Britain, Sazonov, op. cit., 22.

14   Liberal detestation of German militarism: Lloyd-George, I, 5.

14   Tsarist regime as "unpopular as Bolshevism today": ibid, 66–67.

14   The kaiser a "popular figure": "The Times", 21 May 1910.

14   American dislike for the tsarist regime: "Britain and France never quite realised the handicap to their propaganda in neutral countries which was

Page

involved in their alliance with the tsarist regime. America shuddered at the idea of any close association with the government of Russia ... and that went far to neutralise the horror felt at the Belgian tragedy": Lloyd-George, II, 659—660.

15   The Bourtsev affair: Buchanan, 1, 238; Paléologue, I, 156 and 275—281; Pares, 217—218.

16   Isvolski's "amour propre": Poincaré, 1912. References to the Russian Foreign Minister, subsequently ambassador in Paris, are frequent. He was a particular thorn in the French flesh politic. Corroborative comments on his personality are to be found in Sazonov, who was his assistant for a time.

16   Goremykin's ridicule of the Duma: "Memoirs", 69.

17   Isvolski on French obligations: Poincaré, 1914.

17   Tsar and his pro-German faction: ibid.

17   The war as a "contest of autocracies": Lloyd-George, I, 66—67.

17   George V thought a Naval Convention with Russia would be a "capital thing": Poincaré, 1914.

17   Prince Louis of Battenberg to visit St Petersburg: Sazonov, op. cit., 131, also mentioned in passing by Churchill.

18   "Strips of colonial territory": Poincaré, 1912.

18   French alarmed by British tepidity: ibid, 1914, 242.

18—19   Curragh Camp mutiny: Churchill, I, 109; Lloyd-George, I, 54.

19   Russians besiege British Embassy: Buchanan, I, 212—213.

CHAPTER 3: "... FOR FAITH, TSAR AND COUNTRY"

Most of the information and statistics on the Russian armies comes from Golovin or Knox.

20   The "Russian steamroller", the origin of the term is untraceable. It occurs frequently in contemporary British accounts of the Russian army. The French called it "le Moulin à rouleau", the rolling mill.

20   "Asiatic hordes": the phrase appears habitually in most German and Austrian writers. Hindenburg, Falkenhayn, Hoffman and Conrad all use it or a parallel term.

20   Cossack organisation: Golovin and Knox.

21   The mystical troika: Golovin, 206.

21   Guchkov as leader of "The Young Turks": "Catastrophe", 176.

21—22   Russia had one-twelfth of the railway mileage of Germany: Gourko, 4.

22   French concern at "differences in railway gauge": Poincaré, I, 211—226.

22   Only 679 motor vehicles in the whole army: Ironside, Major General Sir Edmund, "Tannenberg", Blackwood, Edinburgh, 1925, 21.

22   "Russia came into the war unprepared": "Catastrophe".

22   Averages struck for all equipment needs: Gourko, 99.

21—22   Equipment statistics: Golovin unless otherwise stated.

23   Air force "beneath criticism": Brusilov, 17.

23   Orders supposed to have been placed in France never despatched: Rodzianko, 207.

23   Shuvaiev, when War Minister, banned discussion of the air force as criticism would be a reflection on the royal house: ibid, 206.

24   Russian "a natural warrior": "Times History of the Great War", Article on the Russian Army, 1914.

24   Standards of literacy: Golovin, 23; Knox, I, 13.

24   Nagaika-flailing cossacks at the Battle of Krasnik: Knox, I, 76.

24   "Cheery" and "wonderfully patient": Lloyd-George, III, 1581, citing a report to British War Council by General Sir Henry Wilson, CIGS, after visit to Russia.

Page
24   Scarcity of NCOs: Golovin.
24   Training squads organised behind the lines: Brusilov, 93.
24   Officer corps, 3,000 below establishment: Golovin, 29.
24   Life in the Russian cadet academies: Troyat, Henri, "Daily Life in Russia Under the Last Tsar", George Allen and Unwin, London, 1961, Chapter VIII, 108–126.
24   Two officers sharing a camp-bed: Knox, II, 452.
24   Plehve is described by Knox and the tsar in letters to the tsarina.
25   Buying Russian General Staff Plans: "Opportunities".
25   Miassoiedev's German decorations: Knox, I, 22; Gourko, 552–553; Pares, Professor Sir Bernard, "A History of Russia", 472–477.
25   Guchkov's duel with Miassoiedev: Paléologue, II, 300.
26   Miassoiedev organised surveillance of the General Staff: Kokovtsev, Count V. N., "Out of My Past", Stanford University Press, California, 1935, 310.
26   Sukhomlinov ready to order mobilisation before going on holiday: ibid, 345–348.
26   Sukhomlinov before Duma Armed Services Commission: "Memoirs", 125, Rodzianko corroborates.
26   It was impossible to obtain accurate or truthful information from him: both Lloyd-George and Poincaré report this.
26   The tsar's "I trust him entirely": ibid, 151.
26   Did not believe there had been any developments in warfare since 1877. He had not read a military manual for twenty-five years: Knox, I, 278.
27   "The bullet is a fool": "Times History of the Great War", article on Russian Army.
27   The grand-duke was "quite absorbed in his profession": Brusilov, 24–27.
27   "The noble champion of truth": Golovin, 235.
27   "Knew the needs of the rank and file": Brusilov, 28.
28   Anastasia introduced Rasputin into royal family: Nicholas II, "Journal Intime", tr., Payot, Paris, 1925.
28   The "Montengrin Nightingales": Paléologue I, 22–23; Poincaré re-echoes the phrase which was apparently a common one at court.
28   The grand-duke wanted Alexeiev as chief-of-staff, "but the tsar said to him: 'I ask you and even order you to keep the present chief-of-staff [Yanushkevich] and the quarter-master general [Danilov]'.": Pares, 193.
28–29   Yanushkevich and Danilov are described variously by Knox, Golovin and Brusilov. In general, Knox alone has anything to say in their favour (I, 42). For example, Danilov, who to Knox is "a hard worker with a good brain", is to Brusilov "narrow-minded and stubborn" (p. 29).
29   The grand-dukes tears: Polivanov, quoted by Florinski, II, 1320.
30   Plans "A" and "G": Ironside, op. cit., 31–36.
30   Plans for fortresses "modified" by Sukhomlinov: Pares, 196.
30   Plans "A" and "G" represented the whole range of Russian strategic thinking: Brusilov, 98.

CHAPTER 4: MOVEMENTS ON THE BATTLEFIELD

Information on Poland is drawn mainly from Halecki, O., "The History of Poland", Dent, London, 1942 and Benes, V. and Pound, N. G. J., "Poland", Benn, London, 1970.

31   Austria the traditional enemy: Ironside, op. cit., 69–70.
31   Peasant life in Galicia: Tăslăuanu, 90.
32   The grand-duke's proclamation to the Poles: "The Times Documentary History of the War", I, Military, Part 1, London, 1918.
32   Comment on the phrase "under the sceptre of the tsar": Poincaré, 1914, 49.

Page

33   Deputation to Isvolski: Poincaré, 1914, 63.

33   Poles who served in Sokoly legions liable to death penalty: "The Times Documentary History of the War", I, Military, Part 1, London, 1918.

33   Russia expected an early Austrian invasion: Knox, I, 39.

33   Plan "A" activated at outbreak of war: Ironside, 69; Danilov, 147.

34   For details of Russian conversion to "L'offensive a outrance", I am indebted to Tuchman, Barbara, "The Guns of August", Constable, London, 1926, 49 et seq.

34   The text of the military convention annexed to the Franco-Russian Treaty is given by Joffre, General Josephe, "The Memoirs of Marshal Joffre", Bles, London, 1952. It was signed by General Obruchev on the Russian side and General Boisdeffre on the French. It had seven clauses, as follows: 1, if France was attacked by Germany or by Italy supported by Germany, Russia would employ all her available forces to attack Germany. France would reciprocate in the reverse instance; 2, if the Triple Alliance forces mobilised, Russia and France would mobilise simultaneously; 3, the French were to put into the field an army of 1,300,000 men; the Russians one of 700–800,000 men; 4, constant contact to be maintained between forces; 5, neither side to conclude a separate peace; 6, the convention was to run concurrently with the Triple Alliance; 7, all clauses to be kept rigorously secret.

34   An attack on Germans never formed any part of Russian general staff plans: Sazonov, op. cit., 241. This is borne out by Danilov, 147, who says that Plan "A" and not Plan "G" was activated at the beginning of the war, and by Ironside, 69.

35   The average distance a Russian recruit had to travel to his depot was 700 miles, compared with 130–200 in Germany. Germany had 10.6 Km of rail per 100 sq Km, beside Russia's 1 Km per 100 sq Km: Golovin, 34.

35   Sazonov, warns Poincaré that it would be difficult to combine mobilisation and harvesting: Poincaré, 1913–14, 168.

36   French asking "Russia to commit suicide": Golovin, 212.

36   The French army "would have to face the formidable onslaught of 25 German corps": Paléologue, I, 61.

36   Paléologue with the grand-duke: Paléologue, I, 59–62.

37   Russian general staff order: Ironside, op. cit., 39 et seq.

37   Moltke and Conrad's Carlsbad meeting, "Ehe ich ging, fragte ich nochmals General von Moltke wie lang es im gemeinsamen Krieg gegen Russland and Frankreich seiner Ansicht": Conrad von Hötzendorf, Franz, "Aus Meiner Dienstzeit", Ricola, Vienna, 1922, 673.

38   Austrian army "inherently unfitted" for the feats Conrad was to attempt, Liddell-Hart, 107.

39   The French considered Austria "negligible": Pares, 196. Pares goes on to comment: "No doubt [it was] for France, whom Austria could not attack, but by no means so for Russia".

40   The French Alsace-Lorraine attacks: Ironside, op. cit., 30.

40   The French general staff's urgings to Russia: Poincaré, 1914, 55.

40   French blame Russia. In 1913, Joffre had visited that country and pointed out the need for fast mobilisation. "The grand-duke assured me my requirement would be satisfied": Joffre, op. cit., 58–59.

40   Baranochi and Stavka, described by Knox, I, 46 and Paléologue, I, 304–305.

41   The grand-duke to Joffre: "With full confidence in victory. . .": Joffre, op. cit., 140.

41   "Chivalrous improvisation": Lloyd-George, I, 359.

41   "Eleventh hour preparations" against East Prussia: Ironside, op. cit., 57–58 and 69–70.

65   opposed to the mad plunge into war with the Serbian slavs".

65   German attempts to succour their Austrian allies described in detail by Hoffman, Hindenburg, Ludendorf, Falkenhayn, "Weltkrieg".

CHAPTER 7: FORWARD – TO BERLIN

66   "The surest way to beat Austria": Poincaré, 1914, 159.

66   "We lost 110,000 men at Soldau": the remark is reported by both Paléologue and Poincaré. But Poincaré says: "Paléologue should have answered, 'We would have made the same sacrifice etc. . .'" (Poincaré, 1914, 163). This makes it sound as if the riposte given by the ambassador in his diary was actually a respond d'escalier.

66   British proposal for sending "three corps to west, via Archangel": Poincaré, 1914, 123; also Danilov, 233.

66   "With Austria hors de combat. . .": Poincaré, 1914, 177.

67   An advance on a wide front in the direction of Pozen and Breslau, Sukhomlinov to Paléologue; Poincaré, 1914, 163; Danilov, op cit., 259.

67   The Russians short of everything from "clothing to great guns": "The Times History of the Great War", 1915, 202.

67   Troops marched barefoot: Golovin, 178.

67   Gathering up the rifles: Agourtine, Leon, "Le General Sukhomlinov", Clichy, Paris, 1951, 34.

67–68   The grand-duke's appeal to tsar: Golovin, 144.

68   "No cause for alarm" over artillery: Buchanan, I, 219.

68   Troops improvised weapons from empty tins, shell-cases, gas-pipes, etc: Gourko, 90.

68   Ivanov reports shell stocks exhausted; figures for output of Russian munitions factories: Knox, I, 220.

68   Balloon observation impossible because of German air superiority: Knox, I, 464.

68   One reason why Russians suffered unduly in artillery bombardments was because their trenching was not good: Knox, I, 233. Brusilov reports similarly (pp. 139–145). He often found his orders to entrench totally ignored. When he went to inspect positions he found some of the trenches which had been dug were entirely filled with snow. Usually there were no communication trenches.

68   Failure of bread supplies: Knox, I, 131.

68   "The position of the wounded is pitiable in the extreme": Brusilov, 33.

68   No ambulances: Rodzianko, 133.

68   Doctors had no idea of their duties: Brusilov, 51.

69   Wounded left out in the open: Rodzianko, 119.

69   Shortage of railways and rolling stock: Knox, I, 186–187.

69   The grand-duke asks about French intentions: Poincaré, 1914, 177.

69   On 15 September Paléologue made "extravagant demands to Sazonov" for whom he drew up the formula: "As soon as the Austro-Hungarian armies in East Galicia are put out of action a direct offensive of the Russian armies against Silesia will be developed": Pares, 205.

69   The grand-duke orders his southern armies to hold good all along the line: ibid, 201.

70   The advance on Berlin begins: Paléologue, I, 136.

70   Galician mud: Hindenburg, 116.

70   "The grand-duke's greatest plan": Hindenburg, 118–119.

71   The Russians did "what few other troops in the world could have done": Falls, Cyril, "The First World War", Longman's, London, 1960, 55.

71   "The battlefield of Warsaw was abandoned to the enemy": Hindenburg, 120.

Page
71   The King of Saxony: "Opportunities", 150.
72   Cholera in the Austrian forces: Tăslăuanu, 93.
72   Dankl's memorandum to Conrad: "Letzter Kreig", I, 492.
73   Germans proposed bringing the Austrian First Army under Ninth Army Command: "Der Weltkrieg", 1914–18, Reichsarchiv, Berlin, 1929, VI, 38.

CHAPTER 8: ONSET OF WINTER

75   Ludendorf in Berlin – "People did not seem to realise the seriousness of our position in the war": Ludendorf, 95.
75   The German command reshuffle: "Der Weltkrieg", VI.
75   "Oberost's" pleas for reinforcement: ibid.
78   14,000 men sent to line without rifles: Knox, I, 215.
79   Scheidemann's "I am surrounded" message to Ruszki and reply: Pares, 208.
79   German transports trying to escape: Gourko, 86–87.
79   Petrograd alive with stories: Paléologue, I, 200.
80   Russians found mountain fighting difficult as they were mainly plainsmen: Knox, II, 483.
81   Rennenkampf loses command: Gourko, 70.
81   Leaves army: Tsar, 12.
81   The conference at Siedlce: Danilov, 317.
81   Paléologue reproaches Goremykin in Kazan Cathedral: Paléologue, I, 223.
82   Anti-British feeling and Sir George Buchanan's address to the English Club: "Dissolution", 109.
82   "The grand-duke upset": Rodzianko, Pavel, op. cit., 178.
82   "How can the grand-duke stand on the defensive?" and Joffre's "local attacks": Poincaré, 1914, 265–267.
83   Some divisions in Eighth Army down to 3,000 men: Brusilov, 104.
83   800,000 men in depots could not be used for lack of rifles: Golovin, 127.
83   Drinking hot tea and keeping feet warm: Rodzianko, Pavel, op. cit., 177.
83   Shortage of boots: Golovin, 178; Rodzianko, 119.
83–84 Correspondence between Yanushkevich and Sukhomlinov, cited by Lloyd-George, I, 441–444, from letters in his possession.
84   News of Russian artillery shortages "a bolt from the blue": Buchanan, I, 219.
84   The first winter of the war: "Dissolution", 108.
84   "The Russian colossus": Bülow, Bernard, Prince, von, "Memoirs", Boston, 1931, 233.

CHAPTER 9: A CRY FOR HELP FROM THE GRAND DUKE

86   British submarines in the Baltic: Woodward, 167.
86   "The age-old dream of Russia placing the Orthodox cross on the cupola of the Saint Sophia": Sazonov, op. cit., 129.
87   Enver's "Pan-Turanian ambitions": Churchill, I, 312.
87   Britain invited to put Turkish navy in order: Sazonov, op. cit., 129.
87   Germans offer to sell "Göben" and "Moltke" to Turkey: Poincaré, 1913–14, 184.
88   Sir Edward Grey's "regrets": The British Blue Book, II, Nos 1–4.
88   The seizure of the "Sultan Osman" and the "Reshadieh", the British version is given by Churchill, I, 314, and the Turkish by Emin, Ahmed, "Turkey in the World War", Yale University Press, 1930, 65. It seems never to have occurred to Churchill that any kind of moral issue could be involved.
88   The Turkish Cabinet took the German treaty for a rough draft and were

Page

highly critical of it: Emin, op. cit., 68.

88   Rifat Pasha's message of caution from Vienna: Emin, op. cit., 74.

89   Russia prepared to guarantee Turkish territorial integrity: Poincaré, 1914, 56.

89   The flight of "Göben" and "Breslau": main sources are Souchon, Admiral V. "Der Kreig zur See', Reichsarchiv; Corbett, Sir Julian, "Naval Operations", History of the Great War, I, London, 1921; Churchill; Tuchman, Barbara, "The Guns of August", Constable, London, 1962.

90   4,000 German soldiers and sailors in Constantinople: "The Times History of the Great War", III, 151.

90–91   The bombarding of the Russian Black Sea ports: inter alia, Churchill, I, 323.

91   The Turkish note to Russia after the bombing: Poincaré, 1914, 233.

91   Difficulties of communicating with Russia after the closing of the Dardanelles: Pares, 119 and 215.

91   Russia "mesmerised by the Byzantine mirage": Paléologue, I, 294.

92   Sazonov "Felt the pressure of public opinion" urging that the international situation should be used to satisfy Russian dreams of the Straits: Sazonov, op. cit., 242.

92   Talk of making Constantinople a new southern capital of Russia: ibid, 250.

92   Pressure in Duma: Sazonov, op. cit., 242; Paléologue, I, 268.

92   King George's "Constantinople is yours": Paléologue, I, 295; Poincaré, 1915, 51.

92   Sir George Buchanan tells Sazonov that Britain agrees Turkish question must be solved in accordance with Russian desires: Paléologue, I, 187.

92   Britain's quid pro quo for Constantinople: Paléologue, I, 299; Poincaré, 1915, 63.

92   Paléologue at Tsarskoe Selo: Paléologue, I, 192; Poincaré, 1915, 83.

92   Expelling the Turks from Europe: in the tsar's formula Turkish power was to be abolished north from the "Enos-Medea line" as it was then called (Sazonov, op. cit., 252). The Enos-Medea line had been drawn under the terms of the Treaty of London which concluded the 1913 Balkan War. By this Turkey-in-Europe was confined to a piece of Eastern Thrace within a boundary line from Enos to Medea.

93   "Before all we must beat Germany": Poincaré, 1914, 232–233.

93   Enver is described by Churchill as: "A would-be Napoleon, in whose veins surged warrior blood, by his individual will, vanity and fraud he was destined to launch the Turkish Empire upon its most audacious adventure": Churchill, I, 313.

96   Attack on the Suez Canal "impending": Churchill, I, 323.

96   Lloyd-George's memorandum to the War Council: Lloyd-George, I, 374, et seq.

96   Churchill's plan: "I pointed out to the Foreign Secretary . . . that a Russian Army Corps could easily be brought from Archangel, from Vladivostock, or with Japanese consent, from Port Arthur to attack the Gallipoli Peninsula": Churchill, I, 319.

96   Colonel Hankey's report of the "Dardanelles' Commission": Churchill, I, 360.

96   Letter from Kitchener, 2 January 1915: Churchill, I, 361.

97   Admiral Fisher's plan for landing on the Pomeranian coast: Woodward, 167.

97   "CELERITY": Churchill, I, 263–264.

98   Armenians "supported Entente": Emin, op. cit., 215.

98   Ottoman Army had no part in Armenian massacres: Nogales, General Raphael de, "Four Years Beneath the Crescent", Scribner, New York, 1926, 26. (The author was a Venezuelan who, after offering his services to the Entente, who refused them, was accepted in the Turkish Army.)

Page

98   The War Council decision of 13 January 1915. "The words in which the decision was formulated was an epitome of their confused thought – 'to prepare for a naval expedition in February, to bombard and take the Gallipoli peninsula, with Constantinople as its objective'. The suggestion that ships were to 'take' a part of the land is delightfully naive": Liddell Hart, 162.

CHAPTER 10: THE JACKALS CLOSE IN

99   Life at "Oberost": Ludendorf, I, 111–112.

99   "Up to this point our battles had saved us for the time being, but they had not brought us final victory": Hindenburg, 129.

100   Tsar Ferdinand even bought himself the dress uniform of Emperor of Byzantium from a theatrical company: Sazonov, op. cit., 229–230.

100   The Archduke Frederick's letter to the Emperor: "Letzter Krieg", II, 94–95.

100   The importance of Przemysl to Austrian prestige: ibid, II, 165.

101   "In the west was that enemy whose chauvinistic agitation against us had not left us in peace even in time of peace etc": Hindenburg, 131.

101   Four corps sent to "Oberost" from army reserve: Falkenhayn, 59.

102   Ludendorf sent to Linsingen's South Army. 'I . . . asked my Emperor to cancel the order. His Majesty graciously approved": Hindenburg, 135.

102   Detailed plans drawn up: "Letzter Krieg", II, 94–95.

103   Russian High Command had no overall plan once their early ones came to grief: Brusilov, 98.

103   The grand-duke asked the French if he should go on the defensive?: Poincaré, 1915, 43–44.

103   The tsar insists on his determination to "fight to the finish": Poincaré, 1915, 15.

103–104   Descriptions of Ruszki and Ivanov: Knox, I, 351–352; Brusilov, 29.

104   Vienna was 400 Km nearer than Berlin: Danilov, 353.

104   Shortage of rolling stock: Knox, I, 186.

105   Casualties at the Battle of Bolimow "smelt of formalin": Gourko, 193.

105   "The chief effect of the gas was destroyed by the intense cold": "Opportunities", 85.

105–106   Development of poison gas: Hansliau, "Der Chemische Krieg", Berlin, 1939, and Meyer, J., "Der Gaskampf und die Chemischen Kampfstoffe", Leipzig, 1926.

106   The sufferings of the Austrian armies in the Carpathians are graphically described by Tăslăuanu. (The author is an Austrian Rumanian, his sympathies are with Rumania rather than Austria.)

108   Russian losses in Augustovo Forest: Knox, I, 241. He describes it as the worst disaster since Tannenberg.

109   Ruszki retired and was replaced by Alexeiev: Knox, I, 281.

109   "The Winter Battle of the Masurian Lakes", the kaiser was responsible for the title: Hindenburg, 137.

109   Joffre's communique: "Our Action in Champagne": Poincaré, 1915, 61.

109   French losses: Ibid, 63.

109   Open francophobia in Petrograd: Paléologue, I, 238.

110   Lloyd-George's plan for an attack by way of Salonica: Lloyd-George, I, 369 et seq.

110   No troops for Dardanelles: Lloyd-George. "Lord Kitchener told us he had no troops to send to the Dardanelles. We had to accept it on his authority for he never condescended to details".

110   The 29th Division released for Salonica: Churchill, I, 419. The discussion over the sending of this unit lasted for weeks and when on 16 March they

Page

were embarked for the Mediterranean their transports were organised in such a way they could not fight on arrival. Horses were on one ship, harness on another, etc. All cargo had to be unladen and rebulked before they could be ready for action. This was the cause of considerable delay.

110   The grand-duke promises a "contingent of his best troops" for Salonica: Poincaré, 1914, 41.

110   The naval bombardment of 19 February: Churchill, I, 420 et seq: Liddell-Hart, 163.

110   The attack of 25 February: Churchill, I, 422.

110   Toasts drunk to Royal Navy: Knox, I, 259.

110   Churchill's telegram to Carden: Churchill, I, 424.

110   "In the Balkans the effect of the naval operations was electrical": ibid, 427.

110–111   Relations between the Entente Powers and Greece and Venizelos: ibid, 318 et seq.

111   Tersztyanski: Ludendorf, 231.

111–112   Przemysl and the operations there: "Letzter Krieg".

112   The Austrian troops were jubilant because they thought the country would have to sue for peace: Washburn, Stanley, "Victory in Defeat", Constable, London, 1916, 8.

112   The grand-duke "breathless and with tears in his eyes": Tsar, 39.

CHAPTER 11: THE TSAR VISITS HIS NEW DOMINIONS

114   "We, the old ones, may not live to see the decisive battles of the coming resolution": Payne, Robert, "The Life and Death of Lenin", London, 1964, 252.

114   "I do not know whether I shall live to see the next rise of the tide": ibid, 244.

115   "For the success of the revolution war is essential": Sazonov, op. cit., 232.

115   The Carpathian battles: inter alia, Brusilov, 101 et seq and Pares, 228 et seq.

115   French experts in Russia: Knox, I, 257.

115   "I was very much in sympathy with the idea of French and English troops driving a wedge between Turkey and the Central Powers": Sazonov, op. cit., 255.

115   Sazonov threw his weight in on the side of an all-out effort in Salonica: ibid, 233.

115–116   "I had difficulty in concealing how painfully the news affected me": ibid, 255.

116   Session of Duma opened, 9 March: Paléologue, I, 268.

116   Paléologue in audience with the tsar: Poincaré, 1915, 83.

116   "I could not admit my right to impose on my people the terrible sacrifices of this war etc": Paléologue, I, 294.

116   The question of the Straits and Constantinople should be settled in conformity with Russian desires: Churchill, I, 427.

116   Russia could not consent to Greece's participating in operations in the Dardanelles; Russia intriguing at Athens and the fall of the Venizelos government over this issue: Churchill, I, 429–432.

117   Russia "preferred to choke": Liddell Hart, 163.

117   Russia "failing, reeling backward under the German hammer": Churchill, I, 429.

117   Paléologue suggests detaching Austria from the Teutonic alliance: Paléologue, I, 235–236.

117   Poincaré's dismay: Poincaré, 1915, 3–4. He believed Russia would lose interest in Germany if Austria was defeated.

Page

117   Witte's interview in "Novoie Vremlia": Paléologue, I, 185.

117   Prince Yussopov in France: Poincaré, 1915, 19.

118   Prince Gottfried von Hohenlohe's letter to the tsar: Paléologue, I, 314.

118   Sazonov wanted Italy's entry into the war prevented: Poincaré, 1915, 57.

118   Dmitriev had asked for reinforcements, but got none: Brusilov, 124.

118   Line 150 miles long held by 300,000 men: Pares, 229.

119   An informal truce to allow each side to fetch water from the Dunajec: "The Times History of the Great War", IV, 435.

119   Austrian officer-prisoners invited to dine in the Russian officers' messes: Rodzianko, Pavel, op. cit., 153.

119   Russian troops gave up their rations to Austrian wounded: ibid, 171.

119   The Easter Truce, 1915: "The Times History of the Great War", V, 95 et seq.

119   "Our Friend would have found it better etc": Tsaritsa, 65.

119   Tsaritsa furious because "Nicholasha" was going to accompany tsar: Tsar, 43.

119   Grand-duke insisted on accompanying tsar: Danilov, 393.

119   Visit "worse than untimely": Brusilov, 131.

119   Mikhail Rodzianko also in Galicia: Pares, 226.

120   "Coldness and indifference" of troop to visit: Paléologue, I, 333.

120   Tsar did not confirm the promises to Poland; the Poles were dissatisfied and embittered: Brusilov, 38; Paléologue, I, 164.

120   Council of Ministers decided it could not discuss the question of Poland in wartime: Sazonov, op. cit., 314. This was an excuse repeatedly used from 1914 onwards to avoid ameliorating injustice.

120   Even Ruthenian clergy favoured Russia: Brusilov, 102.

120   Bobrinski: Brusilov, 69; Paléologue also criticises his conduct.

120   The Orthodox archbishop of Lemberg worth "an extra additional four army corps to the Austrians": quoted by Knox, without giving source, I, 290.

120   Szeptcki harassed: Brusilov, 58.

120   Tsar at Zloczov: Danilov, op. cit., 393.

120   Meets Irmanov's III Caucasian Corps. This unit had distinguished itself in the fighting round Ivangorod fortress in the previous October, forcing the line of the German and Austrian attackers at Kozenice, across the Vistula, under heavy fire: Pares, 206–207 and 226. Hoffman also pays tribute to their bravery when he speaks of their artillery in a rearguard action across the Vistula, keeping up fire with their "gun-trails in the water".

120   Tsar at Sambor: Brusilov, 131–133.

120   Tsar's dislike of Brusilov: ibid.

121   Grand-duke given jewelled victory sword: Danilov, 393–384.

121   Tsar at Przemysl: Tsar, 48.

121   At Odessa and Sebastopol: ibid, 51.

121   Plans for the descent on the Bosphorus: Churchill, I, 427; Danilov, 397; Woodward, op. cit., 176.

121   Germans bombed the rear first to destroy communications: Pares, 230.

121   Germans and Austrians fired 700,000 shells from 1,500 guns on 2 May: Knox, I, 282.

121   The III Caucasian Corps sent up: Brusilov, 136.

122   The German troops "swept the unwieldy enemy before them in the exuberant joy of the attack": Falkenhayn, 87.

122   Paléologue dining with Putilov: Paléologue, I, 348–349.

CHAPTER 12: FALKENHAYN ASCENDANT

123–124   "The moment had come when decisive actions in the east could be delayed

Page

134   Some infantry companies to be armed with long-handled axes: Golovin, 127.

134   Russians had to rail reinforcements to rear before they could send them forward: Falkenhayn, 81.

134   Soldiers' letters full of the word "exasperation": Pares, 232.

134   One village lost twenty-four of twenty-six men called up: Knox, I, 371.

134   "Getting empty in the villages": Pares, 253.

135   Unrest in Moscow: Knox, I, 268.

135   Rioters called for removal of Sukhomlinov group: Tsar, 62, editor's note.

135   Three days before order was restored: Paléologue, II, 12.

135   "You have no ammunition to fight Germans": Lloyd-George, I, 458.

135   Voluntary surrenders becoming common: Golovin, 227.

135   German bribes: Knox, I, 233.

135   Men reported sick at the least excuse: Knox, I, 350.

135   Desertions increased: ibid, 349.

136   Fifth Caucasian Corps sent up from Odessa: Knox, I, 286; Danilov, 387.

136   Indecision over Przemysl: Gourko, 113.

136   Falkenhayn's offensive had gained it own momentum: "Opportunities", 106.

136   German advance renewed: Knox, I, 292.

136   Lemberg falls: Knox, I, 293; Falkenhayn, 103.

CHAPTER 13: CHANGES IN PETROGRAD

137   "The incapability of the government was rendered even more noticeable by the poor ministers it chose. And this . . . was an outgrowth in the social process which was going on . . . The better elements were held in suspicion for they were looked on as opponents of the Government": Golovin, 156–157.

137   The police department directive of 16 December 1914: "Memoirs", 134.

138   Rising prices: Knox, I, 279.

138   Officers' wives lived on supplies sent out of army rations: Knox, II, 388.

139   Prohibition on vodka helped to discourage mouzhiks from growing food: "Catastrophe", 83.

139   No refrigerators in government possession: shortage of tinplate: Golovin, 165.

139   Port of Murmansk ice free, but had no rail connection: Golovin, 198.

139   Russian shipping figure: Knox, intro. xxxiii.

139   Russia suffered "even more than Germany from the isolation imposed on her by the war": "Catastrophe", 81–82.

139   The grand-duke complained of the corruption and incompetence of officials to French military attache: Poincaré, 1915, 150.

139   Railway officials needed bribes: Knox, I, 335.

140   Supplies at Archangel piled "mountain high": Golovin, 200; Rodzianko confirms this.

140   Railways from Archangel converted from narrow to standard gauge: Golovin, 200.

140   Twenty-five per cent of supplies did not reach army: ibid, 189.

140   Few prosecutions for corruption: Knox, I, 335.

140   The party "struggled against patriotic feelings": Pokrovski, M. N., edit., "Essays on the History of the October Revolution", Moscow, 1927, 203.

141   "Socialist" propaganda in Petrovski and Volhynian Regiments of the Guard: Paléologue, II, 25.

141   Birth of the Special Council: Pares, 242; Rodzianko, 132–133; Golovin, 154–155.

142   Miassoiedev's arrest and trial: Paléologue, I, 300. But his execution was not

Page

announced until 3 April: Paléologue, I, 322.

143   The Central War Industries Committee: Golovin, 156; Rodzianko, 135.

143   Sukhomlinov publicly denounced: Pares, 460.

143   Sukhomlinov dismissed: Knox, I, 277.

143   Polivanov cheered as he climbed the tribune to address the Duma: Paléologue, II, 39.

143   The Duma decides to call to account all persons to blame for the equipment shortages in army: Rodzianko, 145.

143   144   The character of the tsarina: "Dissolution", 43.

144   Tsar "living" at Stavka: Sazonov, op. cit., 237.

144   Tsarina's hatred of Guchkov and Rodzianko: Tsaritsa, entries under 28 March, 1916; 15 September 1915; 24 September 1915; 17 January 1916.

145   French technical instructors in Russia: Paléologue, I, 307.

145   Hampered by hostility of Sukhomlinov's minions: Lloyd-George, I, 451.

145   The Okhta factory explosion: Paléologue, I, 329.

145   "It would be impossible to form new factories, as there was already a want of personnel": Lloyd-George, I, 449.

145   Skilled workers called up: Golovin, 70–79.

145   2,500,000 exemptions: ibid, 71.

145   Kitchener appointed as official agent by grand-duke: Pares, Prof Sir Bernard, "A History of Russia", 459; Knox, I, 274; Lloyd-George, I, 449. It was while he was en route for Russia in connection with these responsibilities that Kitchener was drowned when the "Hampshire" was torpedoed.

145   Russia "infuriated" at British failure to meet delivery dates: Knox, I, 275.

146   Austin armoured cars sent to Putilov works and result: Knox, I, 257.

146   "The perfect gas-mask was never invented": Lloyd-George, I, 467–468.

146   Never enough gas-masks for more than front line troops: Gourko, 166.

146   Russian chemists "forgot" research on new explosive: Lloyd-George, I, 467.

146   Polivanov warns Duma: "There is no ray of light": Golovin, 229.

CHAPTER 14: THE GREAT RETREAT

147   The disagreements at "Oberost": Hoffman was led to comment, ruefully: "When one gets a close view of influential people – their bad relations with each other, their conflicting ambitions – all the slander and hatred, one must always bear in mind that it is certainly much worse on the other side, among the French, British and Russians or one might well be nervous": "War Diaries", 73.

147   Hindenburg and Ludendorff wanted to advance on Vilna, via Kovno: Falkenhayn, 115; Hindenburg, 140.

148   Belt of marshland from Osowiec to Grodno: Hindenburg, 140.

148   Hindenburg favoured the more easterly thrust: ibid.

148   Kaiser's conference, 2 July: Falkenhayn, 116.

148   "Our pursuit began to lose its force in incessant front actions": Hindenburg, 141.

148   "Clearing the way to Vilna": ibid, 142.

148   Shavli the centre of the tanning industry: Knox, I, 325.

149   Among critics of the delay in retreating was Golovin: 222.

149   Alexeiev reluctant to give up the fortress line: ibid, 223.

149   Council of Ministers could not understand the need for retreat: Golovin, 230, though this was accepted with much greater equanimity by the Armed Forces Commission of the Duma, ibid, 234.

149   Dragomirov had "lost his nerve": Tsar, 54.

150   Troops threw away arms to lighten load: Golovin, 193.

Page

150   The Statute of Field Administration: Pares, 254. Under this authority was exercised by Yanushkevich, who took a pride in defying the civil authorities: ibid, 255.

150   The Ukase of Catherine the Great: Paléologue, I, 286–287.

151   Jews in Polish units fought well: Knox, I, 231.

151   Friedmann, Jewish deputy for Kovno, attacks anti-semitic policy: Paléologue, II, 41–42.

151   Jews driven from Lodz, Kielce, Petrokov, Ivangorod, Skiernevice, Suvalki, Grodno and Bialystok: Paléologue, I, 173.

151   A Jew hanged for "helping German officer escape in a sack": Knox, I, 231. Knox comments that he must have been a very strong Jew or else the German officer was abnormally small.

151   Lithuanian Jews forced to leave frontier zone: Paléologue, I, 315.

151   Expulsions from Kurland and Lithuania: ibid, 23–24.

151   Newspaper "Volga" incited anti-semitism: ibid.

151   "Reopen the Jewish question in wartime?": Paléologue, III, 19.

151   Germany exploited US anger at anti-semitic policy: ibid, 173.

152   Evacuation of factories: Knox, I, 292.

152   Some hid in forests to return later: Ludendorf, 187.

152   "Only those who have actually seen the flight etc. . ." Gourko, 124.

152   Description of the plight of the refugees: Knox, I, 305; Pares, 253.

152   Feeding points established along the roads: Gourko, 124.

152   Russian soldiers kindness: Knox, I, 322.

152   Cholera, typhoid, typhus rife: Gourko, 129.

152   The loss of cattle: in 1913 Russian had 52 million head throughout empire, increasing by 9 million per annum. In 1914–15, the army took 5 million head; a further 4 million was lost in the retreat; and 9 million killed for home consumption (the equivalent of the pre-war increase). The total loss was, therefore, 18 million head, leaving 44 million. But this gave an annual increase of only 7 million, although the actual wartime demand was 14 million. Instead of introducing stringent rationing to save stock the government actually slaughtered an extra 7 million a year, thus gradually reducing the total herd. (Figs from Golovin, 164.)

152–153 "Curses, disease, grief and poverty are spreading all over Russia": Golovin, 230–231, quoting memorandum from Krivoshein, Minister of Agriculture.

153   The mass movements benefited the Germans, who did not have to feed the inhabitants of the deserted territory: "Opportunities", 106.

153   Argument with Austrian GHQ about the help for the Fourth Army: Falkenhayn, 119.

153   Falkenhayn hoped the Russians could be prevented from escaping eastward: Falkenhayn, 125.

154   Hindenburg and the kaiser enter Novogeorgievsk: Hindenburg, 142.

154   The grand-duke's popularity with the men eclipsing tsar's: Buchanan, 239.

154   Empress believes scandal about grand-duke: Pares, 250.

154   Anna Virubova corresponded with irresponsible young aides-de-cape at Stavka, picking up unsavoury rumours: ibid, 250.

154   Sukhomlinov behind agitation against the grand-duke: Poincaré, 1915, 214.

154   Goremykin tried to stop agitation: Golovin, 232.

155   Polivanov broke the news: ibid.

155   "God be praised! The tsar releases me from a task which is wearing me out": ibid, 235.

155   Danilov demoted: Knox, I, 350.

155   "Alexeiev was not the right man": Brusilov, 171.

155   A giant was needed: Falls, op. cit., 105.

155   Order of the Day announces the tsar's takeover of command: Paléologue, II, 70. The dismissal of the grand-duke had been made official on 23 August (Old Style).

Page
155   "This is dreadful"; Rodzianko, 151.
156   Poincaré's unsent telegram: Poincaré, 1915, 214.
156   "I mean to be the victim": Paléologue, II, 65.
156   The tsar's fatalism: "Dissolution", 45.
156   "Get Nicholasha's nomination quicker done": Tsaritsa, 115.
156   Stavka in a house, one wing of which occupied by tsar: Gourko, 152.
156   Boredom at Stavka: Brusilov, 226.
156   Films only diversion: Gourko, 155.
156   The tsar's reading matter, referred to in letters between royal couple.
157   Rasputin attacked in press: Paléologue, II, 61.
158   The letter of 21 August warned that his decision "menaced Russia, yourself and your dynasty with grave consequences". Many of the signatories were men who had vilified the grand-duke previously: Golovin, 233.
158- 159   Goremykin given order to prorogue the Duma: Paléologue, III, 154.
159   Fury of Duma: Rodzianko, 150.
159   Strikes at Putilov works and Baltic shipyards: Paléologue, II, 75.
159   "I won't have my ministers going on strike": ibid, 85.
159   "I told them my opinion sternly": Tsar, in letter 29 Sept.
159   Tsar had broken with the "conservative-liberal majority": "Memoirs", 146.
160   The Tarnopol "victory": Tsar, 73. "This happened immediately after the declaration of my appointment".
160   Petrograd in danger. Arrangements had to be hurriedly made for the removal of museum treasures, archives and gold reserves to Moscow. Plans were also made for the evacuation of war factories, many of which were in the capital: Gourko, 121.
160   The tsar and tsarina were fearful of Germans coming to Petrograd: Paléologue, II, 51.
160   Something like panic in the capital with people rushing away: Poincaré 1915, 225; also refers to this on 192. He must have gained some satisfaction from this for there had been similar reports of panic from Paris in 1914.
160   "The Russians always succeeded in escaping": Ludendorf, quoted by Pares 235.

CHAPTER 15: THE OFFENSIVE ENDS

162   "If only God would grant that the British and French began now": Tsar 81.
162   "Hecatombs of the slain": Poincaré, 1915, 109.
162   "They're lost in admiration of the Russian army": Knox, I, 319.
162   "For heaven's sake, get your government to give us rifles": Knox, II 36- 40.
162   "We will go on fighting": Lloyd-George, I, 459.
162   The War Office tried to get Knox recalled: Lloyd-George, I, 457.
162   "I considered it essential to afford immediate ... aid to our Russian allies": Joffre, op. cit., 352.
163   Joffre used the excuse of relief offensive to keep troops from the Dardanelles: Poincaré, 1915, 180.
163   British Cabinet wanted to go on the defensive in the west. General French was opposed to this. He told Joffre that "a great enveloping attack on the French front was the best way of helping Russia": Poincaré, 1914, 146. Liddell Hart comments: "Sir John French, of course, objected to any effort outside his own command in France" (161).
163   The July conference at Calais: Churchill, II, 577; also 283.
163   The Chantilly meeting: Paléologue, II, 31—32.
163   Joffre recalled the Russian sacrifices in 1914: Danilov, 449.

Page

163   The Russians "feverishly impatient" for French to resume activity: Poincaré, 1915, 189.

163   An offensive in France greater in scale "than anything ever before conceived": Churchill, II, 578.

164   Kitchener believed the Germans were transferring "immense forces" from eastern to western front: Churchill, II, 538.

165   Gallipoli: Liddell Hart, op. cit., 170–178; also Churchill, more lengthily.

166   History would "despise England and France": Knox, II, 352–353.

166   It was possible "for the Germans to throw in all their forces without running any risk, against Russia": Golovin, 219–220.

167   French were asking when Russia could resume the offensive?: Poincaré, 1915, 188.

167   Doumer in Russia: Paléologue, II, 199; Tsar, 83.

167   "Our offensive is slowly coming to a standstill": Hoffman, 85.

167   "The great anxiety of those September days had once again resulted only in a tactical success": Pares, 247, citing opinion of Ludendorf.

167   Some corps down to 5,000 men: Knox, I, 314.

167   Losses of campaign: 1,410,000 or an average of 235,000 a month: Golovin, 222.

168   "The professional character of our forces disappeared": Brusilov, 93.

168   Russians outnumbered two to one along the whole line: Knox, I, 363.

168   The educated middle class could easily evade military service: Golovin, 278.

168   Seventy per cent of all Russian officers were drawn from the peasant classes: Golovin, 278.

168   So badly trained special tactical schools had to be set up in the rear: ibid.

168   Paléologue was told there could be no troops for Salonica. This decision was, however, reversed by tsar: Poincaré, 1915, 250.

168   Many batteries had to be withdrawn for lack of shell: Knox, I, 314.

168   "The Russians had been beaten along the whole front": "Opportunities", 120.

168   "It was repeatedly pointed out that it could not be considered possible to annihilate finally an enemy etc.": Falkenhayn, 135.

169   German peace feelers: Paléologue, II, 135–137; Buchanan, I, 251.

169   Madame Vassilichikova: ibid, 139; Rodzianko, 169.

169   "An increase in hostility to Germany": Falkenhayn, 155.

169   Bulgaria's conduct: Churchill, II, 584.

169–170   The Czernowitz action: Knox, II, 84; "Opportunities", 125.

CHAPTER 16: THE RECOVERY

172   Orlov had been tsar's friend for twenty years: Paléologue, II, 69.

172   The isolation of tsar increasing: ibid, 43.

172   Sazonov not attending meetings of the Council of Ministers: Tsaritsa, 143. "This man's behaviour is beginning to drive me mad": Tsar, 83.

173   The Duma "playing the game of representing the people": "Memoirs", 146.

173–174   Meeting at Kerenski's flat: Paléologue, I, 145–146.

174   "Civil war – not civil peace, that must be the slogan": Payne, op. cit., 251.

174   French and British governments aghast at reversion to absolutism: Poincaré, 1915, 257.

174   Erzerum "the Turkish Siberia": Nogales, op. cit. 43.

175   Polivanov's achievements: Knox, I, 414.

175   Special Council overloaded with members: Golovin, 168. The Central War Industries Committee was buying in competition with the War Minstry; attempts to "militaries" the factories rejected: Golovin, 157–158.

Page

176   Only 650,000 rifles in all at beginning of winter: Knox, I, 348.
176   1,139,000 rifles imported: ibid, 417.
176   Number of guns had risen to 3,973: ibid.
176   Lloyd-George's offer and Kitchener's fury: ibid, 367.
176   Russian borrowing began in the second week of the war: Poincaré, 1914, 50.
176   Allied credits to Russia: Lloyd-George, I, 426.
176   "Neither the text nor the spirit of our alliance led us to foresee Russia would at some time ask us to lend her our credit": Poincaré, 1915, 57.
176   Inspectors were chosen nepotically and had no technical training: Knox, I, 272.
176   British asked to arbitrate: ibid, 411.
176   Murmansk railways: ibid, II, 511.
177   Skibotten to Karungi sledge route: ibid, 509.
177   Lack of rifles made it necessary to postpone call-up of 1916 class: ibid, I, 284.
177   "A fine pick of well-built, soldierly men": Pares, 354. Many begged to be allowed to participate in the most dangerous assignments, ibid.
177   Abandonment of the Polish salient shortened the Russian line: Knox, I, 320.
177   Falkenhayn's Christmas report to the kaiser: Falkenhayn, 209–218.
177–178 "We found an opinion prevalent that the Russian's losses in men and materials had already been so enormous that we should be safe on our eastern front for a long time to come": Hindenburg, 148.
178   Attacks on Polivanov continued in the tsarina's letters from January to March 1916.
179   Stürmer considered by tsar as mayor of Moscow: Kokovtsev, op. cit., 339.
179   "Had left a bad memory wherever he had occupied an administrative post": Sazonov, op. cit., 306.
179   Tries to have his name changed: Tsar, 128.

CHAPTER 17: DISTANT ECHOES FROM VERDUN

187   The fourteen-inch shell on the Archbishop's palace: Churchill, II, 662.
183   The Verdun battle described: Liddell-Hart, 217–226.
183   Paléologue shows films at Tsarskoe Selo: Paléologue, I, 203–204.
184   "It has been decided to take the initiative into our own hands": Tsar, 154.
184   The creation of North and West Fronts: Pares, 275.
184   Departure and death of Plehve: Knox, II, 393.
185   "I hope . . . Kuropatkin will prove a good commander-in-chief": Tsar, 131.
185   Evert, personality and background: Knox, I, 352.
185   Russian troops en fete: Brusilov, 191.
185   "The word 'rest' was practically a mockery to both officers and men": Hindenburg, 150.
187   The two sides evenly matched in matériel: Knox, II, 411.
187   Alexeiev's guerilla bands: Brusilov, 195.
188   "Such an expenditure of ammunition as we have not yet seen in the east": "Opportunities", 131–132.
189   Three men had to be hacked out of the ice: Knox, II, 409.
189   "Our allies had one law for their advances, and another for our advances": Gourko, 146.
190   The Russians "waded through swamp and blood": Ludendorff, 211–212.
191   Bruchmuller was "quite a genius in his way": "Opportunities", 135.
191   Tsar saw gas-masks demonstrated in February: Tsar, 143.
191   The Narocz attacks were carried out "under pressure from the Western Allies": Falkenhayn, 241.

Page

191–192   "We Russians are so noble": Knox, I, 409.

192   "The Allies did not repay Russia in coin of equal value": Golovin, 218.

192   "France is letting Russia carry the whole burden of the war": Paléologue, II, 133.

192   Boris Vladimirovich's outburst: ibid, 278; Knox, II, 128; Tsar, 215.

193   "I have at last found a successor for Polivanov": Tsar, 155.

193   War Office cars supplied to Rasputin: Pares, 326.

193   Polivanov dismissed without Imperial Rescript: Rodzianko, 184.

193   Shuvaiev: Knox, I, 415.

CHAPTER 18: THE GLORIOUS FOURTH OF JUNE

194   Brusilov's rule to attack vigorously "whenever there was the slightest possibility": Brusilov, 60.

194   Suggests attacking in concert with Evert and Kuropatkin: ibid, 214.

195   Discouragement from his brother-commanders. One told him: "You will break your neck": Brusilov, 217.

196   "Tapping on the wall": Hindenburg, 157.

196   "Unorthodox methods" surprised colleagues: Brusilov, 223.

197   Uneasiness at headquarters about Alexandra and Rasputin. Rasputin was believed to be in the pay of Germany: "Memoirs", 160.

197   Tsarina gave Brusilov a painted medallion of St Nicholas: Brusilov, 227.

197   Italy was within "days or even hours" of capitulation to Austria: "Opportunities", 136.

197   Alexeiev telephone Brusilov: Brusilov, 235.

197   Evert to attack on 13 June: ibid.

197–198   Tsar wanted change of plan: ibid, 235–237.

201   Russian attacks at Baranovichi repulsed: "Opportunities", 142.

201   Ragosa on reason for failure at Baranovichi: Brusilov, 223.

201   Hindenburg's hunting: Hindenburg, 148.

201   Kaiser at "Oberost": "Opportunities", 137.

202   Germans reinforce along the Stokhod: ibid, 142.

203   "Never has a mere demonstration had a more amazing success": Liddell Hart, 229.

203   Stürmer stopped supply columns: Rodzianko, 200.

203   "Our Friend sends his blessing. . .": Tsaritsa, 346; "Alexeiev and I decided not to attack in the north": Tsar, 200.

204   Empress in possession of a map of front: Tsar, 203, editor's note.

204   Admiral Grigorovich fed Rasputin false information about ship movements: "Memoirs", 160.

204   Unlikely Rasputin actually took German bribes. The German author of an otherwise over-sensationalised book on Rasputin, "Rasputin – A New Judgment", puts forward the view that he was not a paid German agent, but a pro-German anxious for conciliation between the two empires, a view not inconsistent with his opinions about tsarist absolutism in Russia.

204–205   Hoffman on the Russian decision not to attack in the north: "Opportunities", 140.

205   Germans had 127 divisions in France, etc.: Knox, II, 457.

205   Haig believed Brusilov's success would enhance his own chances: Churchill, II, 731.

206   Somme and British "tactics of attrition": Falkenhayn, 266.

206   "One third of the Somme guns and ammunition transferred to the banks of another river. . .": Lloyd-George, II, 538.

206   Russian apathy towards war: "Russian society now believes their country is finished": Paléologue, I, 217.

206   Lives thrown away "fighting across the same ground again and again":

Page

Knox, II, 493.

206   Prices: ibid, II, 425; also Paléologue, III, 44.

207   Carcasses being sent to soap factories: Golovin, 170.

207   Ministerial squabbles stopped building of refrigerators: ibid.

207   1916 War Loan brought in practically nothing: "Catastrophe", 100.

207   Meat rotted in Siberia: Golovin, 194.

207   War material on quay at Archangel: Paléologue, II, 277.

207   US shipments at Vladivostok: Golovin, 200.

207   Rail traffic between Moscow and Petrograd stopped for six days: Paléologue, III, 159.

207   Army requisitioned railway carriages for billets: Golovin, 193.

207   Armies set up factories in the rear: ibid, 189.

207   No attempts to organise prisoner-of-war labour in Russia: ibid, 73.

208   Putilov sought government subsidy: Paléologue, III, 159–160.

208   Plan by Naumov to organise food supply with zemstvos: Rodzianko, 200–201.

208   Pamphlets urge strikes for peace: Paléologue, III, 65.

208   Alexeiev proposes a military dictatorship: Rodzianko, 195; Golovin, 171.

208   Stürmer "appointed dictator with full powers": Rodzianko, 200.

208   According to Buchanan (III, 64) the man chosen as dictator was Ivanov who was at that time personal military adviser to the tsar (after Brusilov's succession as command, South East Front). This is not mentioned by any other sources and leads to the supposition that the British ambassador had confused names.

208   Zemgor calls for "a government worthy of a great people": Paléologue, III, 130.

208–209 It was said in Petrograd that "the emperor reigns – the empress governs, under Rasputin": ibid, 306.

209   "Now a correspondence between Alexeiev and that brute Guchkov" – in his reply the tsar, surprised, asks how she knows of this? She does not tell him. But the reason for her knowledge was that she was seeing the reports of the secret police which opened mail, even that destined for General Head-quarters. In August Guchkov had written to Alexeiev: "The government is decaying at its foundations". (Golovin, 245). It is obviously to exchanges of this type she is referring.

209   Sukhomlinov: the tsarina wrote on 1 and 2 May (Old Style): Tsaritsa, 333. Empress's interview with Khvostov: Rodzianko, 199.

209   Twelve-member commission appointed to draw up plans for Polish autonomy: Pares, 247.

209   Sazonov's scheme: Paléologue, I, 298.

209   Scheme outlined to French and British ambassadors: ibid, II, 314–315.

209–210 Nicholas's approval: Sazonov, op cit 305.

210   "I have won all along the line": Paléologue, II, 314.

210   Sazonov goes to Finland on holiday: ibid, 270.

210   "How the papers are down on Sazonov": Tsaritsa, 373.

210   Order of the Bath for Sazonov and Buchanan's anger with Stúrmer: Pares, 345.

210–211 Albert Thomas in Russia: Paléologue, I, 252; Knox, II, 417; Golovin, 171.

213   The Guards as a "personal reserve": Tsar, 99.

213   Plan for Guards' attack was "ridiculous": Rodzianko, Pavel, op. cit. 209.

213   Guard Army generals were appointed by tsar himself: Brusilov, 256.

213   "May God help our brave troops": Tsar, 229–231.

214   "As sorry a looking lot as one could wish to see": Knox, II, 469.

214   The grand-duke Paul attacked frontally instead of on the flank: Rodzianko, 205.

213–214 "Physically the finest human animals in Europe": Knox, II, 472.

215   Rodzianko rebuked for interference: Rodzianko, 209.

Page
215   Kaledin's protest: Rodzianko, 202.
215   "Guard Army" renamed "The Special Army": Knox, II, 475.
216   South West Front losses: ibid, 461.
216   Shuvaiev's letter: Golovin, 68.
218   Alexeiev against Rumania coming into war: Knox, II, 484.
218   Rumanian army figures: Churchill, II, 759.
218   Lloyd-George on Rumania's actual strength: Lloyd-George, 545–546.
218   France angered by Stürmer's secrecy: Poincaré, 1915, 107.
218   Stürmer's ultimatum: Sazonov, op. cit., 259.
219   Austria had only five "tired divisions" in Transylvania: Churchill, II, 759.
219   German moves in Rumania; ibid.
220   Prince Leopold of Bavaria appointed c-in-c, east: "Opportunities", 152.
220   Army of the Danube formed under Sakharov: Knox, II, 504.
221   Twenty infantry and seven cavalry divisions on former neutral ground in Rumania: ibid, 502.
221   400 Km added to Russian line: ibid.
221   Russian officers claimed they would have been in Lemberg by October, but for the Rumanian intervention: ibid, 487.
221   The balance of forces in the Brusilov offensive: Golovin, in an article in the "Slavonic Review," Vol XIII, No 39.
221   Eighteen German division sent from west to east: Golovin, 241.

CHAPTER 20: COMING OF THE STORM

223   Russians entirely dependent on Donetz coal: Pares, 331.
223   Bakers sold rye flour to horse owners: Knox, II, 529.
223–224 Petrograd police report: Pares, 384.
224   Mutinies in Marseilles: Paléologue III, 16–17.
224   Troubles in Russian navy: Woodward, 170–171.
224   Renault factory affair: Paléologue, III, 73–83.
225   "You brought me the unpleasant news of Manasevich-Manuilov's arrest": Rodzianko, 211.
225   "It is the first time I leave you with a feeling of sincere pleasure": Pares, 348. He is quoting from A. A. Khvostov's deposition to the post-revolutionary commission.
225   Protopopov in England conducted himself with "tact and dignity": Rodzianko, 193; "Memoirs," 171.
225   Went to Rasputin for a "cure": Pares, 378.
225   Rasputin had promised him he would be a minister. He had told him, "You will be a minister; you will be a minister": "Interrogatoires," 189.
225   "He is one of the Duma, it will have a great effect on them and shut their mouths": Tsaritsa, 395. "It shall be done": Tsar.
226   Kerenski describes Protopopov as "a normal, elegant and well-bred man": "Memoirs," 171.
226   "I feel I shall save Russia": Rodzianko, 219.
226   Protopopov dressed in the uniform of a chief of gendarmes: "Memoirs", 170. His giant ikon, ibid.
226   The empress "had a radio on the roof of Tsarskoe Selo": Dissolution, 130.
226   Rumour was gaining ground that Protopopov and the empress were provoking food riots: Rodzianko, 258; Paléologue, III, 66.
227   One man suggested keeping Rasputin permanently drunk: Paléologue, III, 58.
227   Rodzianko urges improvements in government on tsar: Paléologue, III, 89.
227   Duma session opens: ibid, 93.
227   Protopopov seeking to reorganise the "Black Hundreds": ibid, 89.
227   Miliukov's "Is this folly or is it treason?" speech: Pares, "A History of

CHAPTER 21: THE RISING OF THE SUN OF FREEDOM

Page
250   Observation posts crowded with pressmen, "soldiers delegates", etc.; Knox, II, 643.
251   Kerenski behaved as if it had been a magnificient victory: Knox, II, 647.
251–252   The July uprising: inter alia, Catastrophe, 237–239.
252   Arrest warrants out for Trotski and Lenin: Golovin, 277.
252   Kornilov appointed as commander-in-chief: "Memoirs", 296.
252   The 81st Czech Regiment surrenders en bloc: Knox, II, 645; also cited by Lloyd-George, who obviously heard of it from Knox.
252–253   The Women's Battalion: "Dissolution", 233.
253   The Iron Division refused to dig in: Golovin, 271.
253   Restoring discipline: Golovin, 276.
254   Losses of the "Kerenski Offensive": Knox, II, 645.
255   Knox's "Six Points": ibid, 661.
255   Food supplies; plan to reduce the army to 5 million; Golovin, 159–176.
255   "Russia cannot make peace or war": Paléologue, III, 253.
256   Buchanan and Knox's message to the Foreign Office: ibid, 225.
256   Clemenceau: "If all the celestial powers asked me to give Russia back her word, I would refuse": Wheeler-Bennett, op. cit., 76–77.
256–257   The Kornilov affair: Memoirs, 368–369; Golovin, 280–281.
257   The Bolshevik radio message: Golovin, 282.
258   Hoffman's reception of message and his conversation with Ludendorff: Hoffman, 203–204.

Besides sources mentioned, the following were among principal works used, providing background or other material:

Allen, W. E. D. and Muratoff, Paul. "Caucasian Battlefields." Cambridge University Press, 1953.

Benckendorf, Count Paul. "Last Days at Tsarskoe Selo." Heinemann, London, 1927.

Bonch-Bruyevich, M. "Poterya nami Galitsii v 1915." Moscow, 1920. (In German as "Der Verlust Galiziens, 1915".)

Bryce, Viscount. "Report of the Turkish Atrocities in Armenia." New York, 1916.

Carr, E. H. "A History of Soviet Russia." Cassell, London, 1966.

Charques, Richard. "The Twilight of Imperial Russia." OUP, London, 1965.

Czernin, Count Ottokar. "In the World War." Cassell, London, 1919.

Deniken, General A. I. "The Russian Turmoil." Hutchinson. London.

Djemal, Pasha. "Memoirs of a Turkish Statesman, 1913–19." New York, 1922.

Gilliard, Pierre. "Thirteen Years at the Russian Court." Hutchinson, London, 1921.

Guse, F. "Die Kaukasfront im Weltkrieg." Leipzig; n.d.

Morgenthau, Henry. "Ambassador Morgenthau's Story." New York, 1918.

Nezmanov, A. "Strategiski ocherki voini, 1914–18." Moscow, 1922. (In German as "Strategischer Uberblick des Krieges, 1914–18".)

Regele, Oskar. "Feldmarschall Conrad." Vienna, 1955.

Seton-Watson, Hugh. "The Decline of Imperial Russia." Methuen, London, 1952.

Steed, Henry Wickham. "The Hapsburg Monarch." Constable, London, 1919.

Toynbee, A. J. "Armenian Atrocities." London, 1915.

Toynbee, A. J. and Kirkwood, K. P. "Turkey." London, 1926.

Turkish Official History. "La Campaigne des Dardanelles." 1924.

Index

294